The Miami Riot
of 1980

The Miami Riot of 1980

Crossing the Bounds

Bruce Porter
Marvin Dunn

LexingtonBooks
D.C. Heath and Company
Lexington, Massachusetts
Toronto

Library of Congress Cataloging in Publication Data

Porter, Bruce D.
   The Miami riot of 1980.

   Includes index.
      1. Miami (Fla.)—Riot, 1980.   2. Miami (Fla.)—Race relations.
I. Dunn, Marvin, 1940–   . II. Title.
F319.M6P67   1984   975.9'381063   83–49201
ISBN 0–669–07663–5 (alk. paper) Casebound
ISBN 0–669–09174–X (alk. paper) Paperbound

Copyright © 1984 by D.C. Heath and Company

Published simultaneously in Canada

Printed in the United States of America on acid-free paper

Casebound International Standard Book Number: 0–669–07663–5

Paperback International Standard Book Number: 0–669–09174–X

Library of Congress Catalog Card Number: 83–49201

*For Shanreka Perry, who at age ten
became one of the first victims of the riot*

Contents

Figures and Tables

Preface

This book is the result of research commissioned by the Ford Foundation and could not have been done without its financial and logistical backing. In this regard, we would like to thank Mitchell Sviridoff, vice president for National Affairs when the project began, who conceived the project and brought the two authors together; Thomas Cooney, then a Ford Foundation program officer, and Roy Winnick, reports editor, both of whom provided much-needed counsel in the research, writing and editing of the manuscript; and Alsie Falconer, also of the Foundation, who patiently guided us through a variety of crises.

It also could not have been done without the cooperation of more than 250 people who agreed to talk to us about their roles in the riot, to provide us the benefit of their expertise, or open doors to us that would otherwise have been closed. Many of these individuals are named in the text, but special thanks are due the following: Chief Kenneth Harms of the Miami Police Department and Director Bobby Jones of the Dade County Public Safety Department; Matthew Schwartz, chief of advanced planning for the City of Miami Planning Department; Tom Petersen and George Yoss, assistant state's attorneys for Dade County; Jeffrey Silbert, director of the Dade-Miami Criminal Justice Council; Archie Hardwick, director of the James E. Scott Community Association; Ernest Martin, executive director of community and economic development for Dade County; Dorothy Fields, director of the History and Research Foundation of South Florida; and Paul S. George, Florida historian. Special thanks should also go to Willie Matthews, proprietor of Willie's Grocery in Coconut Grove, for his help in gaining insight into the psychology of the community.

We would like to thank Chief Joseph McNamara of the San Jose Police Department in California, Dr. William Rose of the University of Miami, and Prof. Penn Kimball of the Columbia University Graduate School of Journalism, whose critical reviews of the manuscript led to its substantial improvement.

Valuable assistance was also provided by our research staff, consisting at various times of Delores Dunn, Kathleen Fanjul, Robert Loring, Sue Martin, Bentone Witner, Ronit Small and Bettye Wiggs.

We are particularly grateful to Craig Rose, a 1980 graduate of the Columbia Journalism School whose taped interviews with merchants, rioters and riot victims added considerably to our understanding of the event.

Although we relied on the help of many people and agencies, the findings and interpretations in this book are solely the responsibility of the two authors.

Introduction

The Miami or "McDuffie" riot in May 1980 was a dark urban episode that captured the momentary attention of U.S. public already surfeited by war, terrorism and other social traumas and catastrophes. With the flickering television images of fires, looting and people lying dead in the street, Miami took its turn on the billboard, then faded from recollection as new horrors competed for people's attention.

The bare statistics of the riot—18 dead, $80 million in property damage, 1,100 arrested—do not in themselves set Miami apart from similar disturbances in Watts, Newark and Detroit a decade earlier. What was shocking about Miami was the intensity of the rage directed by blacks against white people: men, women and children dragged from their cars and beaten to death, stoned to death, stabbed with screwdrivers, run over with automobiles; hundreds more attacked in the street and seriously injured. In contrast, the disturbances of the 1960s could be regarded as "property riots," wherein blacks directed their anger largely against buildings. The deaths that did occur during those disorders were overwhelmingly those of blacks killed by white policemen and National Guardsmen. The few white deaths—of the 101 victims in Watts, Newark and Detroit, only two or three were white people killed intentionally by black rioters—occurred as a byproduct of the disorder. In Miami, attacking and killing white people was the main object of the riot.

Another thing about Miami was that the riot occurred in the sunbelt, along the new growth vector of the nation, rather than in one of the faltering cities of the North. For policymakers in Washington, this geography should be of considerable significance. For if one accepts the proposition that the deep roots of rioting lie in poverty and social despair—the well-off, after all, do not riot, no matter how sorely provoked—the Miami disturbance illustrates the pervasiveness of poverty, even in that part of the country that is relatively prosperous. This should give pause to those who think that generalized economic growth will be sufficient to pull poor black people into the mainstream of the social and economic system.

But poverty, though of course a necessary cause for rioting, is certainly not a sufficient one. Something else must provoke people to take to the streets. In Miami this something was clearly the failure of the Florida criminal justice system to obtain criminal sanctions against the police officers whose beating of Arthur McDuffie resulted in his death. This was only the most recent of several police transgressions against blacks—instances that had resulted in little or no punishment of the offenders. Others included the molestation of a black girl by a state trooper and the killing of a young black man in neighboring Hialeah. Indeed, had the McDuffie killing been seen as the exception rather than the rule of police conduct, it seems doubtful that the riot would have occurred. Poor blacks, like other human beings, harbor a great capacity for putting up with prolonged economic misery—are resigned, if you will, to the proposition that life is unfair. But when the law enforcement system is perceived as being discriminatory and the courts unjust, then those delicate bonds that preserve public order and keep in force the social contract become frayed and no longer serve to hold things together. The killing and burning and looting in Liberty City provided us all a brief glimpse of anarchy.

In the following pages we attempt to set down what happened during the Miami riot of May 17–19, 1980, and to examine several of the reasons why. We recognize that, considering the chaotic nature of such disorders, it is foolish to claim absolute accuracy for every episode in the chronology. Like the three blind men encountering the elephant, each participant sees things differently depending on his or her experience. By talking to a great variety of those involved, however, we hoped that somehow the discrepancies would cancel each other out and that the overall picture would represent a fair account of what occurred.

Along with tracing the history of race relations in the city, we review the events that led up to the riot and describe how the disorder began and how it ran its course. We look at the event from many perspectives, from that of the rioter, the police officer, the public official, black and white merchants, community residents and white and Hispanic citizens of Miami. We try to identify which members of the black community went into the streets and which ones stayed home; we examine what the police did to contain the riot and what they might have done. We review the damage and the cost to the city and county, and report on how public and private agencies responded to the riot after it ended.

We also show the ways in which the Miami riot differed from other racial disorders in this century—indeed, why it should be regarded as a turning point in race relations in the United States. And we examine what made the city a particularly fertile ground for an outburst of such violence. Finally, we try to point out the danger signals that other cities should heed to avoid having a similarly disastrous experience of their own.

The Miami Riot
of 1980

Black workers helping to clear the land for the city of Miami, 1896 (photo courtesy of the Historical Association of Southern Florida)

1

The Past: A Racial History of Miami

From the beginning, the history of race relations in Miami, Florida, has been one of serious problems between blacks and whites. Reviewing the available evidence, one can easily conclude that blacks have been systematically excluded from the social, economic and political life of the city ever since it was founded around the turn of the century out of coral rock and mangrove swamp. One can also conclude that the physical abuse—both threatened and actual—of blacks by whites, including white policemen, was an integral part of the city's beginnings, and that during the early decades of the city's history, whites who threatened, beat and even lynched blacks were rarely brought to justice.[1] Through the mid-1950s, this was the way of life.

Like so many other Southern communities, Miami underwent significant changes during the activist civil rights movement of the 1960s. The decade of the 1970s was also a period of significant changes, one of which was a marked increase in violent reactions by blacks to real or perceived injustice, especially at the hands of the police. From the "rotten meat" riot of June 1970 to a nearly forgotten riot in the Liberty City section of Miami in 1979, there were no fewer than thirteen significant episodes of violent confrontations between blacks and whites in Dade County, Florida. Most often, the episodes involved attacks on police officers. Given this well-established pattern of rioting in response to perceived or real police brutality, it might have been predicted that the verdicts of acquittal handed down on May 17, 1980, in the trial of four white police officers for the murder of Arthur McDuffie would result in the carnage that followed.

Today, Dade County, which includes Miami and twenty-six other municipalities, is a thriving metropolis of more than 1.7 million people. Relatively few of them were born in the area, most having migrated to south Florida during the past thirty years, primarily from the northeastern states and from Cuba.

The city of Miami was founded by Henry Flagler, a former partner of John D. Rockefeller in the Standard Oil Company, and formally incorporated in 1896. Flagler became interested in railroads in the mid-1880s and acquired a line that ran between Jacksonville and St. Augustine in north Florida. In 1896, he extended his Florida East Coast

1

Railroad southward, first to Miami and then to Key West. In so doing, he brought hundreds of laborers to south Florida, many of them black.

According to Florida historian Paul S. George, the first blacks to come to the south Florida area were slaves from South Carolina who, in the early nineteenth century, worked on the scattered plantations that dotted the region before the arrival of Flagler's railroad.[2] The primary source of income for the plantation owners was the manufacturing of "coontie starch" from the "coontie root," which was most probably introduced into south Florida by Escalante de Fontenada, a Spanish nobleman and the first white man known to have landed in the area now called Dade County in 1545.[3] Blacks had also been arriving from the Bahamas to work in rural fields and in the rich agricultural groves around the Coconut Grove section of Miami. Their presence gave the Grove's black community a distinctively island character that is still evident.

The railroad, however, started the shift of south Florida's economic base from agriculture to tourism. Construction of hotels and other tourist facilities drew more blacks from Georgia, South Carolina and other areas of Florida; these blacks made up a significant portion of Miami's first citizens. When on July 28, 1896, the vote was taken to incorporate the city, 162 of the 368 persons who participated were black—a fact not mentioned in most early accounts of the event. A city council was elected at the same time, as were a city clerk and city marshal. All these officials were white.

Most of the land within the original boundaries of the city was contained in two sections acquired by Julia Tuttle and Mary Brickell. The deeds to these sections contained restrictive clauses consigning blacks to a segregated quarter northwest of town that came to be called "Colored Town," and today is known as Overtown. Charles S. Thompson, a black educator in Miami, wrote in a 1942 article in *Crisis,* the magazine of the National Association for the Advancement of Colored People: "Whites were given all property on the Bay of Biscayne and both banks of the Miami River. The Colored were allocated property on the west side of the railroad . . ., one settlement several blocks north of the river Nazarene, near Lemon City, and another several blocks south of the river on SW 8th Street [now the main thoroughfare for Miami's Little Havana]."[4] The practices of the time forbade whites to live or operate businesses in the colored section and the colored to live or operate businesses in the white section. For blacks, Thompson reported, these restrictions were rigidly enforced. Whites, however, though they never lived there, were allowed to have many business establishments in black Miami, some of which were very large.

It was in Overtown, in 1898, that some of the earliest confrontations between blacks and whites occurred. The U.S. Army, then engaged in fighting the Spanish-American War, had built a camp adjacent to Colored Town, called Camp Miami. White soldiers occasionally amused themselves by terrorizing residents of the growing black settlement. Historian George describes what happened in the summer of 1898:

> In June and July, soldiers killed one black and severely injured several others for no apparent reason. This terrorism reached its climax later in July when a canard spread through Camp Miami that a black had killed a soldier. Soon several hundred soldiers were in Colored Town, forcing many blacks to flee under the threat of death. At no time in the brief history of Camp Miami was any soldier arrested by public authorities. Only the end of the war and the evacuation of the camp in August, 1898, averted additional violence.[5]

After the war ended and the soldiers left, blacks had to contend with the Dade County sheriffs. The first one, R. J. Chillingworth, vigorously tried to prevent them from voting in municipal elections. A successor, Dan Hardie, campaigned for sheriff on a platform that advocated "arresting suspicious characters first, and letting them explain afterwards." Hardie referred to his pack of bloodhounds as "nigger hounds," and the black community became the primary source of "suspicious characters."[6] According to George, of thirty-five inmates in the county jail in September 1904, thirty-four were black.[7]

In 1903, Miami first experienced a phenomenon common in the South since the end of the Civil War—an outpouring of white rage against blacks over the alleged rape of a white woman, culminating in the hanging of a black man. The victim was Richard Dedwilley, who was arrested by the sheriff and accused of raping a woman named Rose Gould. The alleged crime so enraged whites that there was talk of an assault on Colored Town. The *Miami Metropolis,* the city's only newspaper, reported the capture of the "unholy fiend of hell" and then added, somewhat hopefully, that many Miamians planned to "treat him to a necktie party."[8] As it turned out, the punishment meted out by the city was just as swift. After a fifteen-minute trial, Dedwilley was hanged in the yard of the county jail.[9]

This case was followed in 1905 by the murders of two whites, C. E. Davis and his daughter, as they slept. After it was determined that the girl had been sexually assaulted, police investigators turned to Colored Town to find the murderer. The *Metropolis* again tried to whip up passions by suggesting that "lynching law may be applied to the perpetrators when located."[10] On January 23, 1903, in an article entitled "Fiendish black brute brings home to us the question of what can be done with these black sons of hell," the *Metropolis* expanded on its theory of race relations:

> All kinds of remedies have been resorted to including hemp, tar and torch, and yet it seems that it is all of no avail . . . and occasionally the demon in human form breaks loose, fearing neither God nor man, bent upon the commission of a crime worse than the foulest murder. For such beings no punishment is mete. No wonder that lynchings and roastings are resorted to and such things will continue to take place North and South, East and West as long as these devilish attempts upon the virtue and lives of white women are made. If white men of Miami had gotten their hands upon him they would have made short work of putting out his worse than worthless life.[11]

The police did arrest two black men, but they were later released when a grand jury found insufficient evidence upon which to proceed against them.

While blacks tended automatically to be accused of crimes committed against whites, the records of coroner's juries early in this century show that Miami courts were quick to exonerate policemen and other whites accused of killing blacks.[12] And general harassment by the police was an everyday fact of life. In 1908 Judge John Grambling of the Miami Municipal Court complimented the recently formed Miami Police Department for having "handled the Negro population in such a manner that Miami is given credit for the most respectable and law-abiding class of Negroes of any city in the South."[13] The judge was especially impressed because he felt that before being given the lesson in manners by the police the "great number of Nassau Negroes . . . upon their arrival here considered themselves the social equal of white people."[14] The police had earned the judge's approval by imposing a 6 p.m. curfew on blacks in the city outside Colored Town, by showing tacit approval of the frequent beating of blacks by white civilians for its violation, and by beating the violators themselves.[15] Police officers were also in the habit of entering Negro dwellings without search warrants, sometimes forcing blacks out of their beds and making them pay a "tax" of $3 or face arrest.[16]

In addition, blacks in Miami were subject to constant verbal attacks in the city's press. First the *Miami Metropolis* and later the *Miami Herald*—today the city's largest paper—regularly referred to blacks with such characterizations as "darky," "coon," "fiend," and "ham-fat," and regularly ran racially degrading stories.[17] In one article discussing the need to rid the city of those blacks who were seen as loafers, the *Metropolis* noted that a certain Mr. Savage, a white man, had helped "clean out the town of the hamfat as the loafing, gambling negroes are called."[18]

By 1910, Miami's blacks numbered 2,258, nearly 42 percent of the city's population, and residential boundary conflicts were becoming increasingly common. The major problems occurred as the blacks of Colored Town tried to move north into north Miami and northwest into a white area known as Highland Park. White residents of north Miami met in November 1911 and agreed, with the support of municipal leaders, to draw a color line along certain streets and avenues near Colored Town that would have the effect of restricting black expansion.[19] Although the color line did not have the force of law, the practice was carefully adhered to, thus effectively excluding blacks from white residential and commercial areas. "The advance of the Negro population," the *Miami Herald* wrote, "is like a plague and carries devastation with it to all surrounding property. . . . What the remedy is, does not now appear, but the fact is that Miami is being badly injured and badly disfigured by the growth of these Negro sections."[20] By 1915, a few blacks had moved beyond the color line but in that year, according to the *Metropolis,* six masked whites raided several black dwellings and warned the inhabitants to abandon their homes. Most of them immediately complied. Although the Miami police investigated the incident, none of the masked assailants was ever apprehended.[21]

In 1917 several blacks, attempting to circumvent the commercial restrictions on black business, started up chauffeur services catering to white customers. In response, white chauffeurs "chased negro drivers through the streets while the police looked on."[22] In July, after a black chauffeur named Fred Andrews was assaulted by several white chauffeurs, Andrews searched out one of his assailants and stabbed him. The black was subsequently arrested, tried and convicted for the offense; his attackers were never caught.

A few days after Andrews' conviction, rumors of an imminent black uprising raced through the white community. Counter rumors spread through the black community, among them that whites were getting ready to shoot up the black residential area. Miami came dangerously close to a major race riot when a group of whites dynamited the Odd Fellows Hall, then the largest building in the city's black section. The dynamiting, which occurred late on the night of July 15, brought many blacks rushing into the streets with guns and other weapons. Violence was averted, in a preview of similar scenarios fifty years later, when several black clergymen pleaded for people to stay calm, and white police officials assured everyone that the dynamiters would be caught. A reward of $50 was offered by the police for information leading to the arrest of the dynamiters. The reward was later increased to $200 after blacks complained of a halfhearted investigation. The dynamiters, however, were never apprehended.[23]

In the end the black chauffeurs won a victory of sorts when it was agreed that blacks would have a monopoly on the operation of buses and automobiles-for-hire in black areas. The parties to the agreement were the Miami police chief, William Whiteman, other white civic leaders and the Colored Board of Trade.

During the 1920s, black militant groups, among them the Negro Uplift Association of Dade County, became active in Miami. First gaining prominence in 1919 after protesting the exoneration of a white police officer accused of the death of a black man, the association charged that officers on duty in Colored Town were inhumane. The group said the police had been seen to beat and club black men and women while making arrests, often after blacks were handcuffed and even when offenses were minor. It further charged that the police rarely obtained a search warrant before entering homes of black citizens and that a double standard of justice prevailed in the courts. In October 1919, in response to the activism of the association, police in Miami reported that they had discovered "dangerous propaganda" in a number of black homes.[24] One tract, a newspaper published by a black nationalist group, reminded blacks that they had "shouldered guns to free the people overseas" during World War I and exhorted them to "use the same guns to free yourselves."[25] Although the appeal seems to have fallen on deaf ears, the discovery of the radical literature caused considerable alarm throughout the white community.

The following summer there was the Henry Brooks case. At 5 a.m. on July 30, a white woman was working alone in her kitchen when, according to newspaper accounts, a black man casually walked in and asked her for food. Suddenly, as the story went, he grabbed the woman around the neck and dragged her into the back yard. Although there was some question as to the nature of the assault, whites were convinced the women was then raped.

Brooks, a fifty-five-year-old black immigrant from the Bahamas, was arrested several hours later in his home a few blocks away by detectives who had tracked him with dogs. The white woman positively identified Brooks as her attacker. That night, as a mob of some 500 white men formed nearby, the local judge decided that for Brooks's protection he should be moved some 300 miles north to Jacksonville. Trailed by white vigilantes, the prisoner was taken the first 100 miles by the police and at Fort Pierce was placed aboard a northbound train. Brooks never made it to Jacksonville. Around noon, just north of the town of Ormond, he was said to have jumped head first through the window of the moving train. His death was ruled a suicide.[26]

Believing that Brooks had been killed by the mob, about 400 of Miami's Bahamians assembled in the Coconut Grove area on the evening of August 3. Next day, the *Miami Herald* printed the following description of what happened next: "Four hundred or more alien negroes from the Bahama Islands gathered on the streets of the colored settlement yesterday morning, and becoming greatly excited, made numerous threats of what they proposed doing to avenge Brooks' death. Some people professed to believe he had been killed by the mob which pursued him from Miami to Ft. Pierce and beyond. . . ."[27]

The gathering of angry blacks alarmed officials to the extent that for the first time in the city's brief history they got an order issued for the mobilization of the National Guard. Whites were not allowed into the area, or blacks out of it.

A few days later, the grand jury investigating the alleged assault of the woman and the circumstances of Brooks's death found that the woman had indeed been assaulted, that her attacker was unquestionably Brooks, that Brooks had met his death by jumping from a train near Ormond, and that there were no marks of violence on his body other than those caused by his fall. The black community apparently accepted these findings. With no further disturbances, Brooks's body was put aboard a ship bound for Nassau.[28]

The Ku Klux Klan officially arrived in Dade County on May 24, 1921, with a parade attended by hundreds of Miamians and followed shortly by a series of attacks on blacks. On July 2, a black minister from Coconut Grove was kidnapped by the Klan for espousing racial equality, intermarriage between whites and blacks and violence as a weapon against white oppression. The minister was released only after promising to return to the Bahamas. Blacks in Coconut Grove reacted with outrage. Believing the minister had been lynched, hundreds poured into the streets of the black section. A large group of policemen and members of the local chapter of the American Legion descended on the community and restored order. The kidnappers were never caught.[29]

Less than two weeks later, the Klan attacked another minister for preaching racial equality, this time a white one named Philip Irwin who served as pastor of a black church. He was beaten, tarred and feathered, and, after being ordered to get out of town, was thrown from a speeding car onto the street in downtown Miami. The pastor left town, thankful to be alive. No arrests were made.[30].

Two years later, a mob in the town of Homestead, south of Miami, lynched two blacks whom they were convinced had killed a United States marshal. No one was arrested.[31]

The rise of Klan influence in the early 1920s had largely been a response to efforts by blacks to move out of areas to which they were restricted by the color line, principally into Highland Park, a small white subdivision located just northwest of Colored Town. When a group of about fifty whites shot up parts of Colored Town after several black families moved into Highland Park, blacks threatened to strike back. Again, in an attempt to keep the peace, a large number of police were rushed to the scene, and only the intervention of black and white leaders averted a violent confrontation.[32]

Peace was not kept for long. On June 29, 1923, several whites hurled two bombs from a speeding car into an unoccupied black home. A crowd of 3,000 angry blacks was drawn to the scene, and the rumor spread that they were arming themselves for a raid on the nearby white community. The mayor of Miami quickly dispatched his entire police force to Colored Town, along with what was becoming a sort of auxiliary army, the American Legion. By late evening, more than 300 armed white men were patrolling Colored Town, and all streets leading into the city were closed. After several hours, most blacks returned to their homes, but the community was occupied by police for several days. The guilty parties were never apprehended.[33]

The earliest case of police officers being so much as formally charged with killing a black occurred on March 1, 1928, when a grand jury indicted three Miami police officers, Lieutenant M. A. Tibbits and detectives John Caudell and Tom Zazworth, for beating to death a man named Harry Kier three years earlier. The killing occurred after Kier's arrest for supposedly insulting a white woman in a downtown hotel. It is not known why it took nearly three years to hand down the indictments, but they came as a result of testimony from William Beechy, a white former Miami policeman. Partly because of Beechy's testimony, the grand jury denounced the policies of the Miami police as "torturous."[34] The *Miami Herald* joined in the criticism, especially of the police chief, H. Leslie Quigg, who was subsequently also indicted for the killing.

During the trial Beechy made it clear that what happened to Kier was a routine matter for blacks considered troublesome by officers. "We stripped them and beat them and ran them off," Beechy said. "We took them outside the city limits in a . . . car and fired once or twice to see how fast they could run."[35] After deliberating for three hours, the jury acquitted Quigg and the three other officers,[36] but a subsequent grand jury report on the police department led to the chief's dismissal.[37] The document cited twelve cases of police brutality, but did not distinguish between white and black victims. It maintained that the police department was dominated from within by a "well constructed organization of known strength, slowly but surely destroying the freedom of our citizens, mean and cruel, practicing habits destitute of moral or civic virtue and serving only to satisfy a malignant passion."[38] The grand jury pronounced Quigg "wholly unfit for the office of Chief of Police, because of shortcomings in the control and direction of those men in his department, his behavior as a chief executive . . . and his apparent contempt for the serious responsibilities resting under him."[39]

Quigg's replacement was Guy Reeve, who proved to be less tolerant of abusive behavior by his officers. The department dismissed an officer who beat a black during a raid staged in November 1928. And the following January the coroner's jury, for the first time, found a policeman guilty of unjustifiable homicide in the killing of a black citizen. His punishment was dismissal from the department.

It was not until 1944, however, that blacks finally persuaded the city to hire its first few black officers. They were assigned to patrol only in black areas.

The Creation of Liberty City

Living conditions in Colored Town went from bad to worse in the 1920s. As the population grew, row upon row of crowded, ramshackle houses sprung up along the district's dusty, unpaved streets. There was little or no running water and no indoor plumbing. Electricity, fast becoming commonplace in white residential areas, was practically unknown in Colored Town. Children and young adults died of tuberculosis and other contagious diseases at a high rate. Crime, primarily bootlegging, prostitution and gambling, thrived. These worsening conditions, combined with white resistance to expansion of the city's black population into white residential areas to the east and south, led to the creation of a new black district to the north and west that later became known as Liberty City.

As recorded by the Black Archives Foundation of South Florida, in 1929 the Reverend John Culmer, priest at St. Agnes' Episcopal Church, one of Miami's leading black churches then and now, became disturbed over the deaths of several of his young parishioners from tuberculosis and started a crusade to improve conditions in his community. He brought his concerns to the attention of the Greater Miami Negro Civic League, of which he was a member, and volunteered to serve as chairman of the league's fact-finding committee. In the early

1930s, his citywide campaign for better housing and sanitation for blacks won the support of the editor of the *Miami Herald,* who agreed to publish a series of columns on the unhealthy conditions in Overtown.

The *Herald*'s exposé, published September 14, 1934, brought national attention to conditions in Miami, and eventually President Franklin D. Roosevelt himself sent officials from the Works Progress Administration to visit the area. As a result, plans were layed for constructing the first federal public housing project in the southeastern United States. Consisting initially of thirty-four units, the project was erected between Northwest 62nd and 67th streets and given the name "Liberty Square."

The Liberty Square Housing Project was opened for occupancy in February 1937, with James E. Scott, a tough-minded and respected black businessman, as its first supervisor. The project, which had a long waiting list from the start, included a central community building containing a nursery school, a doctor's office and children's playground facilities—all unheard of back in Overtown. Tenants had modern kitchens and bathroom facilities, hot and cold water, gas and electricity; in Overtown, residents were still using tin wash tubs, oil lamps, wood stoves and iceboxes. It was not unusual for relatives and friends of those living in Liberty Square to visit the project and ask to take a bath in a real bathtub or to drink a glass of water containing ice cubes.

Whites who lived near the housing project, however, insisted that a wall be built on 12th Avenue from 62nd to 67th Street to separate the black neighborhood from the white. Parts of the wall can still be seen today, although the area is entirely black.

While some blacks were able to escape from their overcrowded enclave, others were still being harassed when they set out to vote in local elections. At a large rally held in May 1939, white extremists launched a campaign to discourage black participation in the approaching primary election for seats on the city commission. The *Miami Herald* vividly described the terrorism against blacks in its issue of May 3, 1939:

> The park rally, last of the primary campaign, was attended by more than 2,000 persons. It was followed by a Klan parade and lighting of more than 25 fiery crosses in the negro section—hundreds of red-lettered warning cards were spread through Miami's negro section Monday night as the Ku Klux Klan staged an automobile protest against negro voters in today's primary election. The crosses carried on a huge truck at the head of a parade of 75 cars bearing uniformed and hooded men were dropped at one-block intervals. A dummy dressed to represent a negro was suspended in a noose from a power pole. On the front of the figure a large, red-lettered sign read: "This nigger voted." . . . The hooded occupants of one automobile . . .

dangled a hangman's noose from the window of the car. . . . Warning cards thrown from the windows read: "Respectable negro citizens are not voting tomorrow. Niggers keep away from the polls." The warnings were signed in inch-high letters "KKK."[40]

The Klan campaign, however, ended up having the opposite effect of the one intended. Several black leaders, among them an activist named Sam Solomon, responded to the threats by informing city officials that Negro voters intended to challenge the Klan by going to the polls in even greater numbers than usual. In no previous election since the founding of the city had more than 50 black votes been cast. On election day in 1939, under heavy police protection led by Chief Quigg, the former terrorizer of blacks who had since been returned to power, nearly 1,000 blacks went to the polls, marking the first time in Miami's history that blacks made a concerted effort to register and vote.[41]

The voter drive succeeded despite a good deal of squabbling among black leaders over the best tactics to use against white oppression. Some leaders, most notably the Reverend Culmer, criticized Solomon for taking too much credit for the success of the drive, which had had support from a large number of whites as well as blacks, and also from the city's main newspaper. Culmer had aired his views about leadership problems in a letter he had written the year before to the editor of the widely read *New York Amsterdam News,* and again in 1940 in an article in the NAACP's *Crisis.* In his letter to the *Amsterdam News,* Culmer talked about an issue that is as alive today among Miami blacks as it was then. "Negroes," he wrote, "could receive more consideration than they do if there were more unanimity of opinion and action on their parts. Petty jealousies and leadership rivalries do more to impede this progress of Negroes than anything else."[42]

By 1950, Liberty City was a bulging community with a large proportion of middle-income blacks, including many homeowners who had moved north from Overtown to the new development. The demand for housing in the area was met in part by white developers who built tracts of cheap two- and three-story apartment buildings that today are known as the "concrete monsters" and are badly deteriorated. But movements of blacks anywhere but into black areas was still fiercely resisted. When in 1951 blacks from Overtown tried to move into an all-white area nearby called Carver Village, they were greeted by explosions of dynamite. On the evening of September 23, 1951, a hundred pounds of dynamite exploded behind an unoccupied, sixteen-unit apartment house in the northwest 6800 block of 10th Avenue in Carver Village. The blast was meant as a warning to blacks scheduled to move into the building the next week. A few days later, another bomb was placed in a mailbox in the area. Blacks began to refer to Carver Village as "Little Korea." At 3:57 a.m., Sunday, December 3, 1951, three more dynamite blasts rocked Carver Village. A crowd gathered of 400 to 500 angry blacks awakened by the blasts. The *Miami Herald* described what happened:

> Tear gas and guns were called for as most police patrol cars on duty were sent to the scene after a crowd of several hundred Negroes threatened two policemen. When two Negroes became abusive and were arrested, the crowd demanded and forced their release, the police said. . . . Police patrols were increased in the Carver Village area Sunday afternoon; additional patrols had been assigned there after the Friday explosions.[43]

Three weeks later, on Christmas night, a bomb exploded in a house in Mims, Florida, 200 miles north of Miami, killing Harry T. Moore, the state executive secretary of the NAACP. Two days later, Walter White, then national executive secretary of the NAACP, issued a statement from New York charging that Moore's death was linked to the terror bombings in Miami. Although the FBI was called in to help the newly formed Dade County Criminal Investigation Bureau and other local agencies, neither the Carver Village bombers nor Moore's killers were ever found.

The period of the 1960s civil rights movement was marked by several significant events. First was the admission of three black students to the private University of Miami in June 1961. (The city's public schools, after much resistance, had been integrated in 1959, five years after the U.S. Supreme Court desegregation ruling.) Then, in the autumn of 1962, several members of the Florida State's Rights Party, a far-right organization, were arrested, tried, convicted and jailed for their part in a series of bombings and bomb threats against supporters of integrating the county's Community Relations Board. And in June 1963, the first joint professional meeting of white and black teachers was held at Convention Hall in Miami Beach.

An event that was to have a much greater influence on black life in the city—the migration of Cubans to Miami—began in earnest in December 1965, with twice-daily "freedom flights" from Varadero, Cuba. During the first year of the flights, more than 100,000 Cuban refugees arrived in Miami, a phenomenon that was touched upon when Dr. Martin Luther King, Jr., appeared at a rally attended by more than 1,200 people in April 1966. King noted that his Southern Christian Leadership Conference had detected a good deal of racial hostility and alienation in Miami, along with growing black unrest, and he warned against the pitting of Cuban refugees against blacks in competition for jobs.[44]

The Miami Riot of 1968

The riot in Miami during the week of August 5, 1968, was similar to other major U.S. racial explosions during the general turmoil in the 1960s. (Our account is based on a report done by the Miami Study Team and submitted to the National Commission on the Causes and Prevention of Violence on January 15, 1969.) It occurred in grotesque contrast to the Republican National Convention held that week across Biscayne Bay in Miami Beach, at which Richard Nixon was nominated for his first term as president. Four people died in the disturbance, which began in the same few blocks of Liberty City's Northwest 62nd Street, near the Liberty Square Project, where the McDuffie riot began twelve years later.

Much of the racial tension that led to the riot, as pointed out in a study issued in August 1968 by the University of Miami, had been caused by the city's police force:

> The City of Miami Police Department did appear to believe that continuous forceful displays and confrontations would elicit fear and respect on the part of the black community and secure civil order.
>
> Of particular concern to blacks was the Miami Police Department's new stop-and-frisk practice, which was employed frequently with young blacks for no apparent reason except as a means of intimidation. Word spread through the black community that the police were regularly hailing black males on the street, addressing them as "boy" or "nigger" and requesting identification and disclosure of the purpose of their being where they were. Patrols with shotguns and dogs regularly entered predominantly black clubs and bars and demanded identification and purpose of their presence from all patrons.[45]

For nearly thirty years, up until 1949, the department had been run with an iron hand by Chief Quigg (with a brief time out after his temporary dismissal in the brutality case). During the 1930s he had hired dozens of whites literally off the streets of rural Georgia towns, transported them to Miami, given them badges, nightsticks and guns and without providing any training whatsoever sent them into the streets of Miami with orders to keep the peace in any manner they saw fit.

His successor was Walter Headley, a strong, hardworking police chief who carried generally unchanged into the late 1960s Quigg's style in dealing with members of minority groups. At one point late in 1967,

Headley became incensed over the level of criminal violence in Miami's black ghettos. After considering the matter for some time, he concluded that he had been too soft on crime. Accordingly, on the morning after Christmas 1967, Headley held a press conference at which he announced that the time had come for his men to get tough. From then on, he vowed, Miami's black communities would be policed by double patrols armed with shotguns and accompanied by dogs. People caught committing a felony would be shot if they attempted to escape arrest. "We don't mind being accused of police brutality; they haven't seen anything yet," the newspaper quoted him as saying to a confidant after the press conference. "They'll learn that they can't get bailed out of the morgue." In announcing his get-tough policy, Chief Headley warned against a local outbreak of rioting then rampant throughout the country. "When the looting starts," he said, "the shooting starts."[46]

As we discuss in later chapters, racial disturbances are usually preceded not only by an immediate, precipitating incident but also by events that may have happened months or even years earlier. One of these occurred the evening of February 4, 1968, when two white officers of the Miami Police Department arrested a seventeen-year-old named Robert Owens and charged him with carrying a concealed knife. On the way to the police station, the officers took Owens to a half-finished span of bridge of the new Dolphin Expressway where it crossed the Miami River at 4th Avenue. There they forced him to strip naked, then dangled him by his heels more than a hundred feet above the river. The incident was reported in the press. It was also reported that in a meeting several weeks before the Owens incident, a delegation of blacks had asked Headley to remove from his Liberty City beat one of the officers involved in the bridge incident because of conduct they regarded as antiblack. Headley was quoted in the *Herald* as telling the delegation he thought that their complaint was "silly."

In addition to problems with the police, there were complaints about the failure of the Dade County business community during the summers of 1967 and 1968 to provide jobs for black youths, despite a widely publicized promise to do so. As the tension increased, black leaders, who had been counseling their followers against violence on the basis of expected retaliatory actions by whites, began to lose their influence to militant black activists.

It was at this point that the Republicans came to Miami Beach. Although there was no direct link between the convention and the riot, the presence of the Republicans inspired black political groups in Miami such as the SCLC, the Congress of Racial Equality and the Black

Panthers to organize political rallies in the black community. The largest of these rallies was set for 1 p.m., August 7, at a community center in Liberty City. Rumor had it that the professional basketball star Wilt Chamberlain would attend.

Between 1 and 2 p.m., about thirty people, most of them teenagers, gathered at the site of the rally to see Chamberlain. Chamberlain never arrived, but several reporters, including two from television networks, were present. A few uniformed Miami police officers looked on from a parking lot south of the rally site. Unknown to the rally participants or to the Miami police, two black intelligence officers from the Dade County police also mingled in the crowd.

By 2:30, some 150 people had gathered for the rally and the crowd overflowed into the street. As the crowd grew, it became more and more restive. A few rocks were thrown at passing cars, prompting the police to call for five more squad cars and a canine unit. As the units arrived, they became the target of the crowd's hostility.

By 4 p.m., the crowd had grown considerably and had virtually taken over 62nd Street. Teenagers were now throwing bottles, rocks and other objects at passing cars. At 5 p.m., two roadblocks were set up, reducing traffic through the area. The police withdrew to reorganize. The crowd in the area continued to swell. By 7 p.m., nearly 300 people had gathered at 62nd Street and 17th Avenue.

Then came an ideal target of opportunity—a white man driving east on 62nd Street in a pickup truck decorated with a bumper sticker that read "George Wallace for President." The truck was bombarded with rocks. The driver panicked and lost control of the truck, which struck another vehicle and came to a halt. With shouts of "Get whitey!" the crowd, now a mob, swarmed over the truck, trying to get at the driver. A group of black men who had been standing in a doorway pulled him to safety inside a nearby bar, while his truck was overturned and set afire by a group of black youths. The Miami Riot of 1968 was now in full swing.

Almost immediately, other groups of black youths moved east along 62nd Street breaking into and looting white-owned businesses. Word of the disorder was spread by radio reports. These broadcasts brought hundreds of residents, primarily from nearby apartment buildings, into the riot area.

Although the vandalism and looting were started by groups of young black males aged fifteen to twenty, they were soon joined by adults, both male and female. The police had no plan for coordinated action. Regrouping at a nearby command post between 7:10 and 8 p.m., police units with sirens blaring rushed from scene to scene trying to arrest looters. Rioters merely waited for them to leave an area before moving in to resume looting. By 8 p.m., with more than 200 officers massed in the area, the police appeared to have restored order, and many people drifted away. Vandalism and looting became sporadic.

Around 8:30 or 9 p.m., however, the riot, which had all but died out, was inadvertently reignited when Miami Mayor Steve Clark and Florida Governor Claude Kirk arrived, accompanied by an entourage of assistants, security personnel and reporters. Their presence brought people back into the street. At various street corners, Mayor Clark and Governor Kirk addressed different groups, asking them to go home. But those who came out to see what was going on had already been home. Why had they been called out of their homes, only to be told to go back? A rock was thrown at a police vehicle, and an officer fired a warning shot into the air. The riot was on again.

At 9:30 p.m., various officials, including Governor Kirk, the Reverend Ralph Abernathy of the SCLC, Dade County Mayor Charles Hall and Melvin Reese, city manager of Miami, met with area residents at the headquarters of the Liberty City Community Council at 62nd Street and 13th Avenue, to discuss problems and grievances. The officials promised to send representatives to a meeting set for 11 o'clock the next morning, August 8. Black leaders then helped the police disperse the crowd.

The following day, three hours before the meeting was to begin, groups of teenagers began gathering near 13th Avenue, where the meeting the night before had been held, and threw rocks at passing vehicles. Again, traffic was rerouted by the Miami police. By 11 o'clock, the crowd in the area numbered nearly 300, but the officials had not arrived. The governor sent Macon Williams, a black member of his staff who handled matters relating to blacks and economic opportunity issues, to represent him. But council leaders considered him merely a messenger with no authority to act, and refused to confer with him.

At noon, still no other representatives or officials had appeared. The crowd, noting the absence of officials, was growing angry and the situation was deteriorating rapidly. The police, supported by fifty highway patrolmen, used a riot truck and tear gas to disperse crowds along 62nd Street. Receiving what they took to be sniper fire, they fired warning shots from shotguns and semiautomatic rifles in the air. Some of the rioters responded by throwing rocks and bottles at the police. People ran wildly for cover. When the several minutes of shooting were over, a young black child had been wounded, and two black men had been shot dead. At approximately 5 p.m., in the wake of the injuries and deaths, the governor called in 950 National Guardsmen and gave the Dade County sheriff's office overall command of antiriot operations. A 6 p.m. to 6 a.m. curfew was set for the area, and all bars and liquor stores in Liberty City were closed. Two more black men were killed by police over the next two days before order was finally restored.

The "Rotten Meat" Riot of 1970

Between June 15 and 19, 1970, in Miami's Brownsville section adjacent to Liberty City, a major racial disturbance occurred that became known among Miami's blacks as the "rotten meat" riot. The riot began with picketing by blacks of a white-owned Pic-and-Pay store, which they accused of selling spoiled products to poor blacks in the Brownsville area. Blacks had long complained about the store. They had given its owner, Fred Weller, a white former public school social studies teacher, a list of complaints that included customer dissatisfaction with the quality of the store's meat, its high prices and its extra charges for cashing any welfare or Social Security check that was over $50. Among the five black groups signing the complaint was the Black Afro Militant Movement, headed by Al Featherstone, who called himself a black revolutionary.

Picketing of the store began June 12 following an altercation between Weller and a black woman, Gladys Taylor, who was head of the Dade County Welfare Rights Organization. Taylor claimed that Weller called her "a nigger" when she complained about being charged $1.25 to cash a welfare check for $157. In an interview with the *Miami Herald* after the riot, Weller denied that he used the term "nigger": "She said, 'I'm going to put your white ass out of business,' and I told her, 'You take your black ass and go somewhere else and shop.' "[47]

After three days of peaceful picketing and an unsuccessful meeting between blacks and Weller, sheriff's deputies appeared at the store and, according to black witnesses, fired tear gas at the pickets. More black juveniles were drawn to the area and began pelting a police car with rocks and bottles. Two white motorists were pulled from their cars and beaten, their vehicles set afire. Molotov cocktails were thrown into other cars and through store windows. The rumor spread that snipers had taken up positions on roofs and in apartment windows. The police responded by sealing off the area and arresting several rioters.

On June 16, Weller's attorneys persuaded Dade Circuit Judge Henry Balaban to issue a temporary injunction forbidding picketing at the market. But the violence continued, first spilling over into Liberty City, then, the following day, into the black section of Coconut Grove.

Although the Pic-and-Pay store was guarded by police units during the rioting, some damage was done when a fire was set in the rear of the building.

Neither of the two persons shot by the police during the disorder turned out to be rioters. Lison C. Morris, the white owner of a construction company located a few blocks north of the Brownsville riot area, was shot as he and four other men watched the disturbance from the rooftop of their building. Police officers said they thought they were burglars and reported that the men had fired on officers as the police approached the building. Morris said the officers stormed in, firing at him and his friends.

An eighteen-year-old black youth, George Curtis, was shot by police in the neck and shoulder. The police accused him of being a sniper, although they never found a gun. In April 1971, Curtis was convicted by an all-white jury of assaulting police. At Curtis's trial, seven white policemen testified that Curtis was a sniper; there were no other witnesses. He was found guilty and sentenced to five years in prison.

In preparation for the trial, the youth had passed two lie-detector tests regarding the shooting, and during his appeals Dade Circuit Court Judge Alphonso Sepe let him stay free on a $1 bond. In 1975, after five years of legal proceedings, the state finally dropped the charges when a reporter for the *Miami Herald* found witnesses who testified that Curtis had not been armed and had not been in the apartment from which the police claimed he had fired at them.

Miniriots in Dade County during the 1970s

Between July 1970 and January 1979, Dade County experienced thirteen outbursts of racial violence.

July 9, 1970. One month after the "rotten meat" riot, scattered and minor rock-throwing at motorists was reported in Brownsville. The incident occurred as the county police attempted to arrest a traffic violater. According to the police report, as the young black man was being arrested he began inciting the crowd to interfere. Backup officers arrived and restored order.

February 22-24, 1971. Black youths from Coconut Grove pelted cars on West Dixie Highway in the aftermath of the police shooting of Joseph Veargis, a seventeen-year-old black who was found to be riding in a stolen car. According to the police, Veargis was shot after he pointed at them what they believed to be a pistol. It turned out be a chrome-plated tear-gas gun. Police sealed off the black area of Coconut Grove and placed sharpshooters with rifles atop key buildings in the area. This occurred after firebombs were tossed at white motorists, injuring one man seriously. The violence spilled over to Coral Gables High School, a predominantly white and Hispanic school that serves students from Coconut Grove. Police reported that twenty-five to thirty black students assaulted several white boys and three white girls.[48]

March 23, 1971. In Opa-Locka, a suburban area ten miles north of Miami, police sergeant James W. Teppenpay shot Joseph Lee Scott, a black bystander during a shootout with robbers. The next evening, an angry crowd of about 600 blacks gathered in front of a local bar. According to news reports, acting Opa-Locka City Manager William S. Griffiths, yielding to the crowd's demand that Teppenpay be suspended, told them: "You can watch me type out the suspension notice on the policeman who shot the man last night."[49] Griffiths also heard blacks call for the ouster of Opa-Locka's police chief, Herbert Chastain, and several other shouted grievances, primarily claims of mistreatment of blacks by the Opa-Locka police. Griffiths said he would take their complaints under consideration but the promise wasn't enough. That night, sniper fire, car stonings and store looting were reported. Stahl's General Store, a white-owned business, was gutted by fire. The next day, Opa-Locka officials declared a 7 p.m. to 7 a.m. curfew. Police continued to receive reports of sniper fire. The following night, two white-owned nightclubs in the black area, the Park Bar (a liquor store), and the Harlem Gardens (a deserted former nightclub) were burned. At the Park Bar, some looters used hand trucks to carry away cases of liquor.

By March 25 an uneasy truce had been established, and the Opa-Locka City Commission agreed to appoint two lawyers acceptable to blacks to investigate their complaints. Frank A. Howard, Jr., a white, and Jesse J. McCrary, Jr., a black, prepared a twenty-four-page report, which they submitted on May 10. The report criticized the Opa-Locka police for "insensitivity" but did not substantiate specific complaints of police abuse of blacks. It was also critical of the Opa-Locka city government, which Howard and McCrary accused of "playing ostrich." Black leaders were described in the report as "less than candid" when they reported to their followers that the police chief had ignored their grievances. Blacks who participated in the disturbance were also criticized for having resorted to violence.[50]

May 7, 1971. Opa-Locka was again the scene of racial trouble when the police used tear gas to break up a crowd of blacks who threw rocks at county police officers attempting to arrest a black man for speeding. The man's car was eventually stopped by a police roadblock at the corner of Ali Baba and Northwest 22nd Avenue, in the heart of black Opa-Locka. The driver had meekly surrendered, police said, but when a crowd gathered he allegedly turned and swung at two officers. Six backup officers were called in to subdue the man, who was thrown into the back seat of a cruiser. The crowd reacted by pelting the police with rocks and surging into the street, where they erected a barricade of large stones and bus benches. The crowd was eventually dispersed with tear gas.

Spokesmen for the black community appeared at city hall soon after the incident to protest the use of excessive force in the arrest of the man.

May 26, 1971. Liberty City experienced minor rock-throwing as Miami police arrested two black juveniles suspected of burglary. Two dozen police officers were called to Betty's Market, at Northwest 62nd Street and 12th Avenue, where ten youths had broken in and set a kerosene fire. Police captured two of them, and fire trucks were called to the scene. Police and firemen were pelted with rocks by some black youths who had gathered there. Other police officers arrived with police dogs. By 11 p.m., order had been restored.

December 15, 1974. Opa-Locka again experienced incidents of rock-throwing, sniper attacks and at least one major fire as blacks reacted to the arrest of two black teenagers by two black Opa-Locka police officers at a traveling carnival. According to the police, a sixteen-year-old boy was arrested after he blew marijuana smoke at Larry Houston, one of the officers. Later, a fight broke out when another officer, Raymond Owens, tried to arrest a seventeen-year-old girl who, Owens said, kicked him. The disturbance was reported to have involved several hundred people. Police Chief Stanley Eshuk said that no police officers used their guns during the disturbance. According to Eshuk, the incident was not racially motivated, since both the girl arrested and the arresting officers were black.

February 27, 1975. Once more, Opa-Locka was taken to the brink of riot when the county police attempted to arrest William Harris, who, according to police, became belligerent and refused to move on when asked to do so. Police had dispatched two units to check on a group of young men who had gathered in front of Mac's Lounge, the scene of several purse-snatchings and muggings, at Northwest 160th Street and 27th Avenue. Police reported that Harris resisted the order to move. As he was being arrested, the crowd became unruly. Other youths were arrested, but after the scene cleared about fifteen black youths moved north along 27th Avenue, where, according to the police report, they beat up and robbed two white youths who were on bicycles. The incident escalated as the gang threw rocks at motorists and smashed large plate-glass windows in a shopping center nearby. They also stole merchandise from an auto parts store. Twenty county units restored order that evening.[51]

August 3, 1977. In Goulds, a rural community in south Dade County, a traffic accident at Southwest 112th Avenue and 216th Street, across from a black apartment complex, caused a crowd to gather. At some point, a county policeman shot Kenneth Akins, a twenty-year-old black man who, police said, attacked at least three officers with a police flashlight that Akins allegedly had taken from an officer during the struggle. Police reported that as they tried to disperse the group of 100 to 200 people, rocks and bottles were thrown at them.[52]

August 15, 1978. A disturbance at the sprawling James E. Scott Housing Project in Liberty City involved county police officers and a crowd of 150. Three arrests were made, including that of a seventeen-year-old who was charged with inciting to riot. Officer Bill Turner was seriously injured when he tried to arrest a black youth for throwing a five-foot-long piece of lumber through a window, showering glass over a one-year-old child. A crowd gathered. According to the police report, officers then tried to arrest another youth, this one involved in a fight with a man in the crowd. The youth began yelling at the crowd, telling them to throw rocks at the police.

October 4, 1978. South Miami, a community five miles south of Miami, was the scene of another civil disturbance in Dade County that year. Early in the afternoon of October 4, a South Miami rookie police officer was flagged down by a twenty-five-year-old black man. According to the police report, as soon as the officer got out of the car, the man began an argument. He was arrested but broke and ran. Two other police units were called in, and the man was caught and charged with battery on a police officer, resisting arrest and encouraging a riot. The rumor spread through the black sections that the man had been abused by police officers as he was arrested. The incident touched off a rock-throwing melee that lasted several hours and injured at least seven white people. The police worked through local black leaders to dispel the rumor that the man had been abused. Order was restored about 8:30 that evening. In November 1978, Jack Present, South Miami's city manager, cleared the officers of the charge of using undue force in making the arrest.[53]

January 24, 1979. On the afternoon of January 24, two county police officers saw a thirty-five-year-old black man involved in what the officers said was a drug sale on 62nd Street in Liberty City. The man fled as the officers attempted to arrest him. After a two-block chase, they caught, subdued and handcuffed him; but the chase had drawn a crowd. The police report of the incident indicates that another black man interfered with the arrest and, after a brief chase, was also arrested. William McLeod, a black witness, told the *Miami Herald* the next day: "The police had [the first man] down on the ground, and [the other man] said, 'Hey, man, you ain't got no business kicking the man like that.' And the cop said, 'When I finish here, your ass is going to jail.' And they chased him down the street and arrested him."[54] Several Liberty City residents insisted that one of the men was clubbed and kicked repeatedly after he was handcuffed. The sight of the police chasing people back and forth angered the crowd, which was still growing. Groups of young blacks started throwing rocks at the police officers and white passers-by, and some twenty units were called in. The disturbance lasted two and a half hours. One of the officers accused of abuse in the case was Alex Marrero, who in the spring of 1980 would be named by three other police officers as the one striking the blows that killed Arthur McDuffie.

July 8, 1979. The black-run Palace Bar in Liberty City was the scene of a confrontation when the police tried to arrest two black men who had run into the crowded bar. The officers suspected them of involvement in a drug sale. According to several reports, a police officer drew his gun in the bar after catching up with one suspect. In their reports filed after the incident, the officers said they had to force their way through the crowd in the bar. As they tried to leave the bar with the man in custody, the crowd surrounded them and started punching and shoving. Other officers arrived and the police closed the bar. After the incident, Ernest Ferguson, the black owner of the bar and himself a former county policeman, maintained that police officers "have a way of creating their own problems. We were taught that in a crisis situation, you make your arrest and get out and write your report someplace else. You don't stay around, agitating people. I used to come in here all the time to check it out, and I never had any problem like this, and neither did anyone on my squad."[55]

Notes

1. Paul S. George, "Policing Miami's Black Community, 1896-1930," *Florida Historical Quarterly* 57 (1979), pp. 434-450.

2. Paul S. George, "Colored Town: Miami's Black Community, 1896-1930," *Florida Historical Quarterly* 56 (1978), p. 432.

3. T. Hollingsworth, *History of Dade County, Florida* (Coral Gables, Florida: Glade House, 1949), p. 34.

4. "The Growth of Colored Miami," *The Crisis* (New York: Crisis Publishing Co., 1942), p. 83.

5. "Policing Miami's Black Community, 1896-1930," p. 435.

6. Paul S. George, "Criminal Justice in Miami, 1896-1930" (unpublished doctoral thesis, Florida State University, 1975), p. 157.

7. Idem.

8. "Fiendish Black Brute Brings Home To Us the Question: What Shall Be Done With These Black Sons of Hell?" *Miami Metropolis,* January 23, 1903, p. 4.

9. George, "Criminal Justice in Miami, 1896-1930," p. 161.

10. Idem.

11. See Note 8.

12. George, "Criminal Justice in Miami, 1896-1930," p. 159.

13. Ibid., p. 158.

14. Ibid., p. 159.

15. George, "Policing Miami's Black Community, 1896–1930," p. 439.

16. George, "Criminal Justice in Miami, 1896-1930," p. 159.

17. Idem.

18. "Chris Savage Murdered Last Night," *Miami Metropolis,* Dec. 11, 1903, p. 1.

19. "Mass Meeting to Determine Color Line," *Miami Metropolis,* November 20, 1911, p. 1.

20. "Disfigures the City," *Miami Herald,* October 5, 1911, p. 2.

21. "Ku Klux Klan Methods Used to Make Blacks Move From a Vicinity of Ave. J and 4th," *Miami Metropolis,* August 14, 1915, p. 1; "A Record of the Darker Races," *The Crisis* 40 (New York: Crisis Publishing Company, December 1915), p. 74.

22. George, "Policing Miami's Black Community, 1896–1930," p. 436.

23. George, "Criminal Justice in Miami, 1896-1930," p. 178.

24. Ibid., p. 184.

25. Idem.

26. *Minutes of the City Council,* Miami, July 30, 1920, p. 353: "Endeavoring to Trace a Negro Who Assaulted a White Woman,"

Miami Metropolis, July 30, 1920, p. 1; "Militia is Ready for Trouble in Negro Quarter," *Miami Metropolis,* August 2, 1920, p. 1.

27. "Jury Will Investigate Attack White Woman," *Miami Herald,* August 4, 1920, p. 1.

28. "Brooks Positively Identified as Assaulter of White Woman," *Miami Herald,* August 4, 1920, p. 1.

29. "Kidnapped Negro Preacher Cause Race Riot Alarm; Bridge Guard Shoots Two," *Miami Herald,* July 2, 1921, p. 1; "Kidnapping Bares Plot to Kill Whites in Key West," *Miami Herald,* July 3, 1921, p. 1.

30. "Tar and Feather White Pastor of Negro Church," *Miami Herald,* July 18, 1921, p. 1; "Irwin Refuses to Leave Miami: Declares He Won't Be Caught Napping Next Time," *Miami Herald,* July 19, 1921, p. 1; "Rev. Irwin Goes North, Decides to Heed Threat," *Miami Herald,* July 20, 1921, p. 1.

31. "Negro Lynched Near Homestead, Killed Marshal," *Miami Herald,* June 16, 1923, p. 1; "Second Negro Lynched in Homestead Murder," *Miami Herald,* June 17, 1923, p. 2.

32. George, "Policing Miami's Black Community, 1896-1930," pp. 444-445.

33-36. Idem.

37. "Grand Jury Report Reflects on Police," *Miami Herald,* May 8, 1928, p. 2.

38. George, "Policing Miami's Black Community, 1896–1930," p. 449.

39. "Quigg Accused As Instigator of Death Ride," *Miami Herald,* April 24, 1928, p. 1.

40. "Klan Parades, Burns Crosses to Frighten Off Negro Voters," *Miami Herald,* May 3, 1939, p. 1.

41. "Record Negro Vote is Cast Under Heavy Police Guard," *Miami Herald,* May 3, 1939, p. 1.

42. Black Archives: History and Research Foundation of South Florida.

43. "New Dynamite Blasts Rock Carver Village Synagogue, Action By Police Demanded," *Miami Herald,* December 3, 1951, p. 1.

44. J. E. Buchanan, *Miami: A Chronological and Documentary History 1517-1977* (New York: Oceana, 1977), pp. 53-57.

45. "Psycho-Social Dynamics in Miami" (unpublished report, University of Miami, Center for International Studies, 1968).

46. "Police Chief No Diplomat," *Miami Herald,* December 28, 1967, p. 1B.

47. "Grocery Store Owner Ponders What Went Wrong in Ten Years," *Miami Herald,* June 21, 1970, p. 27A.

48. "Cars Stoned After Slaying of Grove Youth," *Miami Herald,* February 22, 1971, p. 1B; "Firebomb Injures Passenger in Car on U.S. 1," *Miami Herald,* February 24, 1971, p. 1B.

49. "Man Slain, Officer Shot," *Miami Herald,* March 23, 1971, p. 1B.

50. "Opa-Locka To Receive Racial Report Tonight," *Miami Herald,* May 10, 1972; "Black Exclusion Cited in Opa-Locka Report," *Miami Herald,* May 11, 1971, p. 1B.

51. "Arrests in Opa-Locka Leads to Disturbance," *Miami Herald,* February 27, 1975, p. 28.

52. "Crowd Confronts Police: Officer Wounds Man," *Miami Herald,* August 3, 1977, p. 1B.

53. "A South Miami Arrest Touches Off Rampage By Youths Against Drivers," *Miami News,* October 4, 1978, p. 3A.

54. "Blacks Stone Passersby After Arrest," *Miami Herald,* January 25, 1979, p. 3C.

55. "Opa-Locka Disturbance Quelled," *Miami Herald,* July 9, 1979, p. 1B.

Arthur McDuffie, the insurance agent whose death led to the Miami riot of May 1980 (Miami Herald Photo)

2 Prologue to the Riot

In the fifteen months preceding the 1980 riot, a series of five highly sensitive cases reinforced the belief widely held among blacks that they could never expect to get fair treatment from the criminal justice system of Dade County. The first case involved a black junior high school teacher named Nathaniel Lafleur. Shortly after 7 p.m. on February 12, 1979, five white county, or Metro, police officers on a drug raid knocked on the door of Lafleur's home at 9245 Northwest 25th Avenue. According to Lafleur, who was watching a TV news program at the time, this is what happened:[1]

At the knock on the door, he called out, "Who's there?" An unfamiliar name was given in response. Lafleur asked again "Who's there?" and again was given an unfamiliar name. He opened the door and saw several men, one of whom was dressed as a police officer and was pointing a gun at him. Lafleur slammed the door, locked it and awoke his friend, Loretha McCrary, who was sleeping on the living room couch. He ran to the bedroom, closed the door and called the emergency number 911 and reported that police were breaking into his house. The police then broke in. They pushed the woman onto the couch and said they were looking for narcotics. When McCrary told them "You've got the wrong house," a rifle was put to her face. The officers knocked out a panel in the bedroom door as Lafleur cowered beside a closet. He said the officers next threw him on a bed, kicked him in the kidney, pistol-whipped him and, as an officer held a pistol to his head, demanded to know where the drugs were. He said he was told they would blow his head off if he didn't tell them. They then threw a bucket of water over him and called him and his girl friend "niggers."

At this point, according to Lafleur's account, his twenty-year-old son, Hollis, arrived home. Hollis said he asked a plainclothesman on the porch what was going on. He was told that the police had a warrant, but when he asked to see it, an officer later identified as John Mullally pulled his wallet from his back pocket (with his badge in it), hit Hollis in the face with it and struck him in the eye with his fist. Hollis was then grabbed from behind by another officer, who was not identified, and was hit twice over the head with a flashlight.

The search of the Lafleur home lasted two and a half hours. Lafleur was charged with resisting arrest and his son with obstructing a police officer in the performance of his duties. Both were also charged with battery on a police officer. A loaded pistol was confiscated, but no drugs were found.

At 11 a.m. next day, after being treated at a hospital, Lafleur was released on a bond of $2,100. Doctors found white blood cells in his urine, indicating kidney damage. His eye was red and swollen, and he had a badly bruised knee.

As it turned out, Loretha McCrary was right. The police had raided the wrong house. Two days later Metro officers raided a house nearby at 9121 Northwest 25th Street, the one they had intended to search the first time, and confiscated half an ounce of marijuana. No arrests were made.[2]

The police account of what happened at Lafleur's house differs from Lafleur's story. According to the police, Officer James Leggett knocked on the door and told Lafleur they had a search warrant. Lafleur slammed the door on Leggett's hand, causing laceration and swelling. The police burst into the house and chased LaFleur into his bedroom. Officer Vincent P. Farina said he saw Lafleur run over and reach under the mattress of his bed, then run into a closet. The officers pulled Lafleur from the closet and handcuffed him. The officers reported that they found a loaded pistol under the mattress. The police account of Hollis Lafleur's involvement was that he refused to wait outside when asked to do so. He allegedly said, "Fuck you, man, I'm going inside," then pushed Officer Mullally aside. A struggle ensued.[3]

On February 16 four officers were suspended without pay for their part in the raid. Officer Leggett, the only officer in uniform, was not suspended.[4] At the request of E. Eilson Purdy, the director of public safety, State's Attorney Janet Reno dropped the charges against Lafleur and his son, and Purdy wrote a letter of apology to the school teacher. The department also changed its policy to one requiring that at least a sergeant or a lieutenant be present whenever search warrants were served.[5] The Dade County grand jury, however, refused to indict the officers for criminal wrongdoing.

Because of extensive press coverage of the raid and its aftermath, including numerous editorials in the *Miami Herald* and *Miami News,* as well as in the *Miami Times,* the community's leading black weekly newspaper, Lafleur's name became a household work in black and white homes throughout Dade County.

On the evening of September 2, 1979, Randy Heath, a twenty-two-year-old black man, was driving with his sister Theresa through a warehouse district in Hialeah, the county's third largest city, when, according to his sister, he stopped the car and went to urinate. As he stood next to the wall of a warehouse, he was approached by Larry Shockley, a white off-duty Hialeah police officer. With his gun drawn, Shockley ordered Heath to put his hands against the wall. Shockley later testified that he thought Heath was a burglar. In his first account of the incident, Shockley stated that Heath resisted and was shot during a struggle. During an investigation more than five months later, Shockley stated that Heath did not resist and that after placing his cocked pistol behind Heath's head, the gun accidentally went off, fatally wounding Heath.[6]

The day after the shooting, the Hialeah Police Department announced that Shockley had been suspended with pay, pending an investigation by the state attorney's office. A later investigation by a local newspaper of the Hialeah Police Department's records showed that Shockley had not been suspended. Instead, one month after the killing he was given a week's leave with pay to attend the National Police Revolver Championship in Jackson, Mississippi. Two months after the shooting, Shockley received a merit pay increase on the basis of a departmental report that noted that Shockley patroled aggressively and exhibited a high degree of initiative. Where he needed to improve, the report said, was in the "area of tactfulness."

For reasons never clarified, the state attorney required nearly five months to take the Shockley case to the Dade County grand jury, which cited Shockley for negligence in mishandling his weapon but found no evidence of criminal wrongdoing. Some blacks accused the state attorney of racism and of failing to prosecute expeditiously those cases in which blacks were victimized by whites, especially by white police officers. The state attorney denied the charges.

At 3 p.m. on January 9, 1979, an eleven-year-old black girl was walking home from school in rural Homestead, in south Dade County. Willie T. Jones, a white member of the Florida Highway Patrol, stopped her at South Dixie Highway and 312th Street. Jones told her that a girl fitting her description had stolen candy from a nearby store and ordered the child to get in the back of his car. The frightened girl complied, whereupon Jones drove her to a field, parked his cruiser and moved into the back seat with her. Under the pretense of searching her, he fondled the girl's breasts, while the girl quietly wept. She later told her uncle, with whom she was living at the time (her mother was attending college in South Carolina), that the trooper then told her to remove her panties. She said she refused and started to cry out loud. The officer withdrew his demand but proceeded to touch the child's vaginal area through her underclothing. Jones then drove the girl to a spot near her home and dropped her off.

At the time, the girl was so distraught that she told her uncle and aunt only that a policeman had picked her up and accused her of stealing. That evening, however, she told them the whole story, including the words she remembered the policeman saying before he drove off: "We're still friends, aren't we?" Her uncle called the Highway Patrol office to report the incident, and an investigator was sent to his home a few hours later.

The girl remembered a "Thank you for not smoking" sign posted in the car and the trooper's name tag. His last name, she thought, was "Jones." The investigator showed her photographs of several troopers, including one of patrolman Willie T. Jones, whom the girl readily identified as the patrolman who had picked her up.

After more than three weeks of investigation, during which he failed a lie-detector test regarding the incident, Jones was arrested and charged with lewd and lascivious assault on a child. He was allowed to resign from the patrol the same day, although before the precise time of his arrest. Thus the record would show that he had resigned because of "personal problems" and that he was "unemployed" when arrested. At his arraignment he was not required to post bond and was released in his own custody.

The girl's relatives said they were advised by their attorney, Otis Wallace, a black, to keep quiet about the case to protect the child and because he might eventually file a civil suit against the state on their behalf. Publicity, they said he told them, could damage their case. For various reasons, among them to save the child from embarrassment, the Dade attorney's office, the Florida Highway Patrol and, of course, Jones's attorney also kept quiet about the incident. Their silence, however, helped create the later perception among blacks that there had been a conspiracy to suppress publicity.

The state requested that as punishment the trooper be required to seek psychological counseling and that he pay for such help for the child. No jail time was asked for. The girl's uncle agreed to the arrangement. But Dade Circuit Judge Jon Gordon, to whom the case was assigned, was uncomfortable with the case. He viewed it as an arrangement between the state attorney's office and the defense attorney to go easy on Jones and wondered out loud, in open court, whether the matter would have been handled differently if the victim had been white and the offending officer black. He said the case smacked of racism and removed himself from it, whereupon it was turned over to Judge David Levy.

On August 9, 1979, seven months after the incident, Trooper Jones pleaded nolo contendere to the charges and was given three years probation. He was told by the court that he could never work again as a police officer, had to undergo psychiatric care and had to pay for any psychiatric care the girl might require. Less than four months after the trial, Jones, who was married and the father of two children, was pronounced no longer in need of the care—although Jones's doctor had stated that Jones was a borderline psychotic who was suspected of previous similar offenses. Jones made only two monthly payments for the girl's psychiatric treatment. Then living with her mother in South Carolina, she was described by her mother as withdrawn and suffering from frequent nightmares. It was only after the trooper had become delinquent in payments for the child's counseling that the family decided to make the story public.

When the case was reopened as a result of the publicity, Jones contended before Judge Levy that he had made, or attempted to make, the payments for the child's psychiatric care but that the payment procedures—which required paying the money through the state—were cumbersome and slowed the arrival of the money. Under severe criticism from blacks, now that the whole arrangement had been given publicity, Judge Levy and the state attorney explained that they had agreed to the sentence because the girl's family had agreed to it, pointing out that the girl's uncle himself had wanted Jones to receive treatment rather than punishment. Through Jones's lawyer, the judge ordered Jones to resume the payments and to make the ones that were overdue.

In July 1980, Jones was indicted by a federal grand jury on charges of illegally arresting and sexually abusing the girl, both of which were contended to be violations of her civil rights. Before Jones could be arrested, however, he left the county and has not been heard from since.[7]

Dr. Johnny L. Jones was Dade County's first black public school superintendent. As head of the nation's fifth largest school district, he was a suave, intelligent administrator. He had fought his way up through the ranks, and seemed to many of Miami's blacks to represent the ultimate in black success stories.

In February 1980, Jones was charged with attempting to steal nearly $9,000 in gold-plated plumbing fixtures for a vacation home he was building in Naples, Florida. He vehemently denied the charges, and his many supporters in the black community became convinced that a special effort was being made to destroy Jones because of his race. In one of its editorials, the black-owned *Miami Times* reflected the view of a significant segment of Dade County's black community:

The local media has had a field day for the past week lambasting

Dade School Superintendent Johnny Jones in what we see as an unfair attack upon his integrity. The man has been indicted, tried and made to appear guilty of some wrongdoing even though the inferences and implications have thus far failed to pinpoint any misconduct on the part of the school system's chief administrator.

Fortunately, Dr. Jones is no stranger to attacks by the media. . . . Being thick-skinned . . . is an occupational necessity. But we are forced to ask why should it be any more the necessity for him than for any other public official?[8]

On February 23, 1980, in a rare Saturday session, the Dade County grand jury met and indicted Jones. The next day, in an equally unusual Sunday session, the Dade County school board met and with one dissenting vote (from Joyce Knox, the only black on the school board) voted to suspend him.

When the case went to trial, the prosecutors for the state attorney's office used their peremptory challenges to remove all potential black jurors and on April 22 succeeded in seating an all-white panel to hear the case. Anger grew in the black community, many members of which saw the systematic removal of black jurors as inherently racist and as further evidence of the state attorney's antiblack stance. Close attention to the trial was assured by the fact that complete videotapes of the proceedings were televised nightly throughout Dade County on the community's public television station. It made for spellbinding viewing for the thousands of Dade citizens, including many schoolchildren, who followed the story. On April 30, 1980, less than three weeks before the McDuffie riot, Jones was found guilty of second-degree grand theft and was sentenced to three years in prison.

The fall of Jones brought shock, disappointment and turmoil to the black community. This letter to the editor of the *Miami Times*, published just nine days before the riot, was typical:

I cannot recall that in Dade County there has ever been a white person on trial with an all-black jury. . . . The system of justice is . . . a paradox. To a certain extent, the law applies to people of means more than to those without. In a case like Jones, though he is well-fixed, the color issue still comes out.[9]

While all these cases were in various stages of development and were constantly in the public eye, the most volatile case of all was moving through the criminal justice system. It involved several white police officers from the Dade County Public Safety Department, or PSD, and a black man named Arthur McDuffie.

McDuffie's Death

At 5 p.m., Sunday, December 16, 1979, Arthur McDuffie, a divorced, thirty-three-year-old black insurance agent and the father of two small children, left the house in northwest Dade County where he lived with his sister, Dorothy. He was riding a 1973 black and orange Kawasaki 900 motorcycle that he had borrowed from his cousin, George Randolph. He was on his way to the home of Lynwood Blackman, a friend for the past ten years, who lived at 59th Street and North Miami Avenue. McDuffie had promised to tune the engine of a car belonging to a neighbor of Blackman's, but when McDuffie arrived shortly before 5:30 he found he did not have the right tools. McDuffie sat on his cycle, talking to Blackman's two daughters, aged eight and seven. When Blackman came outside at 5:30, he saw McDuffie heading west on Northwest 59th Street.[11] McDuffie then went to visit a female friend for several hours, possibly until as late as 1 a.m. Following this he got on his motorcycle and headed north in the general direction of his sister's home. He never made it.

At 1:15 on the morning of December 17, McDuffie was seen by a white PSD police officer, Sergeant Ira Diggs, heading north along North Miami Avenue. After only slowing at a red light, according to the police, he "popped a wheelie," a stunt in which the cyclist pulls up his front wheel and takes off, then "gave the finger" to the police car parked nearby and raced away. Sergeant Diggs gave chase. Exactly why McDuffie tried to flee, nobody really knows. One theory is that he did so because his driver's license had been revoked. But why, then, would he have attracted Diggs's attention with an obscene gesture? Whatever his motivation, McDuffie was soon being pursued by more than a dozen police cars in a chase that lasted eight minutes and at some points exceeded 100 miles an hour. He finally stopped at the corner of North Miami Avenue and 38th Street as police units swarmed in. The first units to arrive were those of Officers Mark Mier and Charles Veverka, followed closely by William Hanlon and Sergeant Diggs. Mier drew his service revolver, aimed it at McDuffie and ordered him to freeze while Veverka approached McDuffie and grabbed him by the shoulder, pulling him off the motorcycle. Veverka later claimed that at this point McDuffie turned around and, with his right fist, swung at and grazed him.

Additional units continued to arrive, including some from the Miami Police Department. The City of Miami officers present were Sergeant Wayne English and Officers John G. Gerant, Alexander Prince and Richard Gotowala. All the officers on the scene were white.

McDuffie next was violently set upon by no fewer than six and possibly as many as a dozen PSD officers. According to George Yoss, an assistant state attorney who prosecuted the case, McDuffie managed to fight back in the beginning as Veverka held him in a bear hug; but then he was pulled away from Veverka by other officers engaged in the melee. And in three minutes, it was all over: McDuffie lay immobile, his head split open and his brain swelling uncontrollably.[12] He died four days later.

The Coverup

Immediately after the incident, a rescue unit was called and police headquarters was advised that the man involved in the arrest had suffered head injuries. McDuffie, already slipping into a coma, was taken to Jackson Memorial Hospital.

Officer William Hanlon, who later became a key witness for the state, called in to the PSD's Liberty City headquarters with the first version of the incident. Over the radio, he told a lieutenant that McDuffie had been injured falling off his motorcycle. In their attempt to conceal the facts, Hanlon and several other PSD officers tried to make it appear that McDuffie had lost control of his motorcycle when trying to turn a corner, that he was thrown from the motorcycle, lost his helmet and struck his head on the curb. Officer William Hanlon admitted later that he kicked McDuffie's motorcycle, stepped on McDuffie's glasses and placed McDuffie's watch on the road and shot at it with a spare revolver which he kept strapped to his ankle. He committed the last act, he said at the trial, for no other reason than "pure vandalism." (A marked patrol car also ran over the motorcycle to make it look as if it had been damaged in an accident. Officers used their nightsticks to break all the glass gauges on the motorcycle as well, an act that, although designed to hide their crime, ended up being incriminating. The medical examiner and other investigators who inspected the motorcycle wondered how an accident in which a cycle fell on one side or the other would result in breaking the glass on both sides.)

At 4:58 a.m., headquarters ordered Officer Robert Hinman to conduct a routine investigation of the "accident scene." When Hinman arrived he found that the scene had been cleaned up, or "destroyed," in police jargon.

> *Hinman (over the radio to headquarters):* There's no way I can investigate it if the scene has been destroyed. The—I can respond

to the emergency room and sit and hold the guy's hand; but there's nothing else I can do with it.
Headquarters: Why did they tow all the stuff so quick?
Hinman: I have no idea.[13]

At 5:30 a.m., with growing concern among the officers involved that the accident version might not hold up, Sergeant Evans radioed headquarters that McDuffie had, in fact, been beaten with heavy eighteen-inch police flashlights known as Kelites.

Evans: That guy last night?
Headquarters: Yeah?
Evans: He was hit with Kelites.
Headquarters: He was hit with Kelites?
Evans: Uh-hmm.
Headquarters: Oh, shit.[14]

The Investigation

Whenever it is necessary to use force, Dade County police officers must file a routine "Use of Force Report" to their senior officers. In December 1979, the senior officer in charge of the PSD headquarters in Liberty City was Commander Dale Bowlin. The report written by Sergeant Evans on the McDuffie beating reached Bowlin at midmorning on the 17th. The inconsistencies made him suspicious. "We discussed the reports," he said in an interview published in the *Miami Herald* on December 30. "That same day, in the afternoon and throughout the day, we questioned the officers about the accuracy of the reports. We were not satisfied."[15]

He wasn't the only one. The county medical examiner, Dr. Ronald Wright, who was brought in on the case after McDuffie's death, also had his doubts. He did not believe the extensive injuries to McDuffie's head could have been caused by a fall from a motorcycle. McDuffie appeared to have been beaten to death with a galvanized pipe, nightstick, or heavy-duty Kelite. Wright began to work closely with Commander Bowlin, with Bowlin's boss, Major Willie Morrison, a black, and with the department's Internal Review Section, which is charged with looking into police misconduct cases. Their suspicions increased on December 18, after Internal Review had talked to City of Miami officers who were on the scene but not involved in the incident. Interviews with these officers convinced Bowlin and the others that Mc-

Duffie had been severely beaten. At this point, Internal Review notified the state attorney of the case.

On December 24, the first article about the inconsistencies in the reports of McDuffie's death appeared in the *Miami Herald*.[16] On December 26, Officer Charles Veverka became the first broken link in the chain of conspiracy. As he later told a newspaper reporter, he was at home on Christmas Eve with his children, thinking about McDuffie's three children who would face their first Christmas without their father; he decided to turn himself in. Veverka went to police headquarters with his father, a PSD lieutenant, and told his superiors what he knew of the beating. Those present, in addition to Veverka and his father, were Captain Marshall Frank, Captain Frank's immediate superior, Major Willie Morrison; and Hank Adorno and George Yoss, both from the state attorney's office, who prosecuted the case. "We all realized at that point that there was a major police coverup," Yoss said later in an interview. "We knew at that point that it was a high-visibility case."[17]

After hearing of Veverka's account, PSD director Bobby Jones announced to the press that four police officers had been suspended in connection with the death of Arthur McDuffie. Two days later, five more officers were suspended. The nine were Ira Diggs, Michael Watts, William Hanlon, Alex Marrero, Herbert Evans, Jr., Mark Mier, Charles Veverka, Joseph Del Toro and Eric Seyman. "They beat my son like a dog," Eula McDuffie, Arthur McDuffie's mother, was quoted as saying in the *Miami Herald*. "They beat him just because he was riding a motorcycle and because he was black."[18]

On December 28, State Attorney Janet Reno announced that four of the suspended officers—Marrero, Diggs, Watts and Hanlon—had been charged with manslaughter and tampering with evidence. A fifth, Sergeant Evans, was charged with tampering with evidence and leading the coverup.

The Trial

McDuffie was buried on December 29 wearing his full-dress corporal's uniform of the U.S. Marine Corps. The highly emotional funeral—including television images of McDuffie's flag-draped casket, his grief-stricken mother, former wife and eight-year-old daughter—was broadcast that evening. The next day, a gripping close-up picture of McDuffie's mother was carried on the front page of the local section of the *Miami Herald*.

When it was announced that the police officers were being charged only with manslaughter instead of murder, the black newspapers and radio stations ran angry commentaries accusing Janet Reno of being a racist and calling for her resignation. In response, she argued that the facts of the case did not warrant filing murder charges and invited anyone with additional evidence to support more serious charges to come forward. No one did.

On January 1, 1980, however, the state attorney announced that suspended officers Charles Veverka and Mark Mier had been granted immunity and would testify as witnesses for the state. And the following day, with Veverka and Mier now apparently willing to say that Alex Marrero struck the blows that caused McDuffie's death, and with Hanlon saying that McDuffie was handcuffed when Marrero struck him, Reno announced that the charge against Marrero would be raised to second-degree murder. "We increased the charges," says Assistant State Attorney Yoss, "not because of pressure from the black community, which was commonly held to be the reason, but because we now had evidence that Marrero acted in a way that was 'eminently dangerous to another, evincing a depraved mind regardless of human life,' which is second-degree murder."[19]

Reno assigned the case to Adorno, her most experienced prosecutor, who would head a team of what she considered to be her best assistant state attorneys. The state also decided to try all the officers at once instead of independently, a move that drew considerable criticism after the trial.

On January 3, two dozen blacks, joined by a handful of whites, marched in protest of the McDuffie killing in front of the county's Criminal Justice building. They carried signs reading "Justice for McDuffie" and "Right the Unrightable Wrong." A story about the killing and the demonstration was carried in *Newsweek*. The case was now beginning steadily to attract national attention. And local coverage was so intensive that defense attorneys for the officers asked on February 29 that the trial be moved out of Dade County, arguing that it was now impossible for the officers to receive a fair trial. On March 3, Judge Lenore Nesbitt agreed and ordered the case moved to Tampa. "The case is a time bomb," she said. "I don't want to see it go off in my courtroom or in this community."[20]

Blacks in Miami, however, feared that if the trial were moved from the county there would be a greater chance that the officers would be found not guilty. The Tampa branch of the NAACP pointed out that only a few months earlier there had been a strikingly similar case in which a white Tampa police officer had been acquitted by an all-white jury of fatally beating a young black motorcyclist stopped for a routine traffic violation.

On March 28 Judge Nesbitt dismissed the two felony charges against William Hanlon, on the grounds that the state lacked the evidence to proceed against him. The state attorney's office then dropped its lesser charges against Hanlon, provided him immunity from further prosecution and announced that he would testify as a witness for the state, along with officers Veverka and Mier.

The trial began March 31, and immediately the team of defense lawyers began using their thirty-four peremptory challenges to remove blacks from the six-person jury. "We wanted a black on that jury as badly as they didn't want one," said Yoss. "We knew how many blacks were in the group of potential jurors waiting to be called in. We would send someone down to the room to look. By about the third week of jury selection we realized that they had enough challenges left to bump all the blacks waiting to be called. Realizing we were going to have an all-white jury we tried to get the best six we could."[21]

In the early stages of the trial, the state called to the stand Dr. Ronald Wright, the medical examiner for Dade County, who graphically described the force used to inflict McDuffie's fatal injuries:

> *Prosecutor:* Would you describe to the members of the jury, as best you can, what amount of force would be necessary to cause that particular fracture, the one between the eyes?
> *Wright:* It's the equivalent of falling from a four-story building and landing head first.
> *Prosecutor:* On what?
> *Wright:* On concrete.[22]

From the medical examiner's testimony, it became clear that when McDuffie's skull was fractured, he was lying face down with his head against the pavement. There was no possibility of his head recoiling from the blows—thus the extreme severity of the fractures. He was also handcuffed at the time.

The state then brought forth its key witnesses, the immunized police officers. The first was Charles Veverka. Veverka admitted to pulling McDuffie from his motorcycle and exchanging punches with him. He said, however, that as he struggled with McDuffie, within seconds, other officers, including Sergeants Diggs and Marrero, literally snatched McDuffie from him and proceeded to beat him violently with nightsticks and Kel-lites. Veverka described for the jury how Marrero battered McDuffie while he lay helpless on the pavement.

> *Prosecutor:* What did Officer Marrero say?
> *Veverka:* The words I heard were, "Easy. One at a time."

Prosecutor: What did Marrero do?
Veverka: I observed him, with either a Kelite or a nightstick, holding it with both hands and bringing it over his head and come down twice across the top back area of Mr. McDuffie's head.[23]

The prosecutor asked Veverka to demonstrate to the jury the way he saw Marrero strike McDuffie.

Veverka [demonstrating]: I observed him straddle Mr. McDuffie in this manner, Kelite or nightstick, whichever it was, holding it with both hands, bring it back over his head and come down on the side or the back of the top area of his head.
Prosecutor: How hard did he hit him?
Veverka: Oh, extremely hard.[24]

In demonstrating the way he said he saw Marrero strike McDuffie, Veverka said Marrero's blows came down on McDuffie in a chopping motion, as one would swing an axe to chop a log in two.

Veverka: I was standing approximately four or five feet east of Mr. McDuffie and Marrero. I got splattered with blood.[25]

Parts of Veverka's testimony, including his graphic demonstration of the beating, were carried on the evening television news programs in Miami.

The questioning then turned to the coverup. Veverka implicated Sergeant Evans, saying that Evans was the leader in the attempt.

Prosecutor: What happened next?
Veverka: I heard Sergeant Evans say something. These words are not exact, but as best I can recall, it was, "The bike needs more damage." And he looked at Hanlon and said: "Go get in the car and ride up on it."
Prosecutor: What, if anything, did you observe or hear?
Veverka: That would be a crashing sound. When I heard the sound, I looked up. I saw a . . . police unit sitting on top of the motorcycle.[26]

Veverka next testified that Sergeant Evans advised him to write up the incident, making it appear that McDuffie had injured himself in a fall from the motorcycle before he was touched by the officers at the scene. Veverka testified that he complied. Under cross-examination by defense attorneys, Veverka admitted that he submitted several

false reports of the incident and that he had lied to the police investigators in the coverup attempt.

The major tactic in the defense was to raise questions in the jury's
mind about the credibility of the immunized officers, and to have it
appear that the officers were lying to conceal their own involvement
in the incident. Indeed, the defense accused Veverka and Hanlon of
striking the blows that actually killed McDuffie. And as the trial proceeded it became increasingly difficult for the jury to discern who, in
fact, did what in the two or three minutes of the beating.

After getting Veverka to admit that he had lied in his initial report,
a defense attorney asked him if he felt that it had been all right to lie.

> *Defense attorney:* My question is, do you feel that as far as lying
> in that statement, it makes no difference as far as you're con-
> cerned, because they couldn't use that statement against you?
> *Veverka:* My belief at that time was that the statement couldn't be
> used against me to—
> *Defense:* All right, and therefore you felt it would be all right to
> lie under oath, didn't you?
> *Veverka:* I didn't necessarily think it would be all right. I know I
> did lie under oath, yes.[27]

Following Veverka, another immunized officer, Mark Mier, took
the stand. With Mier's testimony, the state's case was jolted in that he
contradicted Veverka on two keypoints.

First, Mier testified that on his arrival at the scene, apparently
within moments of the arrival of Diggs and Veverka, he pointed his
service revolver at McDuffie and ordered him to "freeze." Looking
down the barrel of his gun at McDuffie, thus having a clear view of
McDuffie's actions, Mier testified that he saw no punches thrown by
McDuffie at Veverka. The jury was left to decide for themselves whether
Veverka was lying about the punch in order to make it appear acceptable that he, too, struck McDuffie.

Mier testified that he too saw Marrero straddle McDuffie and
strike him with his Kelite or nightstick. But Mier contradicted Veverka in his description of the way in which Marrero struck the blows.
Mier said that they came not in a chopping, overhead fashion, as Veverka had testified, but in a side-to-side fashion, from right to left. Mier
demonstrated this to the jury, which now had to decide which, if either,
of the two versions they would believe.

As they had done with Veverka, the defense attorneys attacked
Mier's credibility on the grounds that he, too, had at first participated
in the coverup.

Defense attorney (to Mier): Would you tell me . . . is there some way that the members of this jury, or anyone in this courtroom, can tell when you mean it and when you don't mean it, when you swear to tell the truth, so help you God? I mean, is there a little smile on your lip, or are your ears turning red, or is there some way we can tell when you're telling the truth and when you're not? *Mier:* No, sir.[28]

Next, the state called John Gerant, a police officer with the Miami Police Department, who had been present the night McDuffie was attacked but who was not accused of any wrongdoing. Gerant's testimony was crucially important because he was not an immunized witness. Unlike Veverka, who admitted hitting McDuffie, and Mier, who helped in the coverup, Gerant might be presumed to have nothing to hide regarding his own actions that night.

In his initial testimony, Gerant supported Veverka's account of the way the fatal blows were dealt to McDuffie. He said the man who struck McDuffie hit him in a chopping overhead fashion, as Veverka had testified. Gerant, however, seriously damaged the state's case— and shocked the courtroom—by not pointing to Marrero as the man who dealt the blow. He pointed instead to another defendant, Michael Watts.

As chief prosecutor Hank Adorno explained after the trial in an interview with *CBS Reports,* the state's whole case suffered severely from the Rashomon syndrome—the tendency of eyewitnesses to see things from different perspectives and angles and at different times. "The Watts beating occurred at the beginning, before Marrero ever got there; the Marrero beating occurred later on," Adorno said. "I think, any time that you're trying a case . . . based solely on eyewitness recollection of an event, you're . . . going to have three people looking at the same things and seeing different things. And that's what I had to get across to the jury. That doesn't mean . . . it didn't happen; it means that they're looking at it from different [viewpoints]."[29]

In addition to the conflicting testimony from immunized witnesses, another issue to be considered by the jury was the character and possible culpability of the state's key witnesses. Were they any better or worse than the officers against whom they were testifying? In no instance was this issue more straightforwardly presented than in the testimony of William Hanlon.

Judge Nesbitt had granted Hanlon a directed verdict of acquittal of the felony charges against him three days before his testimony against the other officers began. The state immunized him and forced him to take the stand. Hanlon became the third officer to accuse Marrero of

striking the fatal blows. Under pressure from a defense attorney, however, he indicated that he himself was not beyond thoughts of brutality
that night. He described the casual nature in which he suggested to
several officers how McDuffie's legs could be broken. At the time,
McDuffie was lying on the ground—bleeding, unconscious and handcuffed. Hanlon said: "I walked over and I made an off-the-cuff remark.
I said—I had the nightstick with me—I said, 'If you wanted to break
somebody's legs, you could hit him here; you'd probably break
them.' "[30]

Edward Carhart, a defense attorney, told *CBS Reports* after the
trial that this was about the most chilling thing he heard a witness
testify to in a courtroom: "You have a man lying there handcuffed,
semiconscious, and Mr. Hanlon says it popped into his mind, 'You
could break a man's legs if you wanted to.' And he walked over to
demonstrate how it could be done. I find that an incredible thought
process."[31]

In the defense stage of the trial, Diggs and Marrero were called
to testify. Diggs denied hitting McDuffie, but it was Marrero's testimony that added a new element to the trial. Marrero admitted to
struggling with McDuffie, including striking him several times. Marrero
said, however, that he did it because McDuffie was trying to take his
gun away from him:

> *Marrero:* I had the nightstick here. Immediately, a matter of less
> than a second, I lunged at the man. I went like this and tried to
> get him, throw him to the ground.
> *Defense attorney:* Did you know where his hands were?
> *Marrero:* This hand goes right for my gun here.
> *Defense attorney:* Indicating the left hand to the right hip.
> *Marrero:* He grabbed my gun. He didn't touch it, he grabbed it.
> *Defense attorney:* What did you do?
> *Marrero:* I said something to myself.
> *Defense attorney:* What did you say?
> *Marrero:* As I felt that hand on my gun, I said, "Oh, shit!" I went
> back like that and struck the man somewhere in the area around
> him [indicating the right shoulder with his nightstick].[32]

Marrero went on to tell the jury that McDuffie tried again to grab his
gun.

> *Marrero:* It was at this point, as I was holding him here, that we
> both fell to the ground and went down very hard. My elbow was
> giving me tremendous pain. I kind of let loose of the man. He tried

to get up. As he did that, he went again for my gun and he grabbed it the same way he did last time. I went back and I struck him again as hard as I could, and I hit him somewhere—
Defense attorney: Where did you hit him?
Marrero: Somewhere in this area here.
Defense attorney: Indicating somewhere between the forehead and the—
Marrero: And the mouth.
Defense attorney: Okay. But you hit him as hard as you could?
Marrero: Yes, sir.[33]

News reports of Marrero's testimony claiming that McDuffie went for his gun reached a skeptical black community in Miami. Marrero, the only one of the officers to be charged with second-degree murder, was also the only one who claimed that McDuffie tried to reach for a policeman's gun. Testimony from several other officers, including John Gerant, who was not involved, indicated that McDuffie offered no resistance. Members of McDuffie's family, including his mother and brother, also insisted that McDuffie was not the sort to fight policemen.

At 11:52 a.m. on Saturday, May 17, after almost four weeks of testimony, the case went to the jury. In Miami it was a clear spring morning, with temperatures in the mid-seventies. Through news reports, people knew that the case had gone to the jury. After such a long, complicated trial, it seemed doubtful that a verdict would be returned very quickly. Yet, after just two hours and forty-five minutes of deliberation, the jury returned to the courtroom. Radio and television reporters waited to relay the news to Miami. The court clerk read the verdicts:

> We, the jury at Tampa, Hillsborough County, this 17th day of May, 1980, find the defendant, Michael Watts, as to count three of the information, manslaughter by unnecessary killing, not guilty.
> We, the jury . . . find the defendant, Herbert Evans, Jr., as to tampering with or fabricating physical evidence as charged in count five of the information, not guilty. We, the jury . . . find the defendant, Ira Diggs, as to count three of the information, tampering with or fabricating physical evidence, not guilty. We, the jury . . . find the defendant, Alex Marrero, as to count one of the information, second-degree murder, not guilty.[34]

Notes

1. "His Skull Cracked as Police Raid Wrong House," *Miami Herald,* February 14, 1979, p. 1A.

2. "Right Raid But No Arrest," *Miami Herald,* February 15, 1979, p. 1C.

3. See Note 1.

4. "Four Suspended for Raiding Wrong Home," *Miami Herald,* February 17, 1979, pp. 1B-2B.

5. Purdy Called on Carpet in Wrong House Raid," *Miami Herald,* February 16, 1979, p. 2B.

6. "Grand Jury Will Probe Slaying By Hialeah Cop," *Miami Herald,* March 3, 1980, p. 1C.

7. "Florida Highway Patrol Trooper Molested Girl; He's Cured Before His Victim," *Miami Herald,* January 21, 1980, pp. 1A, 16A.

8. "Assassination By Innuendo," *Miami Times,* February 14, 1980, p. 4.

9. "Community Reacts to Jones Verdict," *Miami Times,* February 14, 1980, p. 4.

10. "Cops Role in Death Probed," *Miami Herald,* December 24, 1979, p. 1B.

11. Interview with George Yoss, Dade County Assistant State Attorney, April 14, 1983.

12. "Cyclists's Death Termed a Murder," *Miami Herald,* December 27, 1979, p. 1B.

13. "Miami: The Trial that Sparked City Riots," *CBS Reports,* August 27, 1980.

14. Idem.

15. See Note 11.

16. See Note 12.

17. See Note 11.

18. See Note 12.

19. See Note 11.

20. "Trial Moved to Tampa," *Miami Herald,* March 3, 1980, p. 1B.

21-30. See Note 13.

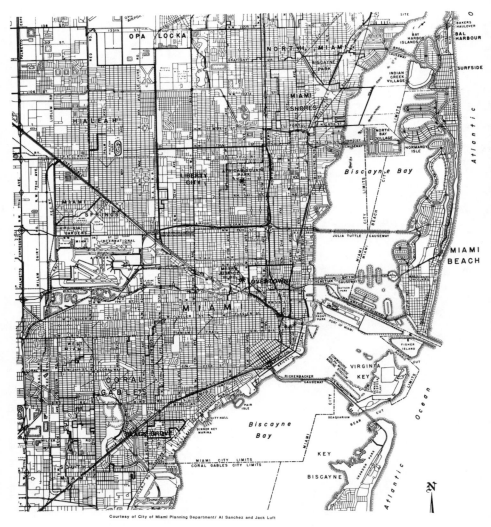

MAP OF MIAMI Liberty City is the squared-off area in the north central part of the map; African Square Park, near the scene of the first killings, is located along 62nd Street in the eastern section of Liberty City; Overtown sits just north of downtown Miami, southeast of Liberty City; the Metro Justice complex is located just to the west of Overtown; the black section of Coconut Grove lies near the southern boundary of the city.

3 The Riot

. . . the general core-area clientele were inflamed and violent.
—From the After-Action
Report of the Dade County
Public Safety Department

It took thirteen minutes for the clerk to read all the verdicts, and although the judge had warned against outbursts in his courtroom, the reading was followed by screams and weeping. The chief defendant, Alex Marrero, who had faced a second-degree murder charge, broke into tears over his acquittal and had to support himself by leaning on a wall. Frederica McDuffie, Arthur McDuffie's ex-wife, who had planned to remarry him before he was beaten to death, led McDuffie's sobbing mother, Eula, through the crush of reporters. "My son, my son," she cried out. "They're guilty, . . . they're guilty in God's sight and they have to live with this."[1]

At 2:42 p.m. that May 17, the news went out over the Associated Press wire, and most Miami radio stations interrupted their regular programming to report the verdicts. Several minutes later WEDR, a disco-music radio station popular among young blacks, began to receive so many angry and hysterical phone calls that Clyde McDonald, the afternoon deejay who goes by the name of "Iceman," became alarmed and called station manager Jerry Rushin at home to ask what he should do. Rushin told McDonald to put him on the air from his house. "I knew all hell was going to break loose because of this," Rushin says. "I thought if I could get them thinking about something else, it might ease things."* In his broadcast, Rushin proposed that the city's black leaders meet on Monday morning with State Attorney Janet Reno "to get some answers."

Many Miamians, whites as well as blacks, were shocked by the acquittals. But for blacks, the trial had a significance that went beyond the McDuffie case itself. It represented the truest, most damning test of the entire legal system—the system they had so often been counseled was their best hope for achieving equal treatment in American

---

*Unless otherwise noted, all quotations in this and subsequent chapters came from the authors' interviews.

society. For them the gray areas of the case—the contradictory testimony, the credibility of the police witnesses, the way the prosecution had been conducted—had little meaning compared to the unendurable fact that a number of white policemen had beaten to death a black insurance man for what amounted to a traffic violation and that not one of them had gotten so much as a slap on the wrist from the courts.

"For outsiders, I think, it would be impossible to appreciate the shock that went through the black community," said Major Clarence Dickson, the highest-ranking black in the Miami Police Department. "I think it is safe to say that you'd almost *have* to be black to understand. All their grievances, all their distrust of the system, all the beliefs people had in the evil of the system, all they had thought was wrong. Suddenly, it all turned out to be true."

That afternoon, Dade County's two top police officials, Chief Kenneth Harms of the Miami Police Department (MPD) and Director Bobby Jones of the Dade County Public Safety Department (PSD), addressed a community rally at Liberty City's African Square Park. The event was unrelated to the trial and was attended by about eighty black community residents concerned about a rise in street crime. The park (see map)[2], which contains two basketball hoops, a children's playground and cement checkers tables used mostly by older men, was built on the site of the 1968 Miami riot on 62nd Street between 12th and 14th avenues. Sixty-second is a broad avenue that had been renamed Martin Luther King Boulevard and was supposed to have been spruced up with plantings and other amenities, although nothing had been done beyond adding several concrete bus shelters. Flanked by cinderblock bars, pool halls, mom-and-pop grocery stores and one-and-two-story public-housing projects, 62nd Street today looks like any other ghetto main drag in the city. Although the area is completely black, the street serves whites, too, as the principal east-west access to I-95, Miami's major north-south highway. Whites also drive into the area on weekend nights looking for cocaine and marijuana, which are sold openly on street corners near African Square Park.

The two police chiefs, who were informed about the McDuffie verdict during the rally, left the area at about 3:30 p.m. A black plain-clothes MPD detective, Sergeant Edward Burke, was assigned to stay around the park to see if he could detect any serious trouble brewing as a result of the acquittal. He could not. "From the way people were reacting, you could tell they were angry and that they might do something," he said. "But I didn't think it would happen that quick—or that big."

Back at WEDR, about two miles away, the Iceman's line was now solidly clogged with angry phone calls. "People were saying they didn't want to wait until Monday morning to do something," Rushin says. By 3:45 p.m., 300 to 400 people were milling around outside the station, talking animatedly about the verdict and shouting out their rage. "They were saying that the white jury had let off those white cops, that they wouldn't take it anymore and they wanted to do something," he says. "Whenever something like this happens, they look to us at the radio station. They think we can do something that other people can't." In what he said was an effort to calm people down, Rushin decided to bring several members of the crowd inside to give them, and himself, an opportunity to express their frustration and anger on the air. Rushin says he forgot to make a tape of that day's broadcast, but at least one listener, Major Dickson of the MPD, was writing down what was said. "Rushin was saying things like 'It's a cryin' shame, that all-white jury turning those white officers loose. How long can we continue to take this nonsense? When are we going to raise up and be heard?' " Often, Dickson said, Rushin's voice cracked, and he appeared to be on the verge of tears. Then the community people, most of them women, came on and there was much sobbing and crying out of "Where can we go? What can we do?"

Another WEDR listener was a twenty-one-year-old black counselor in an ex-offender program run by the city who usually keeps the radio on while she works. "You could feel the tension from the radio," she remembers. "You could hear it building up, and you could feel the hurt in his voice. You knew he felt really mad."

Crowds of young blacks, many with large transistor radios balanced on their shoulders, were congregating near African Square Park and also along 22nd Avenue in the sixties and seventies, site of the largest housing project in the city, the James E. Scott Houses. The anger pouring out over the air echoed their own. "We had watched the trial every night," said one nineteen-year-old youth who was there. "All those pictures and descriptions explaining how they beat the man to death, and they found those guys guilty of nothing? Not nothing? That's like saying the man didn't die." On every street corner the litany of perceived wrongs was repeated: the Johnny Jones case, the Nathaniel LaFleur case, the case of the black youth in Hialeah who was "killed for taking a piss," the constant mistreatment and harrassment of black men by the police, the failure of the city to do anything to fix up Martin Luther King Boulevard.

At about 5 p.m. the first rocks and bottles were in the air, lofted

at cars being driven by whites along 62nd Street. One person who
remembers just when it started was Betty Wiggs, an administrator in
the Haitian Refugee Center on 12th Avenue and 62nd Street.

> I was in my office on Saturday doing some paper work. It was a very
> hot day and quite a few people were on the street. Around four-thirty
> or five o'clock things began to get noisier than usual, so I took a peek
> outside. There were definitely more people than usual on the street,
> and I could hear some of them talking about the verdicts in the
> McDuffie trial. Just as I was turning to go back inside, a small car
> passed down 62nd Street with what seemed like two white people in
> it. Just as it approached the light at 14th Avenue people started
> throwing things at it. Someone yelled, "Get the crackers." There
> seemed to be a lot of tension and anger on the faces and lips of the
> people standing there. I went back inside and gathered my things. As
> I came out I could see some young men standing by the walk light.
> They seemed to be pushing the light to make the cars stop there. I
> could feel that something was about to happen, so I left.

    In Liberty City, as the police well knew from previous distur-
bances, it is not unusual for young blacks to throw objects at cars as
a way to express anger or to create some excitement. "Rocks and
bottles on Saturday night are more or less a common thing here," says
Lieutenant Randall McGee, who was a platoon commander at the
Liberty City precinct of the Public Safety Department that afternoon.
"It was nothing you'd ordinarily get too excited about." At the Liberty
Square Housing Project across African Square Park, some older people had even set up aluminum lawn chairs in front of their whitewashed
bungalows to watch the fun.
    At about 6 p.m., a rumor began to spread that a white man speed-
ing along 62nd Street had shot a black child, variously said to be a girl
or a boy and to be either six or ten years old. No child was ever found.
The City of Miami Rescue Squad, responding to a call about the incident, was told that the child had already been taken to the hospital,
but no hospital has a record of such an admission. Nevertheless, the
rumor added to the existing tension and drew hundreds more to 62nd
Street. By 6:15 p.m. the crowd was so large and the rocks and bottles
coming so thick that the Miami Police Department, which patrols that
section of Liberty City, pulled its few squad cars out of the area and
began—fruitlessly, it turned out, because of a lack of men and wooden
barricades—to set up roadblocks to try to keep out white drivers.
    At about 6:20 the mob set upon its first victim: a white derelict,
name unrecorded, who was beaten and bloodied by young blacks at
62nd Street and 13th Avenue. The police received several calls about
a "man down" at that location, and at 6:30 an unmarked MPD car

driven by Sergeant José Burgos tore down the street, picked up the man and sped off. Before going into the area, Burgos had asked for a backup car to help him out, but he decided to go in to try to save the man on his own before the other car joined him. The action becomes confusing at this point, but what seems to have happened is that in response to Burgos's call for assistance a backup car left its post on 17th Avenue, where it had been guarding the western entrance to 62nd Street, and thereby permitted traffic—including several cars operated by, and carrying, whites—to enter the riot area unaware of what was going on. The way was now open for disaster.

One of these cars may well have been the cream-colored 1969 Dodge Dart driven by eighteen-year-old Michael Kulp, and carrying his brother, Jeffrey, twenty-two, and a friend, Debra Getman, twenty-three. The Kulp brothers, who had come to Miami from Spring City, Pennsylvania, a year earlier, worked in the shipping department of Burdine's Department Store in downtown Miami. They had spent the day at the beach with Debra, a waitress in a fast-food restaurant, who was then asleep in the back seat. Jeffrey sat alongside his brother in the front seat. The car had no radio, and none of the three, according to homicide detectives who later interviewed Debra, had heard anything bout the McDuffie verdict.

As reconstructed by the police and eyewitnesses, the car was suddenly struck by a shower of rocks and bottles as it was going east along 62nd Street at 13th Avenue. A chunk of concrete came through the windshield, striking Michael in the head and causing him to swerve across the center divider strip, across the lanes of oncoming traffic and up on the sidewalk. There, the car struck a seventy-five-year-old man named Albert Perry, fracturing his ankle. It also struck a ten-year-old girl, Shanreka Perry. Moments before, Shanreka had been playing in her yard nearby when she spotted her sister and aunt walking toward a grocery across 62nd Street and started out to join them. Her aunt feared for the girl's safety in the growing chaos, and remembers shouting back to her: "Girl, you better go home." Shanreka turned back, and this was the last thing she remembers. The Kulp car struck her and drove her up against the stucco wall of one of the buildings in the housing project, crushing her pelvis, severing her right leg and smearing the wall with a wide swath of blood. Cries of horror and anger went up from the crowd; women grabbed sheets off a clothesline, wrapped up the bleeding girl and hailed a black taxi driver coming down 62nd Street to take her to Jackson Memorial Hospital.

According to eyewitnesses, the accident further inflamed the mob, which dragged the Kulp brothers from their car and began to beat them savagely. Debra, who had been jolted awake by the barrage of rocks, managed to get away from the car and run through the project to a street on the other side. There, she was helped by blacks into a taxi and escaped with only a few cuts on her face. The Kulp brothers, from all accounts, were beaten continuously by a variety of people for between fifteen and twenty minutes. They were punched, karate-kicked and struck with rocks, bricks, bottles and pieces of concrete, one of which was later recovered by MPD homicide detectives and found to weigh 23 pounds. At one point, someone picked up a yellow *Miami Herald* newspaper dispenser and brought it down on Jeffrey Kulp's head. They were shot several times with a revolver and run over by a green Cadillac, whose driver then came over and stabbed them with a screwdriver.

About 7 p.m. Bernard Coates, a black staff worker for the Dade County Community Relations Board, arrived on the scene. By then, the worst of the beating seemed to be over. The victims were lying in the street, one brother by the curb and the other near the median strip. Someone had placed towels over their heads, perhaps to protect them from the sun, which even in the early evening was still hot—or perhaps just to hide the bloody spectacle. People were milling around. A black woman took pictures of the brothers for a community newspaper. Suddenly a black male approached Jeffrey Kulp with a brick. Coates said he pleaded with him to stop, but the attacker lifted the brick high in the air and smashed it down on Kulp's head. This served to renew the attack by several others, and Coates ran for a telephone to get the police. As he did so, an aged derelict, whom people in the community know only as "Ernest," approached Jeffrey Kulp, reached down and inserted a red rose in his bleeding mouth. When Coates finally got through to MPD headquarters he was told that the police did not have enough men right then to go in and stop the violence. He slammed down the phone and left the area.

Michael Kulp miraculously survived the beating, although able to function in only a severely limited way. His brother, Jeffrey, died in Jackson Memorial Hospital on June 12.

An hour after the Kulp beatings, three other whites—Benny Higdon, twenty-one, his brother-in-law Robert Owens, fourteen, and Robert's friend Charles Barreca, fifteen—were stoned and beaten at almost the same spot and nearly as brutally as the Kulps. Of the three, only Barreca made it alive to the hospital, where he died shortly afterward. "In my thirty years on the force, it was the most violent crime I've ever seen," says Sgt. Mike Gonzalez of the MPD's homicide squad, who directed the murder investigation. "We get a lot of cases where you have extreme violence—people beating up people and stabbing them and what not—but nothing like this." Gonzalez tried three times that night to get to the scene of the Kulp and Higdon murders, only to be driven back each time by angry crowds. "We weren't able to do any real investigation until it was all over," he says. "All we did that night was try to keep score."

The fifth victim, Bertha Rogers, fifty-five, was driving north on 22nd Avenue in her 1966 Chevrolet Malibu when, at about 9:30 p.m., she was struck by a shower of rocks in front of the Scott Houses at 69th Street. Someone reached in and grabbed her purse. Gasoline was then poured over her and she and her car were set on fire. A bystander got her out of the car and drove her to Jackson Hospital. She died of severe burns on May 22. Forty-five minutes later, three blocks away on 22nd Avenue, a car driven by Emilio Munoz, sixty-three, a Cuban-born butcher, was stoned and overturned outside the Scott Houses at 72nd Street. As Munoz lay pinned in the wreckage, the crowd beat and jabbed him with sticks. Then someone threw gasoline over the car and set it on fire. According to the medical examiner, however, Munoz was already dead. Blood from the beating had trickled into his lungs, choking him to death. He would not be extricated from the charred car until the next day, at about the same time a fishing boat from Miami was waiting in the harbor at Mariel, Cuba, to bring his wife and son over to the United States.

The body of Chabillall Janarnauth, twenty-two, a light-skinned immigrant from Guyana who was known as "Shab" by his fellow workers in a Miami drafting shop, was found on 27th Avenue near 50th Street just before 11 p.m. He was so mutilated that a friend could identify him only by his brown boots and his distinctive hair and eyebrows. The police theorized that he had been beaten and then run over several times with his own car, which was never found.

The last victim that night was Mildred Penton, sixty-five, who was returning from the Flagler Dog Track with her husband and daughter when crowds began throwing rocks at her car on 27th Avenue near 48th Street. "We were just driving along and suddenly it felt like a brick building was falling on the car," her husband, John, said later.[3] Mrs. Penton was struck in the head by a brick and lost consciousness. After four days in a coma she awoke briefly but then went back into a coma and died five weeks later.

The white people injured but not killed during the riot ranged from those with superficial glass cuts to those who were shot or beaten so severely that they were left permanently crippled. In all, 417 people were treated at the area's nine hospitals during the three principal days of rioting. No uniform statistics were kept according to race and time of admission, so it is difficult to be precise about victims and injuries at various times during the riot. Dr. Bernard Elser, chief of the emergency ward at Jackson Memorial, the largest hospital in the city and the one to which most riot victims were taken, says that the overwhelming majority of those injured Saturday night were white. The next day, when looting was going on full force, and after the police and National Guardsmen had succeeded in closing off the riot area to white motorists, the color of those injured changed from white to black. And at least half of the black cases, he said, seemed to involve glass cuts and other lacerations that would have occurred as a consequence of looting.

"We normally see a lot of injuries here at Jackson," said Dr. David Bernstein, chief surgeon in the emergency ward. "What impressed me, though, was the severity of the beatings that took place Saturday night. That was impressive. Just the severe skull fractures we were seeing, and the cases of mutilation."

Jackson, which has the fifth largest emergency facility in the country, had all six of its operating rooms going at once on Saturday night. Of 161 patients treated Saturday and Sunday, 50 required surgical operations. The hospital ordered 278 units of blood—nearly 35 gallons—from the city's blood bank. Late Saturday night the hospital became so overloaded that its staff was obliged to turn away all but the most serious cases. "What also impressed me," says Dr. Bernstein, "was the number of totally innocent people who were injured, in particular those caught in the middle of it the first night of the rioting. People who had nothing to do with the situation."

One example was the case of Martin and Ruth Weinstock, a retired couple in their sixties who had driven down from their home in Fort Pierce, north of Miami, to spend Saturday with their daughter, a medical student. Mr. Weinstock, who had been raised in the Hebrew Orphan Asylum in Manhattan, had owned a grocery store in the Bronx, then managed a retail bedding store in New Jersey before retiring in 1969 and moving to Florida. His wife, a registered nurse, still worked part-time. At 6:30 p.m., after visiting their daughter, the Weinstocks decided to see a minor league baseball game at Miami Stadium before heading home. The game, during which the Fort Lauderdale Yankees beat the Miami Orioles, ended at about 10:30 p.m., whereupon the couple got into their green VW Rabbit for the two-hour trip home. They had heard nothing about the McDuffie verdict.

Driving north on Tenth Avenue, then east on 20th Street toward I-95, they noticed large crowds of blacks along the sidewalks and in the street. Suddenly a tall black man in a white shirt ran across their path. "Marty, watch out!" Ruth remembers saying. At the same time, they heard dozens of blacks calling out: "Stop! Stop that car!" Weinstock sensed trouble and jammed the accelerator to the floor. The car was then struck by what his wife calls a "maelstrom" of rocks. The window on her side was rolled up and withstood several direct hits. Weinstock's was rolled down and he was struck in the head with a baseball-sized chunk of concrete that fractured his skull. He remembers driving two blocks more to get out of the worst of it, then stopping the car and turning to his wife. "Look what they hit me with," he said, showing her the concrete. Then he fell back, his eyes closed, his mouth open, and he lost consciousness. His wife thought he was dead.

Terrified, Mrs. Weinstock got out of the car and ran toward an intersection up the street. "Get the police, get an ambulance!" she shouted at the black faces staring at her. "Get the police. You've killed my husband." She started back to her car and got there just as the main part of the mob was coming up the street. A black teenager with a stick approached her car and made a grab for her purse on the seat. She tugged it away angrily. "You don't want that," she recalls shouting. "I remember just feeling mad. Feeling that that boy didn't realize how serious the situation was. He didn't have to get involved in this." Another youth approached the car and also grabbed for the purse. Again Mrs. Weinstock yanked it back and shouted at them to leave her alone. Other cars were now approaching, and her attackers left the Weinstocks to go after them.

As Mrs. Weinstock locked her doors, her husband regained consciousness briefly and mumbled groggily, "We've got to get out of here." He put the car in gear and drove it forward. "I knew we had to get out of there quickly," he recalls. "We were done for if we didn't. I felt that I was out to be gotten that night. I felt that if they got close enough I wasn't going to be there anymore." But his injury had taken all the energy out of him, he says. "I've never been in a fight ring, but I imagine it's like a man in the ring, feeling as if you can't go on any further." He drove the car two more blocks, then passed out. Once more, his wife got out of the car and began screaming for someone to help them. "I felt tremendous shock and alarm, but when Marty said, 'We've got to get out of here,' then I realized it was life and death."

At about this time a black chemist and his wife, Ron and Jackie Malone, were driving through the intersection and saw the Weinstocks in trouble. Malone came over, moved the badly bleeding man to the passenger side and then, with his wife following in their car, drove the couple to Parkway General Hospital in North Miami Beach. On the way he told them about the McDuffie verdict.

Weinstock spent six days in the hospital recovering. Several months after the riot his only physical problem was occasional difficulty sleeping. The couple, who kept the piece of concrete as a souvenir of their experience, harbor no bad feelings toward the rioters. "They should only know that I agree with their anger," said Weinstock, a former member of the NAACP. "If the people who threw the concrete were brought before me in handcuffs, I would insist that the handcuffs be removed, and I'd try to talk to them. I would say that I understand and that I'm on their side. I have no anger at all. But they'll never solve their problems by sending people like me to the hospital."

One of the worst gauntlets whites ran that night was a quarter-mile stretch of Grand Avenue in Coconut Grove, a neighborhood located in the southernmost part of Miami, at the opposite end of town from Liberty City. The Grove is truly a community with a split personality. In the space of twenty-five yards, Grand Avenue changes from the white part of the Grove—a bayside community of million-dollar houses, lavish yacht clubs, branch stores from Fifth Avenue and Palm Beach and restaurants serving $500 bottles of wine—to the Black Grove, a neighborhood of 5,000 people, many of whom are desperately poor. Here the avenue is lined with a handful of disheveled stores, bars and laundromats, along with rows of two-story cinderblock apartments and small white-clapboard houses known as "shotgun shacks." The shacks, three-room structures constructed in the 1920s to house black laborers who built the railroad, got their name from the fact that one could fire a shotgun through the house, from the front door and out the back, without hitting any walls.

White people use Grand Avenue as the most direct route from the waterfront along Biscayne Bay to the University of Miami and the middle-class suburbs south of the city. That night, from about 8 p.m. to the time the police finally erected barricades at both ends of the avenue—about 10 p.m.—no white-operated car made it down Grand Avenue unscathed. Dr. Edward Sofen, fifty-nine, acting chairman of the Department of Politics and Public Affairs at the University of Miami, was driving there with a friend at about 8 p.m. when his car was hit by a shower of rocks. Swerving to avoid hitting people lining the road, Sofen struck a street sign and the car rolled over. Crowds moved in to attack. One man heaved a concrete block through the window; Sofen was struck in the head and blinded with his own blood. The pair were lifted out of the car; their wallets were ripped away. Sofen managed to break free—by then he had lost contact with his friend—and run several blocks to an intersection where the Reverend Theodore Gibson, a black Episcopal minister and a local political leader, was helping white people to get out of the Black Grove. Sofen was driven by a black to the Coral Gables Hospital, where he stayed six days for treatment of an orbital skull fracture.

Roberta Gallagher, a social worker and instructor at Biscayne College, was coming home with two friends from a day of sailing on the bay when the car in which she was riding was struck. The driver sped on through the crowds and Gallagher, lying on the back seat, escaped with only a head wound that required four stitches. "I had no idea what was going on," said Gallagher, who vows never to drive down Grand Avenue again. "It was the doctor who told me about the jury verdict."

Kazuki Ishikawa, twenty-two, a Japanese student at the University of Miami, suffered a fractured skull when a rock came through his open window and struck him on the side of the head. Blood streaming down his face, he stopped the car and exchanged places with a passenger, who drove him to the hospital. While the car was stopped, a black man in his mid-twenties came up and threw a rock at the windshield, Ishikawa said, but no one tried to attack them. "I thought maybe it was because we were Oriental," he said.

One witness to it all was Willie Matthews, forty-seven, a black Grand Avenue storeowner who watched the beatings from inside his store holding an Iver Johnson .38 under his white apron. Matthews had been at home when the rocks and bottles began to fly. "This guy came over to get me when it began. 'Willie,' he said, 'the niggers are throwing rocks at the cars.' I got over here quick, because I got three panes of glass and I wanted them to be here in the morning."

Matthews, who was born and raised in the Grove, has three children, two of them school teachers and one a college student. His store, many of whose customers are older black men in the Grove, serves everything from bacon and grits cooked on a stove in a back room to packages of snuff and chewing tobacco, chilled bottles of Twentieth Century Jinney's Dry Grape Wine and shots out of a vodka bottle to mix with soda from the cooler. A graduate of Fort Valley State University in Georgia, Matthews spent three years in the army and then had a series of what he said were negative experiences working for white bosses, first as a juvenile counselor at the courthouse and then as a staff worker for Big Brothers/Big Sisters Organization. In the latter job, he said, he had built up a successful black branch office of Big Brothers in the Grove, increasing its annual budget from $16,000 to more than $65,000. Then he was transferred to the large downtown headquarters, where he was the only black in the office. "I'd come in all dressed up, looking good all the time, and the white receptionist would ask things like how many suits I owned! It was like I wasn't supposed to have that many suits, being 'just a nigger.' And the white guy that ran the agency, he drove around in a little bitty Datsun, and here I had a great big car, a Pontiac then. So with him it was always, 'See the big car Willie's driving!' " Matthews quit and opened up his store.

The beatings he saw that night horrified him. He is quick to add that he, too, feels bitterly toward white people and saw the riot as an understandable expression of black anger. "Don't think I'm talking in disfavor of what they did," he said. "We didn't do nothing, my generation. I had three jobs in eighteen years and each time I ran into a white man who couldn't agree with me. But what I did was bow off. I just quit."

That night, he said, the beating was carried on by young people, roughly eighteen to twenty-four years old, many of them the children of the people with whom Matthews had gone to school. They pushed garbage dumpsters into the middle of the street so cars would have to slow down, becoming easier targets. "The young people I watched, they had no heart, no heart whatsoever," Matthews said. "A guy on his motorbike came down and the bike skidded. They took him over there by the side of the road and they beat him something awful. They beat him so much that I almost took out my pistol and went over there and said, 'Hey, you beat him enough!' His whole face was all puffed up and bloody. Then they stomped his bike all to pieces. Then there was a little car, a Toyota or something, with a guy and a girl. The driver stopped when something hit his car—I don't know why he did that, because they took them out of there and they stripped the girl and sent her running toward the village all naked. Then they took the guy and beat him. One guy drew back and like in the movies he aimed a karate kick at his head. Then they were trying to set his car on fire, throwing matches at the gas tank. It took ten minutes before they got it right, and then it really blew—whooooosh!

"I would have accepted it all if it had been on TV or in the movies. But right here in front of the store! These kids, they just got no God in them. No God. Now me, I've still got God and Jesus in me. I'm a bitter man, a bitter man. If I get angry at you I'll whip your ass, but then I'll let you go. I'll let you go. They didn't do that. They just beat them and didn't stop."

Sergeant Patrick Burns, thirty, white, of the uniform division of the Miami Police Department, had been raised in Miami, growing up in the now-black Edison Housing Project. As a boy he had been picked up for joy riding in stolen cars and had spent time in a youth rehabilitation program before joining the Marine Corps. Sent to Vietnam, he saw six months of combat before returning to Miami and becoming a police officer.

At about 7:45 p.m., Burns was summoned by Major Dickson, who was in charge of a temporary police command post in a firehouse at 46th Street and 11th Avenue, and ordered to go in and get the bodies reported to be lying on 62nd Street out of Liberty City. With five other officers who volunteered to join him, he headed for 62nd Street. Here is his account:

All we had was that there were bodies out on the street. I guess I thought they were dead, but I was hoping they weren't dead and so I said, 'Okay.' I had picked a couple of guys who were seasoned veterans and could take care of anything, and then three rookies because I knew they thought I was God and they'd jump—whatever I told them to do they'd do quick.

The young cops wanted to go; when you're really young you don't value your life the way you do when you've been through a lot. It's like army draftees, seventeen- and eighteen-year-olds, who'll do anything they're told. An older man's going to say, 'Hell no, I won't go.'

Two of the guys were black officers I knew and respected. One of them had backed me up in a couple of situations where a black perpetrator was ready to kick my butt, and he was there and the black-white thing never came up, whereas there are other blacks in the department who wouldn't help us and vice versa.

We had a paddy wagon that looked sort of like an ice-cream truck with the letters MPD on the side. I put two guys in that and the other two in the squad car with me. Going in I was ad-libbing it all the way. Fortunately I had worked in the neighborhood for quite some time and I have the ability to think a little bit ahead, like a quarterback reading the defense. Also I grew up on the streets so I know what that's all about.

So we took off up 17th Avenue from 46th Street. A lot of things were going on in my head. I wanted to get in and get out quick. I thought a lot about my wife and my brother. We were going down the street, getting shot at; you could hear the shots, even on 17th Avenue before we got there, and we were just flooring it. I didn't have a strategy, but I wanted the element of surprise. I knew I had to get the jump on them because I knew the initial shock of seeing the police wagon and a car all of a sudden would give us a short period of time before they knew they had us outnumbered three hundred to one.

I didn't want to come down 62nd Street from 17th because they would have seen us coming a long way away. They would have been shooting at us before we got in and by then thousands of them would be out and we wouldn't have a chance. So I ducked down 58th Street east to 14th Avenue, going north, and then we came flying around the corner of 62nd Street and we swooped in on them so fast they didn't know what was happening or where we were coming from. I had the mike keyed so no one could talk but me and so I could tell the guys where to put the truck and what to do.

So we came flying around the corner and we saw the bodies. The crowd took off, hundreds of them, and we saw the bodies out there, lying. I remember someone hanging over one of them when we came in and it looked like he was stabbing with something. It was bad. We started taking shots right away. Bullets were bouncing on the sidewalk right in front of us, hitting the truck. I saw this guy up on the balcony of an apartment shooting at us—you could see the muzzle flash. So I was trying to duck him and get to the bodies at the same time. I ran over yelling at this policeman, this rookie. I ran over and grabbed one Kulp brother, the one toward the curb, first. I really can't recall. I grabbed him and he was still fibrillating—sort of jumping, you know. His head had been split open with an axe it looked like. I grabbed him and I was trying to carry him to the truck. The rookie was just standing there, frozen. We're taking shots from the other side. I ran over and rolled the other brother over. His head was looking up but his body was so mutilated it was like all out of the natural way of lying down. He had his head split open too, and he had a rose coming out of his mouth. He was dead, it looked like, and there was just blood all over the place. I reached underneath his arms, and I couldn't hold on to him. He kept slipping out of me, he had so much blood over him. I was trying to get him up and he was just so damn heavy, and the kid, the rookie, was just standing there. I'm pretty strong, but I couldn't get a grip on him, and there was blood all over me and he kept slipping out of me. I was screaming at the rookie, and we're getting shot at even more.

Finally I had Kulp up around my waist, like up around my chest, and the other policeman, I finally kicked him in the ass with my foot, and I screamed at him to grab him, and we ran to the truck. We got him in the truck and I said to get the hell out of here. Suddenly, this dude from the projects came running out with a shotgun, and we're running for it, and he blasted a shot at us. It blew out the light on top of the car. I was running to stay out of range and I couldn't stop for the car, so the driver started taking off and I ran over on the other side of the car and jumped in, and we hauled ass.

Sergeant Burns and his men made three more runs that night to rescue people beaten by mobs, and he also picked up the three victims in the Higdon car. For months after the experience he suffered from a condition, familiar to police psychiatrists, called "freeze-frame think-ing," during which images from the Kulp scene reappeared vividly before his eyes. He began to have trouble with his marriage, eventually separating from his wife. Police work, which he had always loved, began to seem distasteful. When he gave a deposition at the state attorney's office for the prosecution of the Kulp and Higdon murder suspects, he broke down and went into the men's room, where he spent several minutes sobbing before returning to complete his testimony. "Before the riot," he says, "I felt I could handle anything that came my way. But now I've been thinking that there's more to life than all this, and I'm worried that after much more of police work I won't be able to see the other things."

The Metro Justice Building

While Sergeant Burns was speeding the Kulp brothers to Jackson Hos-pital, the riot was about to take a new turn at a complex of four government buildings at 13th Street and 13th Avenue, about five miles south of the action in Liberty City (see map). The complex consists of the Metro Justice Building, which houses county courtrooms and the offices of the state attorney; another building is the headquarters of the Public Safety Department, and two others house the State Health Department and other government agencies. These buildings, plus the Dade County Jail with its 900 inmates awaiting trial, overlook the banks of the Miami River, and are set off from the surrounding area by vast parking lots and an elevated expressway. Although the area bustles with activity during the day, it is usually deserted at night.

Shortly after the McDuffie verdict was announced, officials of the local branch of the NAACP and other prominent blacks thought of holding a rally at 8 o'clock that night at the Metro Justice complex, not just to express their anger at the verdict but also to dissipate energy that might lead to violence. "It was designed," said George Knox, former attorney for the City of Miami, "to be an orderly expression of hostility." Director Jones of the PSD gave permission for the rally, and it was announced at about 5 p.m. over WEDR and WMBM, the city's black-oriented stations, and also over many white stations.

Not everyone thought the rally was a good idea. "I thought it was the worst thing they could do," says T. Willard Fair, president of the Urban League of Miami, who had been watching a Los Angeles Dodgers baseball game when the verdict flashed on the air. "When something happens as emotional as the McDuffie verdict and you want to avoid trouble, you do not bring together everybody to hold a protest. You just don't do that." Nevertheless, when he was asked by rally organizers to come and speak, he said he would.

By 7:45, about 1,000 people stood in the parking lots and sidewalks in front of the Justice Building, mostly young blacks but also some older black people, women, children, even some whites. "In the beginning it seemed fine," said Michael O. Fowler, a UPI reporter who by now had heard reports of bottle throwing at cars but as yet knew nothing of the deaths in Liberty City. "People were talking freely, even joking." More and more people streamed into the area. It got to be 8:15; the speakers had arrived, but it turned out that no one had thought to set up loudspeakers so they could be heard. Fair sought out William Perry, president of the local branch of the NAACP, to ask what was going on. "I was told there was no public address system, no planned agenda, and that those who wanted to speak could do so by using a bullhorn. I said there was no way I was going to be heard with a bullhorn. The crowd was just too large." By now 3,000 people were present, many of them becoming increasingly restless over the lack of action. There were rhythmic chants of "Justice, Justice, Justice," and "Reno Must Go." Someone got them singing "We Shall

Overcome" and the gospel song "Amen," and the crowd swayed in time to the music. But the atmosphere was becoming tense. "I didn't see many people I could recognize," Fair said. "I heard a lot of the kids saying that they didn't come to talk. They were tired of talking. They wanted to *do* something. There was a lot of vocalizing of their anger: 'It was wrong what they did. They shouldn't let those white folks go.' " Many of the young people had their transistor radios with them and news of what was happening in Liberty City was beginning to spill over the air.

The PSD had allotted fifteen officers to monitor the rally, but they shortly found themselves hopelessly outnumbered and considered it prudent to stay out of sight. At about 8:45, Knox ran over to the PSD building behind the Justice Building and frantically asked the officer on duty if they had a public address system he might borrow for the speakers. The officer said they had none. The officer also said there were only five or six people in the entire headquarters building who could help if trouble started.

A Black Muslim minister named Hasan Lateef used his bullhorn to draw part of the crowd away to a public park by the Torch of Freedom, a shrine to Cuban refugees located about a mile away. Part of this group, however, broke away and headed for the front of the PSD headquarters; three or four shirtless young men began gesturing tauntingly at the police inside the building. Egged on by each other, one finally kicked a hole in the glass front door. "That's when I left," said Fair. "When I saw men attack the police headquarters with the police *inside,* then I knew they were really crazy."

The situation was fast getting out of control. While the rally organizers pleaded for order, the crowd was shouting its rage over the injustice of the McDuffie verdict and of white society generally. Two PSD officers who had been watching events from a distance drove their cruiser into the crowd, apparently trying to scatter people, then sped off. The act added another provocation, and the crowd edged closer to destructive behavior.

Even blacks who under normal circumstances would never have done so found themselves being drawn into acts of violence. One such black was a thirty-two-year-old lawyer who worked for the State of Florida and attended the rally with his wife and ten-year-old son. "I remember being consumed with rage," he says, "and feeling that somehow I had to dramatize it." He had felt that way twice before, he says: once after the death of Dr. Martin Luther King, Jr., when he and other black students at an Alabama college had occupied an administration building in defiance of the police, and the other after the death of Robert F. Kennedy. "Now I felt that I had to do something. I didn't want to let the moment pass." The first thing he did was to stand fast when a police car tried to move slowly through the crowd to break it up. "I refused to back down. I refused to move for him. Even though I was a public official in a sense, I didn't identify with anyone official at that time. All I identified with were my black brothers, and all I could think about was how the criminal justice system I had respected put its foot on my neck and face." His anger was so intense that he began ripping antennas off police cars parked nearby, an act of criminal vandalism that continued to shock him weeks later. "I remember thinking what kind of impression I was making on my son—what it meant seeing his father like that. But I also wanted him to know what it was about and why I was angry."

At one point Knox had gotten into a police car and was using its loudspeaker to get the crowd away from the PSD building and back in front of the Justice Building. But then another police car from the tiny suburb of Sweetwater, answering a call from the PSD for outside assistance, came careening up to the edge of the crowd, its siren going and lights flashing. In the resulting confusion, a rumor broke out that the car had run over the foot of a black girl. In response, a dozen men overturned an empty PSD car nearby and two other cars belonging to county officials. Rags were inserted in their opened gas tanks, and, while some blacks present tried to stop them by standing in their way, others tossed lighted matches past them, toward the gasoline soaked rags. At last one car burst into flames, followed by another.

The crowd now erupted into full-scale riot. They smashed the glass doors of the Metro Justice Building and set fires inside its marble lobby, terrorizing the desk clerks on weekend duty. They overturned several more cars and set them on fire. In back of the building, the attack resumed on PSD headquarters. Some men produced pistols and began firing them in the air. Others piled wastepaper against the front door of the PSD to set the entrance on fire. The few policemen trapped inside the building were calling frantically for help. The lieutenant in charge at the Dade County Jail was asked to send over as many guards as he could spare. "I remember the lieutenant saying, 'José, get the shotgun and go over there,' " said José Nadal, a Cuban-born guard who was on duty at the jail's loading dock when the riot erupted. An ex-U.S. Marine, Nadal took the gun and waded into the rioting throngs at the PSD:

> I did not want to shoot, but they were trying to jump me, and this one man was trying to set a police car on fire. I went like so with the butt of the shotgun, like they teach you in drill instructor's school, and hit him on the head. Then I see two men, they are trying to light the papers on fire in the doorway, and I hit one hard, the one with

the lighter, and he dropped his lighter and went down on the ground. Soon I hear the pop, pop of pistols being fired. Then I hear a big caliber. It is a rifle—you can tell—and we hit the ground.

The mob turned from the PSD entrance and began setting fires in the unoccupied state office building across the street, and also began attacking whites who were passing by on foot and in cars. One of these was Fowler, the UPI reporter who was there to cover the story. He had just had his notebook grabbed away by three young black men. He turned around to talk or, if he had to, to fight, he says, and that's the last thing he remembers. He later learned that a man had hit him with a club from behind and that another had punched him in the face as he went down. The next he knew he was in the emergency room of Jackson Memorial Hospital, just up the street from the Metro Justice complex.

Among those caught in the violence were medical people trying to get to Jackson Memorial to help take care of the growing number of injured. "A neurosurgeon was attacked when his car was stopped near the Justice Building. Someone tried to choke him," said Dr. Elser, the emergency room head. "Several nurses had rocks thrown at their windshields. We tried to get other doctors into the hospital, but there was no way they could get through. In particular, there were two surgeons we wanted to have come in, but the police wouldn't let them off Route 836 [an east-west highway that passes overhead near the Justice Building]. One policeman told them he wouldn't take them in his patrol car because they'd be in more danger that way than if they went in on their own."

At about 10 p.m., the Miami police at last mustered enough men—seventy in all—to move in with a credible show of force. As soon as the rioters saw police officers wearing face shields and carrying riot batons marching toward them in echelons ten-deep, they quickly melted away toward Liberty City and other points north.

Having beaten and killed white people and having tried to burn down the seat of the county's justice system, the rioters next turned to the business of destroying the mostly white-owned businesses in their own neighborhood.

The police strategy to quell the riot was, first, to seal off the major riot areas, and then to go in and restore order with a massed force of police and National Guard. The first of these goals was officially achieved at 10:36 p.m. Saturday, more than five hours after the riot started, when, according to the headquarters log of the PSD, an effective perimeter was established along 105th Street to the north, the

Miami River to the south, 37th Avenue to the west and 6th Avenue to the east. Whites, however, were still filtering into the ghetto along side streets, as evidenced by the Weinstocks' encounter with the mob on 20th Street at about 10:45 p.m. A more nearly accurate estimate of when an effective perimeter was established would be midnight or 12:30, when the first Guard units arrived in the city.

The second part of the strategy—taking back the riot area—did not really begin to be put into effect until Sunday night, nearly twenty-four hours later. One problem, as we discuss in Chapter 4, had to do with logistics and with the instructions Governor Bob Graham gave for deployment of the National Guard. Another was that the task of trying to control people who do not wish to be controlled requires such a large force that even with the help of the approximately 1,000 National Guardsmen brought in by early Sunday morning, the authorities were still spread painfully thin.

"First you need enough men to go in and move people out of an area," says Captain Douglas Hughes, commander of the PSD's Central District Headquarters, which is responsible for the half of Liberty City that lies outside city limits in Dade County. "Then you need more men to stay and hold areas that have been taken back. We could do one or the other, but not both at the same time."

Between 11 o'clock and midnight, scattered incidents of looting and burning were also breaking out in other black communities all across Dade County: in Perrine and Homestead to the south, where black migrant farm workers live; in Opa-Locka and Carol City to the north, which house many black middle-class residents. None of these areas, however, suffered rioting on the scale of the impoverished center of Liberty City, where by 11 p.m. thousands of people were in the streets, and where many were furiously tearing apart the commercial fabric of the community. "It looked like the Orange Bowl Stadium," says Clarence Watson, the black owner of a record store on 27th Avenue and 54th Street, in describing the looting and burning of the large Norton Tire Company store located opposite his store. "There were thousands of them. They got all the doors open by backing into them with this little car. Once they broke down one, then they would go to the next. Thousands of people, just waiting for the doors to open. They just stood around waiting, and then they went in." The police, he says, did no more than observe the chaos. "Once in a while a police car would ride by and look at it and keep on going. They didn't stop."

Judging from calls to the police and also the times at which burglar alarms began to go off, the looting started in earnest at about 8 p.m. The burning did not begin until much later. Apart from the fire set at the Metro Justice complex, the first riot-connected fire in the county

portion of Liberty City was reported at 11:13 p.m. at a small grocery
near the Scott Houses on 22nd Avenue and 66th Street. In the city's
portion of the ghetto, the first blaze was set at 11:30 p.m. at the Edison
Furniture Store on 7th Avenue and 69th Street. By Sunday, the city
and county fire departments had recorded 213 more fires in Liberty
City alone, with 21 additional fires in Opa-Locka and 13 in Perrine.
In the dark hours of early morning, the city glowed as if it had come
under a large-scale incendiary attack.

Of all the commercial streets in the ghetto, 7th Avenue, the eastern boundary of Liberty City, was the most thoroughly looted and
burned. Along an approximately three-mile stretch, virtually every
business with lootable goods was hit; many were also put to the torch
and, several weeks after the riot, had to be bulldozed flat. We present
a detailed account of the looting and burning in chapters 5 and 6, but
the pattern of what happened to 7th Avenue was similar to that for
other commerical streets throughout the ghetto.

The riot came to the avenue about 6 p.m., when a black man was
seen running toward 7th from 70th Street repeatedly firing a revolver
in the air, like a cowboy fresh into town from a cattle drive. Generally,
however, rioters were distracted by the antiwhite violence going on
several blocks to the west, and did not begin serious looting until about
two hours later. Susan's Meat Market, a Cuban-owned business at 64th
Street, was the first store to be looted, witnesses said; it went at 8 p.m.
Then the Edison Furniture Store at 69th Street was looted and burned
to the ground. By midnight on Saturday looting victims included Eagle
Discount, an army-navy store at 63rd Street; the U-Totem at 68th
Street, whose safe was carted away; the Pantry-Pride supermarket at
62nd Street, which moved out after the riot; Spelter Electric, a lighting-
fixture store at 67th Street, which was also burned to the ground. At
2:30 a.m. looters cleaned out the display bikes at the Harley-Davidson
franchise at 77th Street.

By 3 a.m. Sunday, the riot entered a lull, common in such disorders, during which rioters took a break from their frenzied activity and
went home to bed. Calls to the county's 911 emergency number concerning arson, theft and assault—the three main riot activities—began
gradually to diminish at that hour, and then fell off even more sharply
between 6 and 9 a.m. (see Figure 3-1), as did the number of arrests of
rioters. Whereas the police had picked up 135 people in the six hours
between 9 p.m. Saturday and 3 a.m. Sunday, they arrested only 30
more between 3 a.m. and 9 a.m.

Looters along 7th Avenue reappeared in force at about 10 o'clock
Sunday morning. It was then that people were seen bringing along
tools with which to break into the Allstate Office Equipment Corpo-

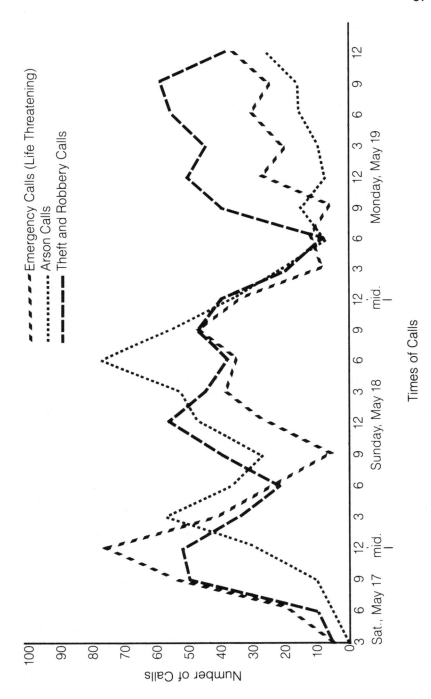

Figure 3-1. Riot Calls to 911 Received at Dade County Public Safety Department, by Number and Time.

ration at 72nd Street, E.J. Liquors at 70th Street and Farrey's Hardware at 72nd Street, which was also destroyed by fire. By late Sunday afternoon, most of the stores along the avenue had been broken into and all merchandise of value carted away. Scavengers continued to pick through the debris until about 9 that night, but by this time the police had become strong enough to make looting a risky activity, and the disorder began to wane.

Sunday: The Meeting at the Community Relations Board

Officials of the Dade County Community Relations Board (CRB) met Sunday morning to discuss what might be done to cool things off. The board, set up in 1968, represents blacks, Hispanics and whites (called "Anglos" in Miami) from major community organizations throughout the county. It not only provides a forum for airing concerns but also acts as a contact point between minority groups and police and city agencies. At the morning meeting the board decided to call a large gathering that afternoon to which it invited police and government officials and black community activists. The meeting began at 1 p.m. at the CRB's headquarters in the wealthy suburb of Coral Gables. Jammed into the organization's board room were about one hundred people, including top-ranking police officials—although the chiefs of both departments were busy with the riot and could not attend—several members of the city and county commissions, Miami Mayor Maurice Ferre, State Attorney Janet Reno, about twenty prominent blacks and reporters from the city's newspapers and television and radio stations.

Not all of Miami black leaders had agreed that such a meeting should be held or, if it were, that they should attend. Willard Fair, of the Urban League, said he considered the riot a justified expression of black anger and that therefore black leaders should not be going into the streets and urging people to return to their homes. Accordingly, he went off to play golf while the meeting took place, shot a score in the mid-eighties, including four birdies, and then issued a statement to the press: "I stated," he wrote later in a diary of his activities during the riot, "that anyone who had any understanding of the ramifications of dehumanization and social isolation could understand the riots and that the Black community's behavior is socially justifiable and understandable. I was criticized. Many whites thought . . . it was irresponsible . . . because they assumed that Black leaders were there to protect them and not to lead Black folks."

Another prominent black who did not attend the CRB meeting

was Archie Hardwick, director of the James E. Scott Community Association, the city's largest antipoverty agency. "People called me and asked me what could be done about the riot and I said there was nothing they could do," he said. "All we could do was to tell people to stay inside. In a riot you have to wait until it goes its course." He said the CRB meeting would produce little more than the familiar shouting match between black and white leaders. "What power does the board have anyway?" he asked. "What can they deliver? Nothing. Outside of us getting into some verbal calisthenics and yelling at each other—'You white folks are full of shit,' 'No, we're not full of shit.'—it doesn't accomplish anything. If they don't know that blacks are angry at them, then they're fools.

"The meeting was called by a lot of different people and groups who want to be recognized by the white establishment as being able to keep it quiet out there. I told my people to cool it. Let the white folks come to us."

The session was held anyway, lasted about four hours and ended in confusion.* At its start, government officials announced a list of things that had already been done to try to stifle the riot. The governor, they said, had declared a state of emergency under which liquor stores, bars and gun shops throughout the city were closed. A curfew had also been imposed within the riot area from 8 p.m. to 6 a.m. Anyone caught on the streets between these hours would be subject to arrest. "I want you to know that the eyes of the world are on Miami," Mayor Ferre told the group. He had already, he said, asked two nationally prominent blacks, Jesse Jackson of Chicago and Andrew Young of Atlanta, to come to the city the following day to talk to local blacks and try to help calm things down.

This was met, first, with stony silence and then with anger on the part of several blacks, who regarded it as a direct slap in the face. Not only did they resent his bringing in outsiders—and doing so without consulting any of them—but also the fact that by calling in Jackson and Young, Ferre seemed to be saying that the Miami riot was not the result of a legitimate grievance among blacks but the failure of local black leadership to lead properly. "It was as if he was asking the big niggers to come in and get all the little niggers into line," Hardwick said afterward.

One by one the blacks in attendance got up to say what they felt should be done. Charles Cherry, head of the state branch of the

---

*Our account of what happened comes from viewing a thirty-minute tape of the meeting recorded by WPBT-TV, the city's public television station.

NAACP, said he thought they should draw up a list of demands. If the white officials acquiesced to these demands, black local leaders could take the list to the streets as an inducement to stop rioting. Otis Pitts, head of the Tacolcy Center, a multiservice social agency in Liberty City, accused a county commissioner of not pushing hard enough for programs that benefit blacks. To give "real hope" to the minority community, he said, "you need to do something very different and dramatic from what you ordinarily do." The commissioner shot up from her seat and said he had no right to criticize her, then made disparaging references to "people who make money from being street leaders."

Clinton Brown, a black IBM executive, said he thought the curfew would only give the police the excuse to push black people around and "is only going to make it worse." Robert Simms, director of the CRB and also black, said that twelve broadcast news outlets had made air time available for blacks to broadcast appeals for calm. There was much talk of having black community leaders put on white armbands and go out on the streets, as they had done in the 1960s, to help stop the riot. Some blacks felt this would be of little avail. "They're not really listening to us at this time," said Francena Thomas, director of the Department of Black Affairs and Women's Concerns at Florida International University. "No one from the black community can go out there and tell them to hold it down, because now their real feelings are coming out." One community worker stood up to announce that, indeed, she supported the riot. The damage the blacks had done was nowhere near as serious as the damage done to them, she said: "I'm for it. I support it. Some buildings were burned, but what the heck?"

The object of most of the blacks' ire was State Attorney Reno, who sat up at the front of the meeting staring back at the speakers, grim and unblinking. The list of famous cases was invoked once more— Johnny Jones, Randy Heath, McDuffie. If she resigned right then, she was told, lives might be saved that night. In response, Miss Reno told them she was as "bitterly disappointed" as they were over the McDuffie verdict and that she would accept any kind of investigation into her conduct of the state attorney's office. But she would never resign. "That," she said, "would be tantamount to giving in to mob rule."

About 5 p.m. Sunday, with the riot outside at full throttle, a retired black social worker named Georgia Ayers got up to talk. In a booming voice that reined the meeting into silence, she said that even if it didn't work it was everyone's duty to get out onto the streets and try to get people to stay in their homes. "Night is coming and we're still here talking!" she shouted. "You all who were here in sixty-eight, you know what has to be done. Get your armbands and get out in the streets. If you don't, a lot of our young are going to get killed."

Sunday Night and Monday Morning

Mrs. Ayers' warning had already come too late. The eight white victims of the riot all died—or, as in the Kulp case, were fatally injured—some time Saturday night. The nine black deaths occurred on Sunday and Monday, as the police and guardsmen began moving in and taking back sections of the city. Four blacks had been killed by early Sunday morning: Elijah Aaron, forty-three, father of five, an irrigation system worker who had to quit his job after two heart attacks and kidney problems, was shot to death on 27th Avenue and 44th Street by a PSD patrolman who claimed Aaron was looting a tire store and that he had pointed a pistol at the policeman. Abram Phillips, twenty-one, father of one, was shot by a Miami police sergeant at 22nd Avenue and 72nd Street after Phillips, according to the sergeant, had fired four shots at him with a pistol. Michael Scott, seventeen, a student at McArthur High North, a school for problem students, was killed by a security guard at the Jet Food Market on 27th Avenue and 54th Street. Kenneth China, twenty-two, was found dead on 26th Avenue and 53rd Street from what a police report said was a "stray bullet."

Late Sunday afternoon, about when the CRB meeting was breaking up, three more blacks were shot by white motorists driving through black areas. One of the victims, fourteen-year-old Andre Dawson, had run after his sister, who had gone to a store on 3rd Avenue and 83rd Street despite her mother's warning to stay where she could call them both in for the curfew. Suddenly what witnesses later said was a blue pickup truck or van raced down 83rd Street and three shots rang out. Two of the bullets struck Dawson in the head; he was dead on arrival at Jackson Memorial Hospital. At about the same time, Eugene Brown, forty-four, a cement finisher and father of three who liked to talk of the day he would open his own construction business, was driving two of his children and his wife, Rosie, to a U-Totem store on 83rd Street at North Miami Avenue to get some orange juice. The store had been partially looted the previous night but was still open for business. While Brown waited in the car, the other three went toward the store. Shots were fired from what eyewitnesses think might also have been a blue truck. Rosie ducked down behind her car. When she raised her head she saw her husband had been hit and was sitting there "with blood all over his mouth." She drove him to Jackson Hospital, where he also was dead on arrival.

The third Sunday afternoon victim was a thirty-five-year-old truck driver named Thomas Reese, who, at about 6 p.m., was drinking beer among a crowd of thirty persons watching the fire at a grocery store on 103rd Street at 13th Avenue that had been burning since early that morning. Up the street two teenage boys were throwing rocks at passing vehicles. Witnesses remember that Reese had just finished telling them to stop when the boys scored a hit on a truck. The vehicle skidded abruptly to a stop, and the driver started firing at the crowd from his cab. Everybody scattered, but before Reese could get behind cover he received a fatal bullet wound in his back.

The most controversial police shooting of the riot occurred Sunday night on the corner of 2nd Avenue and 42nd Street in the Haitian district of the city. There, at about 8 o'clock, a thirty-nine-year-old Haitian minister named LaFontant Bien-Aimé was shot to death by a Miami policeman as he was driving in his van with his thirteen-year-old son, Kensy. The police officer, Karl Robbins, thirty-seven, said he was chasing looters away from a furniture warehouse on the corner when suddenly a van bore down on him as if trying to run over him. As he jumped out of the way, Robbins said later in a police report, he fired his shotgun at the driver. "The van continued west on 42nd Street approximately eight to ten feet, where it struck a parked, unattended vehicle in the street," he said. "The driver expired on the scene." Bien-Aimé's family maintained that he had not been looting, but was only on his way to his church a block north of the shooting scene for his regular Sunday night services. A subsequent grand jury investigation issued no indictment of the officer after the state attorney's office said it found evidence that the minister had indeed been inside the furniture warehouse.

The last black to die in the riot was Allen Mills, thirty-three, a janitor at a luxury apartment house on Rickenbacker Causeway. He was shot to death by two City of Miami policemen at 4:30 Monday afternoon on the corner of 7th Avenue and 54th Street. According to the police, Mills, who had done time for armed robbery and was then on probation for shoplifting, had been riding his bicycle around the area and acting erratically. At one point, they said, he threatened police officers with a four-inch folding knife, then rode off. In another confrontation, the police said, he attacked two officers at a barricade and was shot seven times. He ran twenty feet before he fell. Mills died shortly after at Jackson Hospital.

By midnight Sunday the riot was fast running out of steam. Some 3,000 National Guardsmen were in the area, and although only half this number were actually available for street duty they still gave the police enough manpower to begin shrinking the perimeter and moving in to discourage systematic looting. Many of the arson calls now were instances where fires were blazing up again in buildings that had not been adequately hosed down during the height of the riot. What looting remained was being carried on by scavengers sifting through the ravaged and burned-out buildings in search of goods left behind by the earlier waves. It was also approaching Monday morning, when many people had to get up and go to work.

As dawn broke on Monday, the city was still shaken and full of fear—stores and offices in the downtown section of Miami closed shortly after lunch that day following a false rumor that blacks had burst out of Liberty City and were on the rampage. But the command post log at the PSD's Central District noted: "Situation becoming stabilized."

On Tuesday, burglary calls to the 911 number dropped to their preriot level. The police made only ten arrests all day for riot-related activity. By Wednesday it was over. Most of the Guard troops were being sent home. Barricades at perimeter checkpoints were opened, allowing whites to drive through black areas of the city once again. The public schools, which had been closed Monday and Tuesday, opened their doors and took thousands of children back off the streets. Although the curfew remained in effect until Friday, Director Jones of the PSD extended the evening hours from 8 to 10 p.m. And by the end of Wednesday, for the first time in five days, the PSD log could record: "There were no unusual problems throughout the day."

Notes

1. "Rage at Verdict," *Miami Herald,* May 18, 1980, p. 32A.
2. Map compiled by City of Miami Planning Department.
3. "Riot Takes 18th Life," *Miami Herald,* June 29, 1980, p. 18.
4. Table compiled from calls to 911 number received by the Dade County Public Safety Department.

Miami police officers apprehend a youth suspected of participating in the riot, May 17, 1980 (United Press International Photo)

4   The Police

By the time we had all our tactics together, the riot had run its course.
      —Major Robert Windsor of the
      Dade County Public Safety
      Department.

At one time or another, police officers from all twenty-seven incorporated towns and cities within Dade County saw duty during the May riot. Additional help came from neighboring Broward County, from the Florida Highway Patrol, from the Florida Marine Patrol, even from the Florida Fresh Water Fish and Game Commission. The two departments that saw the most action were the City of Miami Police Department (MPD) and the Dade County Public Safety Department (PSD), which patrols the unincorporated regions of the county. Although some rioting occurred in all black sections of Dade County, the bulk of the violence—some 75 percent of the destruction and nearly all the attacks on whites—happened in the large square area in the north central part of the county known as Liberty City. The population of Liberty City is about evenly divided between poor and working-class blacks. Because its boundaries cut across city and county lines, it is patrolled by two different police departments. The 40 percent to the east that lies within Miami city limits is the responsibility of the Miami Police Department. The rest, lying to the west and northwest of the city, is within the purview of the Public Safety Department.

The differences between the two departments are readily apparent. The MPD, a force of 660 men and women, dress in dark blue uniforms and drive white cars with green markings. They operate out of an impressive new headquarters building on the outskirts of downtown Miami and police an area that is entirely urban, diversely populated and, within the low-rise limits of Florida cities, densely settled. The PSD's force of 1,450 wear brown and tan uniforms and patrol in white cars with brown markings. They operate out of six police stations around the county and rule over a rural and suburban as well as urban population. The mobilization order calling in all PSD officers for riot duty threw together policemen who normally covered ghetto streets in Liberty City with those more accustomed to flat country roads where people are far outnumbered by groves of mango and avocado trees. Not surprisingly, a large share of the PSD crime statistics comes out of its Central District station, which covers Liberty City. Although the PSD's Liberty City beat has less than 5 percent of the county's population, the year before the riot it produced 23 percent of its robberies and 40 percent of the attacks "with knife or cutting instrument."

The reputation of the two departments among black residents of Liberty City is bad or less than bad, depending on which black person you talk to. Neither department enjoys much of a public relations advantage over the other—nor, for that matter, does either seem to have markedly better or worse relations with blacks than do most other police forces in the country. Many police officers in both departments seem convinced, however, that their high commands, by listening to community complaints and by giving close attention to affirmative action plans, have gone overboard to cater to black sensibilities. They argue that this has made the patrolman's job of enforcing the law in Miami more difficult because blacks now feel freer to challenge an officer's authority. As for some of the higher police officials, their conviction that they had done a good job responding to black complaints about police conduct led them to view the May riot almost as a betrayal of the police by the black community.

MPD Chief Kenneth Harms, for one, said after the riot that he was disappointed that black leaders had not done more to cool things off, considering how the department had bent over backwards to befriend the community. "We had what we considered to be a good working relationship with the black community," said the chief. "Hell, that's what I was doing out there at 3 p.m. on Saturday, when I'd much rather have been cutting grass," he said of his appearance in African Square Park on the afternoon of the riot.

MPD Captain Lawrence Boemler, who was working as patrol commander when the first bottles were thrown, shares Chief Harms's view. He points as examples of police involvement with the community to such preriot efforts as organizing police-community groups to discuss problems, placing policemen in schools to help teachers with delinquency, developing of neighborhood crime-watch programs, greatly increasing efforts to hire black policemen (albeit under a federal court order) and holding sensitivity-training sessions between Miami policemen and black civilians. "What the riot showed," says Captain Boemler, who was shot and wounded by a looter on the second day of the disturbance, "was that, when it all hit the fan, the openness of the department and all the efforts at good police/community relations made no difference."

When it came to law enforcement activities, the preference among policemen from both departments in the months before the May riot seems to have been to try to avoid contact with the black community rather than to deal with it aggressively. Patrolmen did little more than answer radio calls; they rarely stopped suspicious people, followed up crime leads, or bothered to serve arrest warrants. Arrests for traffic violations, which is one index of aggressive patrolling, fell in the PSD's Central District by more than 50 percent from January-May 1979 to January-May 1980—from 7,251 to 2,981. The record of field interrogations—reports filled out on suspicious persons encountered during a police officer's tour—went down by 80 percent during the same period, from 3,140 to 656. The PSD had also stopped answering all but the most serious calls from the James E. Scott Houses, a sprawling one- and two-story public project along 22nd Avenue that has perhaps the biggest crime problem in the entire state.

"They were not initiating any actions," says Captain Douglas Hughes of the PSD's Central District. "They were avoiding situations. They weren't doing the 'craft' part of police work at all. They were just answering their calls, putting in their eight hours and then going home. There was a total withdrawal from confrontation with the community. They felt that, God forbid, they should have a conflict with a black citizen."

Part of the problem was a lack of enough officers with which to run an active department. At the MPD, a hiring freeze from 1975 to 1977 had reduced the number of officers from close to 800 to 660, this to handle not only the steady increase in crime over that period but also a rise in criminal activity that in part attended the waves of Mariel immigrants from Cuba in the months preceding the 1980 riot. Homicides in the city rose 80 percent in 1980; purse snatchings and muggings in the downtown shopping district also rose dramatically. Crime became so rampant that in January 1981 the State of Florida lent the city a hundred police officers to handle traffic problems so the Miami police could chase criminals. The freeze was lifted, allowing the department to increase its strength to 814 in the year after the riot. But the department was obliged, under court order, to see to it that 80 percent of the new officers were black, Hispanic, or female, which decreased the pool of people it considered qualified.

"We aren't doing real police work anymore," says Captain George Green, who was in charge of the Emergency Operations Center at the MPD during the May riot. "My officers just go from call to call all day long. I spot-checked my platoon in March and found that on the average they were running ten calls behind. They don't even get a chance to eat." The department used to have sixty-five officers who worked at nothing but stakeouts, playing decoy and doing other plainclothes jobs; they all were dispersed throughout the force and their functions abandoned. It also got rid of the thirty-man warrant squad which spent all day making arrests for the court. "Now we'll serve a warrant only if it's a biggie," says Captain Green.

Another crucial measurement of police efficiency—how quickly they come when they're called—also declined substantially. In a sampling of one percent of police calls, the department found that its response time on the average call increased from 12.4 minutes in 1977 to 19.9 minutes in the early part of 1980. The response time also increased for emergency calls, the "code three's" that indicate an armed robbery, a shooting, or a serious injury, for which there is supposed to be a lapse of no longer than one minute between when the call goes out over the air and when a patrol car is on its way to the scene. Looking at its response time in the first four months of 1980, the department found that 38 percent of its answers to emergency situations were delayed beyond the one-minute limit.

The PSD was plagued by similar problems. By the time of the riot it had more officers than it had in 1975—1,458 compared to 1,226— but this represented only an 18 percent increase, whereas the county-wide population had increased 28 percent. And during the same period, the amount of crime rose even more precipitously. Robberies in the PSD's Central District increased by 57 percent from 1978 to 1979. Homicides rose 47 percent, rapes 37 percent and burglaries 48 percent. In addition, because of the problem of finding qualified new police officers, the department was not able to get itself up to authorized strength. At the time of the riot, the Central District had only 158 out of the 210 men and women it was supposed to have for twenty-four-hour duty. It took them nearly half an hour to respond to the average call.

Another reason for the general pulling back from involvement with blacks was the fear the police had of being mobbed by residents of the community unless they showed up in overwhelming numbers. This is most dramatically seen in the informal policy of the PSD over the years to abandon regular patrol of the Scott Housing Project in Liberty City. No crime statistics are available for the project alone, which stretches along 22nd Avenue from 71st to 75th Streets. But its residents live in such terror of being burgled, mugged, raped, or assaulted that in the hundred-degree nights of summertime—and without any air conditioning—they commonly sleep with their windows shut tight rather than give an opening to an intruder. Criminals often use the project as a hideout because they know the police will not pursue them after they have mugged or assaulted someone along 22nd Avenue. "The project has become a sanctuary," said Chief Dale Bowlin, head of the PSD's uniform division, "because they know that we won't go in there." Unlike housing projects in other cities, Scott has no police of its own, and, because its architecture consists of one- and two-story apartment houses separated by alley ways that twist and turn like a maze, the police cannot penetrate it readily with patrol cars. "At night an officer can easily get trapped in there," said Captain Hughes. "You go in with your car and you can't see around corners once you get into those breezeways, and they push a 'Dempsey Dumpster' into an alley way to block it. Now, if you want to get out fast, you're in trouble. So you begin to behave over a period of time in a way that minimizes your risk."

Before the riot, the police had special rules for answering such calls from the Scott Houses as they chose to bother with. First, a call for the police was answered at all only if it came into the 911 switch-board more than once, on the theory that if it was genuine and dire enough, more than one person would call, or a single person would call more than once. A single call was suspected of being a ruse to get a police officer in for the purpose of hurting him in some way. Once the police decided to answer a call, different policies held for the day and night. In the daytime, because it was theorized that much of what the police refer to as the "problem population" was away at school, calls were answered by a two-man patrol car. At night, calls were answered by three cars: a lead car to open up the way and look out for traps, a middle car that would actually handle the call and the last car to make sure the exit was not blocked by an unfriendly crowd so the whole team could get out quickly if it had to.

For many teenagers (and adults, too), gathering in force to taunt the police is a major form of amusement in Liberty City, particularly in the summer, when young people are home from school and have nothing to do. "What usually happens," says Captain Hughes, a former New York City policeman who has been with the PSD since the early 1970s,

is that you get a crowd of youths, and in the back are the bottle throwers and the "screamers" yelling "Get Whitey" or "Get the mother." Then a bottle crashes somewhere, and no matter what you're doing—usually trying to arrest someone and get him out of there— they start yelling, "He's beating the man! He's beating the man!" Or you get some guy who's assaulted another guy and stabbed him, and they start shouting, "Don't kick that man!" And you've suddenly got your hands full.

I remember once, several years ago, I was sent into a project to serve a homicide warrant on a man, and the man's wife started fight-ing with us and wouldn't let us take him. "He didn't do anything," she starts yelling. Then before I know it I'm suddenly rolling around on the ground fighting with the woman, and the whole project is coming out. We called in four more cars to help us, and when the people saw the PSD brown-and-whites, more of them came pouring out and pretty soon there were 300 or 400 people there. At times like that you need to get out very fast, because with every second of delay the intensity and the size of the crowd increases. We all piled into the cars and drove off and by the time we left, the avenue was filled with blacks. There must have been 750 people there, still yelling, "The cops beat that man!" or "The cops shot that man!"

Such incidents still seem to be almost routine. About a month after the riot we were in Liberty City one night joining on his patrol Sergeant John Carrel of the PSD, a burly former military policeman and a graduate of the University of Florida, who was working the four-to-twelve shift out of Central District. At about 5:30 p.m., while Carrel was on his supper break at a restaurant, he heard a call over his walkie-talkie that two men had tried to rob a pool hall along 22nd Avenue and 44th Street of the contents of its jukebox and that there had been a shooting. Carrel raced his rickety cruiser to the scene, using his siren to clear intersections and stomping alternately on the brake and the gas. There, he found his eight-man squad surrounding the place, training their shotguns at it over the hoods of their cars. One of the robbers had been shot to death by the manager; the other, after pistol-whipping a jukebox route man who was in the place at the time, was thought to have taken a hostage and secreted himself in a crawl space between the roof and the ceiling.

The avenue was blocked off. Carrel was soon joined by his lieutenant, his captain and assorted other brass, along with the county's five-officer Special Resources Team, which is a SWAT-style outfit, and a half dozen more police officers to help control bystanders and traffic. A crowd of some 200 blacks formed on the sidewalk across the avenue from the pool hall. Reporters and cameramen from three television stations arrived. They filmed the scene and the crowd and interviewed a black community-relations officer called in to help control the bystanders. By now the SWAT team, armed with revolvers, riot shotguns and a police dog, were laying siege. Their first act was to pull the dead man, who turned out to be nineteen years old, out of the doorway in a trail of blood. On his stomach was the little bag of jukebox quarters that had cost him his life. Finally, the SWAT team stormed inside. Their quarry, who as it turned out had no hostage, gave up readily after he saw he wasn't going to be shot, and was speedily taken away.

Only now, when the outcome was no longer in doubt, did the crowd start to get restless. Three incidents occurred that might have provoked an unruly reaction. First, a young boy came over to the rescue van, loudly proclaimed that he had been shot in the leg by a policeman several blocks away and demanded treatment. The rescue man found no wound, but pretended to treat the boy anyway. Then a middle-aged black man, who was angry and obviously quite drunk, came over and started to berate Sergeant Carrel for having shot the man in the pool hall. Carrel explained in an exceedingly patient fashion that the pool hall manager, not the police, had done the shooting. The man didn't seem to believe what Carrel said and stormed off, muttering. Finally, something happened in the crowd that prompted a small black women to begin banging and kicking a police cruiser. A patrolman—red-faced and holding a semiautomatic rifle—began yelling back at her. Quickly, Carrel's superior, a lieutenant, came over and tried to have the officer whisked away to avoid an incident. Carrel, however, wanting to back up the men of his squad, told the lieutenant that the man had done nothing wrong. "He goes when we all go," Carrel said angrily.

At last, in the manner of an army platoon pulling itself gingerly out of an engagement with the enemy, the police let the traffic resume its flow, warily got into their cars and left the scene.

Another reason for the negative police attitude toward the black community comes from the general misanthropic view that to one degree or another seems to have been adopted by policemen almost everywhere. Whether their disaffection comes from dealing almost exclusively with poor and hopeless people whose conduct does not always jibe with the police officer's views of morality, or whether it has something to do with the reasons people become police officers in the first place, is open to anyone's speculation. In Miami one of the obvious reasons for the lack of police involvement with the black community has to do with geography and climate. As with black and white citizens generally in Miami, there is little off-the-job contact between police officers and blacks. Officers certainly do not live in Liberty City; a majority of them do not even live in Miami, because the moderately priced housing they can afford lies increasingly in the rapidly expanding Hispanic areas where police officers, sharing a general feeling among Miami Anglos, choose not to live. Instead, they tend to reside in the large suburban housing developments in the south and southwestern parts of the county.

But even during their workday, it is possible for the police to do their jobs almost completely cut off from the community they are hired to protect. Liberty City consists mostly of one- and two-story houses and apartments set back from the sidewalk by a yard and fronted by wide avenues and boulevards on which cars travel at high speed. The manner of police patrol consists of riding up and down the avenue, car windows rolled up, air conditioners blasting, very much as if the police officers were in mobile isolation booths. The only time they leave their cars is to answer a specific call for assistance. At mealtime, county police officers leave Liberty City to eat in Hialeah, in part because they regard lunchrooms in the black neighborhood as unclean.

"It's always easier to shoot people you don't know," says Captain Hughes, who has been fighting a seemingly losing battle to get his men to leave their cars and go out and meet members of the community:

> We've got to get out of the motorized cruiser mentality, somehow. You can talk to people when you're handling a call. You don't have to drive out of the district for a drink of water; go to the local store. They've got to realize they're not occupiers, they're members of the community. When you go into black areas as a policeman you need to develop some credibility with people. You can't just stay in your cars and go zooming up and down.

Not only do the police tend to avoid contact with the community except for the calls they have to answer, but in many instances they actively ignore crimes that are staring them in the face. At one notorious gin mill on 69th Street and 17th Avenue, the prostitution and drug dealing became so rife several years ago that the proprietor was ordered by a local judge to put up a chain link fence around his parking lot to keep the activity outside of his property lines, in at least a gesture of obeisance to state liquor laws. Up and down the two streets flanking the bar, prostitutes lounge along fences in front of one-bedroom shacks, thirty or forty at a time, trolling openly for customers. In the middle of the block sits a pristinely whitewashed edifice housing Walker's Church of God and Christ, whose pastor, Elder Elijah Edwards, erected his own chain-link fence to keep the hookers off church grounds. Edwards, an elderly gentleman who comes from Titusville, Florida, was assigned to the church just before the May riot, and is now trying to get reassigned somewhere else. "If you don't bother them, they don't bother you," he said of the prostitutes. "But when I agreed to come here I didn't realize it was going to be like this. This is a terrible place."

Elder Edwards's live-and-let-live attitude is shared by many men of the PSD. "The law's not enforced around here because it would generate complaints," said one sergeant. "If you get a prostitute who knifes her john, we'll make an arrest. But otherwise we'll arrest prostitutes only if they're blocking traffic."

Part of the problem, he said, was that a PSD vice squad specializing in prostitution and drug activity was disbanded a year before the riot for budgetary reasons. Another reason is that many police officers feel that nothing they do in the ghetto will make any difference in the crime rate anyway, so why try? Indeed, many policemen feel that crime is simply a fixture of life there, like mom-and-pop stores and barbecue stands. It's the way the people *want* to live, they argue. Why else would they mob policemen when they come in to arrest criminals? Said one Liberty City sergeant:

> When we used to get an emergency call in the Northeast District [an all-white area also policed by the PSD], which happened maybe three times a week, you'd go in and find a guy beat up, and do a big crime scene. First-aid, an investigation and all. You'd spend a lot of time on it. Here, we get code-threes [the emergency code] seven and eight times a night. Most of them are stabbings, shootings—usually a drunk blowing off a shotgun. You get there as quick as you can but there's not much you can do. The rescue truck is there for the guy who's hurt. You go to the hospital and all, but that only ties you up and wastes a lot of time. Will the guy press charges? *No.* Mostly, it's some buddy of his. He'll go out and beat the shit out of him next week. You can't get too excited about it. There are some legitimate robberies and assaults, but it's mostly friends and relatives beating up on each other. Our feeling is the prostitution, the drug selling, gambling, battery in the house—let them do it.

His attitude toward fighting crime in Liberty City is the same as it is toward replacing the broken lights at the Brownsville Pool on 48th Street and 24th Avenue. "Why bother to replace them when they'll just get broken again?"

On the reverse side of the coin, the police feel that what actions they do take can only expose them to unfavorable scrutiny by the department and get them into trouble. This strong feeling that their superiors as well as the public are against them grew more intense as a result of the McDuffie case. Not only did the PSD hierarchy move quickly to prosecute the officers involved, but both the PSD and the MPD used the occasion to begin clamping down on all uses of force by police officers, deadly or otherwise. "The word has gone out," said Michael Cosgrove, assistant chief of the MPD, "that if the force is excessive, you're going to pay."

This sort of statement both angers and hurts many police officers. While they, too, generally condemn the killing of McDuffie, they see it not as the purposeful misuse of force, but as a case where a group of men very much—indeed, too much—like themselves had lost control and acted hysterically. It is significant that what police officers seem to criticize most about the "McDuffie cops" is not their beating of a man to death, but their trying to cover it up afterward. That was the bad thing they had done—a stupid and unprofessional act. What the

McDuffie cops did while hysterical is understandable because it was human; what they did after they gained their senses is what they should be held accountable for.

"The McDuffie case comes very close to home," says Dr. Mark Axelberd, a psychologist and director of the Counseling and Stress Control Center in Miami. The center is used by the PSD for the psychological testing of recruits and by the MPD for forty-hour classes in stress management. "It was a case where a group of guys went out of control and 'lost it,' just like a lot of officers could have lost it. Policemen see the McDuffie cops and they say, 'Hey, I could be in that awful mess.' "

This tension between the men on the beat, who must deal with the realities of the ghetto, and their superiors, who must answer to the political authorities for the conduct of their men, is not particularly new. But as urban racial problems seem to get worse instead of better, the tension is likely to become considerably more pronounced. "There's a feeling among the men that the department is turning away from them," says Dr. Axelberd:

> They have to deal with the social issues in reality that society deals with abstractly—on the TV screen or in the newspapers. They deal with the problems that society refuses to deal with, and then they get blamed when they deal with them inappropriately. The cops feel they can't win. A lot of police officers have taken a passive attitude, that there's no sense in getting involved. Anything you do, all it will do is get you into trouble. So it's do what you have to do, keep your mouth shut and look the other way.

The Police Reaction to the Riot

Analyzing the riot with hindsight is a luxury the police departments in Miami did not enjoy on May 17, 1980. But even given the fact that the police had long been out of touch with the black community, it is still surprising how completely they failed to detect the degree of anger attending the McDuffie case—and to prepare at least minimally to confront its consequences. After the riot Chief Harms of the MPD appeared to be saying that he was not surprised at all that the disturbance had occurred. In a broadside against the media in general and the *Miami Herald* in particular, he accused the press of inflaming black passions against the police to such an extent that the riot was almost a logical outcome. Testifying before the governor's commission investigating the riot's causes, Harms said the newspapers should take a major share of the blame for the disorder. "The attitudes and perceptions they have created," he said, "made a significant contribution to the emotions of the community preceding the riot."

If this inflammation of anti-police passion was so apparent to Harms after the riot, why wasn't it so before? And if it was obvious before May 17, particularly considering the city's long tradition of rioting, why didn't he better prepare his department to deal with the results? In trying to explain their lack of preparedness, several police officials argue that the acquittals caught them as much by surprise as it did the general public. "We have been criticized by some for not being prepared," says Robert Dempsey, deputy director of the PSD. "But nobody could have anticipated the disposition of that case. And if you say maybe we could have anticipated it, then the question is how do you estimate the degree of reaction? How do you anticipate how violent the reaction will be?"

Many police officers we talked to were well aware of how shaky the prosecution's case really was, especially because, from their viewpoint, judges and juries are always letting guilty people go free because of some technicality or loophole. "We were talking about it the week before, and my dollar was on these guys not getting convicted," says Captain Michael Mahoney of the MPD, a native of Boston who worked in the command post on the first night of the rioting. "We know what it takes to get a conviction and that a lot of times juries can find people not guilty when we know they're totally guilty." Indeed, the betting among those closest to the case—the lawyers at the state attorney's officer itself—was that the McDuffie policemen would get off. "The word around here," says Tom Petersen, chief administrative assistant to State Attorney Janet Reno, "was that an acquittal was a distinct possibility. What I can't understand is why the cops had no contingency plans. The verdict came down about 2 p.m. on a hot Saturday afternoon. No rain. The start of a weekend. It couldn't have come at a more inopportune time."

Even more puzzling than their lack of contingency plans in the event of an acquittal was why the police remained as if paralyzed even after the verdict was announced—and why, once the bottles started flying through the air, the departments were so slow to respond.

As we noted in the previous chapter, both Chief Harms of the MPD and Director Jones of the PSD learned of the verdict at about 3 p.m. while on the podium of the anticrime rally in African Square Park, barely two blocks from where four persons would shortly be beaten to death. Jones left after he gave his speech. Harms, because the park is located inside his police district, asked Major Clarence Dickson, a black officer and head of community relations, to have his men circulate around and evaluate the emotions of the crowd. Most of the people in the park, however, had come for an anticrime rally, so while they expressed anger over the acquittals, it is hardly surprising that they did not hint of being about to commit serious violence. Chief Harms departed for his home in southwest Dade County.

At the Miami police headquarters, the early evening "B" shift checked in between 3:30 and 4 p.m. Captain Larry Boemler, the shift commander, was told about one or two phone calls to the complaint desk threatening to "get a policeman tonight." But otherwise all seemed quiet. On instructions from Chief Harms, he passed the word to his men to keep a "low profile" that night. "I told them no high-speed chases with siren, no foot chases, no drug arrests. I also told them in the complaint room that we wouldn't handle any domestic disturbances tonight." The only other precaution was to take a car from the southern part of the city and put it in the Liberty City district. The MPD thus had five cars there, instead of four, when the riot broke.

Captain Boemler rode around Liberty City himself to check on the district. One stop was at a Burger King, patronized by blacks, at 7th Avenue and 36th Street. "They had all heard about the verdict," he said. "And we talked about it. 'Yeh, it's too bad,' and everything. They were mad, but I didn't get back that there was going to be any violence."

In the western section of Liberty City, at the PSD's Central District headquarters located in back of a shopping center at 79th Street and 22nd Avenue, the police were no better prepared. Black residents of the area had also been calling up the PSD to talk about the McDuffie case. "It wasn't so much that they were angry at us," says Lieutenant Randall McGee, the watch commander. "It was just that they seemed very emotional and wanted to talk to someone."

When the officers of the Central District assembled for their roll call, nothing was done to prepare them for anything but a normal night. "Upon reporting for duty at 4 p.m.," reads the PSD's After-Action Report compiled after the riot by Captain Bera Pitts, "all Area II police personnel were aware of the acquittal and discussed it freely at roll call. No action was initiated on a District level to develop contingency plans in the event of a reactionary disorder. Each officer was given his field assignment and released to duty."

"We were told at roll call that no one knew what to expect," says Sgt. Robert Edwards, one of three squad leaders who was in the thick of the riot. "They said make sure you have your helmets and night sticks, but as far as being prepared, we weren't prepared. That was it." Of the PSD men in Liberty City, Edwards was the only one who had ever experienced a riot before. In 1968, as a member of the police force in Prince Georges County, Maryland, he had been called in to help out the police in Washington, D.C., during the extensive rioting after the death of Dr. Martin Luther King, Jr. Given that experience, Edwards said, he felt uneasy going out on patrol that night. "I'd seen the King riot and I knew what could happen," he said. "I thought we were definitely going to have some problems, and I remember saying to the guys before we left the station: 'I hope we're all back here again at two o'clock in the morning.' "

On the MPD side of Liberty City, the start of the riot was announced at precisely 6:02 p.m. by Unit 621, a car that normally handles traffic problems, which came on the air to say: "I just got a bottle thrown at me out here at 62nd Street and 14th Avenue."* Unit 210, with squad leader Sergeant José Burgos, immediately came on the radio to warn all police units to stay out of the area, a warning he was to repeat three or four times more during the next thirty minutes. The radio quickly began to crowd up with static calls of alarm as the ghetto slid determinedly into chaos. A motorcycle patrolman called in to say he had just been hit by a rock. A call came in about a child shot in African Square Park, but no one could find her. Unit 212 said he had just got his rear window shot out at 114th Street and 59th Avenue. At 6:18 p.m., the county police got their first call several blocks to the west, on 62nd Street and 18th Avenue: "Two hundred and fifty negro males throwing rocks at passing cars." Unit 212 came back on the air to say he hadn't been shot at, it was a rock that had broken his window. At 6:20 p.m., Lieutenant Allan Schlefstein of the MPD ordered a car to 7th Avenue and 62nd Street to keep out all westbound motorists. "Correction," he said quickly. "That's any *white* motorists."

At 6:23 p.m., twenty minutes after the first bottle, the police got their initial call about a person being beaten. "Attention all units: Be advised a man being beaten at 13th Avenue and 62nd Street by crowd . . ." Sergeant Burgos came on the radio to tell other cars to cut out all unnecessary radio traffic, then ordered two units driven by black policemen to go into the area to see if they could find the victim. Two minutes later came a report of a man shot at 12th Avenue and 62nd Street. At 6:36 p.m., Lieutenant Schlefstein reported that whites were still getting into the area. "We're going to lose this," he said, "if we don't stop that traffic on 62nd."

By then, the men sent in by Sergeant Burgos to look for the victim of the beating had reported seeing nothing, but calls about the beating were still coming in to the central operators at 911. "We were at 17th

---

*All quoted radio chatter came from listening to police tapes.

and 62nd," Burgos recalled later, "and a black passer-by told us a man was being beaten at 14th and 62nd and that unless we got through to him they were going to beat him to death." Burgos and Lieutenant Schlefstein decided to go themselves. Says Burgos:

> I asked for another car to help us, but we were in an unmarked car and I figured we could get in and out without being hurt, so I didn't wait for a backup. We headed east on 62nd Street and as we approached 14th Avenue we saw a white male on the sidewalk. Several blacks were around him, about twenty of them. He was covered with blood. He was in a sitting position and trying to get up, but he couldn't. We pulled the car across the traffic, and when we got to him we saw he was a "ricket" [Miami police jargon for a derelict] that had stumbled into the area. He was moaning, "Why me? Why's this happening to me?" People scattered when we went in to get him but then rocks and bottles started flying. One just missed the lieutenant—a big boulder. We got the guy on a blanket on the floor in the back and took off, rocks glancing off the glass, until we got out of there.

By now it was about 6:40 p.m., and the police were about to lose control of the city. Blacks were pouring out on the streets of Liberty City in increasing numbers. At the PSD, according to Captain Pitts's After-Action Report, men going out on duty at 6:30 p.m. "were briefed by on-duty supervisors to the effect that the general core-area clientele were inflamed and violent."

The MPD had set up a temporary command post at a firehouse, on 46th Street and 14th Avenue, from which to launch missions to rescue people reportedly being beaten on 62nd Street, sixteen blocks away. However, the commander at the post, Captain Mahoney, was having serious manpower problems. "We were really afraid at this point that we didn't have enough men to take charge of the situation," he says, "and we didn't want that to get out to the community." The result was that the police stayed hunkered down at the firehouse listening to the growing riot over their radios. They also started hearing reports of the crowds heading down to the rally that had been called at the Metro Justice Building.

"Here we are," recalls Captain Mahoney, "we're at this damn fire station. Everything's going to hell. Crowds throwing rocks and bottles, motorists trapped, people being beaten, reports of 'man down.' And then we're getting calls about huge crowds heading down to the meeting at the Justice Building. Now I'm really concerned, and I'm saying to myself, 'I'm just not prepared for anything else.' "

Like soldiers on the losing skirmish line, police officers manning roadblocks on the outskirts of the original flare-up on 62nd Street were being pushed back and back by advancing rioters. In the PSD part of

Liberty City, the roadblock set up to stop cars from driving east along 62nd Street had to be rapidly moved westward from 17th Avenue to 22nd Avenue, then to 27th Avenue and, finally, to 37th Avenue on the Hialeah city line. To the north, rioters pushed the police back from 62nd Street to 79th Street and finally to 103rd Street. To the south, the line moved from 54th Street to 41st Street to 36th Street. "Pretty soon," said Sergeant Carrel of the PSD, "we had our ass in the Miami River."

As the perimeter expanded, the police had more and more streets to keep blocked off, and it soon became impossible to seal off the riot area. Whites continued to filter into the killing ground. The situation was complicated by a complete lack of wooden barricades during the opening phase of the disturbance. All the barricades for the city and county belong to the County's Department of Traffic and Transportation. Not only was there a logistical problem in getting them in operation quickly, but once they were handed out the PSD, as a county agency, tended to get the lion's share. By 6:45 p.m., three quarters of an hour after it all began, the MPD still had not a single barricade to put up along 7th Avenue to keep motorists from driving west on 62nd Street.

The perimeter was also porous because the police stationed at roadblocks had a tendency to drive off to answer emergency calls; and when they left, nothing remained to warn whites to stay out. "Some of the guys got a little frantic with all the emergency calls," said Lieutenant McGee of the PSD. "They'd take off and leave their posts. I'd try to raise them on the radio, but they couldn't be raised." To the east, the MPD was having similar problems keeping its people put. Captain George Green, who was at the Emergency Operations Center (EOC) set up at the Miami police headquarters to replace Captain Mahoney's temporary command post at the fire station, said that unless a sergeant stayed at the roadblock with his officers, they tended to disappear. "Unless you keep on them, they're going to go off," said Green, a failing he attributed to lack of discipline among modern police officers. "When I was a patrolman years ago and was told to stand somewhere I would stay there until I died and never move."

On the MPD's side of Liberty City, the problem of sealing off the riot area was compounded by the fact that for a while there were two command posts—one at the EOC at police headquarters and the other at the fire station on 46th Street. "The EOC would take a man away from one post and put him somewhere else and not tell the people in the firehouse," said one MPD lieutenant. "Then the people commanding the firehouse would act as if they had men where they didn't anymore." It was some four hours after the first rocks and bottles were thrown, according to the log of the PSD, that the perimeter was considered secure on the main streets and avenues (although whites could still filter in on small side streets). "If we had moved in and got the perimeter up a little more quickly," said Captain Green, "we would have saved lives."

By 7 or 8 p.m. the streets inside the riot area were in full disorder; wherever the police came into contact with the rioters, they were made to fear for their lives. Sergeant Edwards of the PSD, whose eight-man squad covered an area from 62nd Street north to 79th Street, says he will find the experience hard to forget:

> We were never given any instructions on what to do out there that night. Whatever I did with my squad I did on my own. If we had gone off to Key Biscayne I don't think anyone would have known we were gone. My main concern was the safety of my officers. They were so scared that night; they have never seen a riot and had never had any riot training. If you have training, then you know you have certain capabilities. That feeling of helplessness is not so overwhelming.

When the rocks and bottles started flying, he put two men at the broad intersection of 62nd Street at 22nd Avenue to block eastbound traffic toward I-95:

> That was about 6:30. Five minutes later I rode by the spot again, and there were the two men standing rigid and holding shotguns, back to back, facing east and west, with their one little police car stopped in the middle of the road. They were scared stiff and I don't blame them. Rocks and bottles were whizzing around them, glass was everywhere. People were racing by in their cars blowing their horns and yelling at them. Pedestrians were screaming at them and throwing things. I took them off the post for their own health.

At one point Edwards got a call that a car had struck a building in the Scott Housing Project along 22nd Avenue and that the driver, a white man, was trapped inside and being beaten and stoned by the mob. "There were three cars and my unit, and we tried to get in, but we couldn't," he said. "The bricks and the bottles, the crowds—it was too thick. Someone came out and said they had set the man's car on fire with him in it. So I canceled the call. By the time we'd have rolled he would have been dead anyway. I'll have to live with that for a long time to come."

The victim was later identified as Emilio Munoz, the only Cuban American killed during the riot. And, as it turned out, Sergeant Edwards was right. Even if he had reached the burning car and pulled Munoz out it would have been too late. According to the Miami medical examiner's officer, as we noted in Chapter 3, Munoz was already dead from the beating by the time the crowd set his car on fire.

About 6:30 p.m., around the time the Kulps were being beaten, Police Chief Harms was sitting down to an Italian supper at Anthony's Restaurant in southwest Dade, keeping in touch with his department through a beeper device attached to his belt. During the meal, he received a worried call from the state attorney's office wondering what the police were doing about protecting the Metro Justice Building should problems occur at the impending rally. Harms said that fifteen PSD policemen had been assigned to duty there and not to worry. "People we regarded as responsible were in attendance," he said. "It seemed peaceful. We'd just gotten over handling major demonstrations with the Latins without any trouble. I thought, 'Hey, this is not the end of the world.' "

Indeed, the action of the police to pull back from the riot rather than charge in and try to at least to hamper the rioters' activity had as much to do with conscious strategy as it did with unpreparedness and lack of manpower. One lesson police strategists took away with them from the disturbances of the 1960s was that it was often police heavy-handedness at the start of the riots—Watts and Newark are good examples—that helped turn small disorders into large ones. Thus the policy in Miami had been not to go in and attempt to smother a disturbance but to hang back, try to isolate it and hope it would run out of steam. "It was not unusual for cars to be rocked-and-bottled on Friday and Saturday night—it was business as usual," said Chief Harms. "If you stand there and make a confrontation, you'll escalate it; it can easily get out of control. Our typical response is that if there's any significant violence, stop the traffic and keep people out instead of officers going in and stopping and chasing kids. Time and time again when making arrests within a black area, the possibility of conflict is escalated."

Like soldiers trained to fight the last war, however, the Miami police forces—and who could fault them?—had failed to perceive that the disorder they were watching develop had already taken a much different course than the ones of the past.

Harms finished his meal and then drove to a church to attend his secretary's wedding, scheduled to start at 8 p.m. As the ceremony was beginning, the people at the Justice Building were bursting into riot, and three more persons had been fatally beaten on 62nd Street. Harms's beeper went off again. "I went to a phone, called the department and saw that significant problems were developing," he says. Among his instructions to Assistant Chief Michael Cosgrove was an order to gather up as many officers as possible and try to lift the siege of the Justice complex.

A diminutive but tough ex-commander of the MPD's SWAT unit, Cosgrove had served as a military police sergeant doing liaison work with the Saigon police during the Vietnam War; at only thirty-two years old he had risen swiftly in the department. His assignment to clear the Justice Building, however, was easier given than executed, considering that it involved trying to stop a riot by 3,000 people with only a handful of police.

His first move was to leave police headquarters and go up on to Route I-95, an elevated highway that overlooks the Justice complex, to have a look. "I saw ten to fifteen police cars that were overturned and on fire," he said. "I saw a fire in the State Office Building. It looked like a fire was beginning in the ground floor of the PSD Building. A mob had broken through the doors of the Justice Building. Some people were shooting in the air with what appeared to be Saturday night specials. It looked like we'd have our hands full." Luckily for Cosgrove, the C shift had just reported for duty, which gave him more men—a total of seventy counting the fifteen that had been sent over from the PSD. He ordered the officers to gather at a staging area at 12th Avenue and 11th Street, a site that was a block and half from the Justice center but screened from the rioters by the superstructure of I-95.

In thinking how to take back the Justice complex, Cosgrove was worried about two things: the safety of the people he had seen trapped in the Justice Building, and possible injuries to his men from sniper fire. Normal police crowd-control maneuvers are meant to break up and move unarmed masses of people engaged in normally peaceful actions such as strikes and demonstrations. "If you go into crowd-control formation and order them to disperse, and they don't, and you have snipers firing at your men," he said, "there's no way your men are not going to return the fire, and you're going to have a lot of people hurt." To try to pick out and "neutralize" possible snipers, he ordered the Special Threat Response Unit, the MPD's SWAT force, to meet him at the Justice Building within fifteen minutes. He then organized thirty of his men into three lines of ten men each stretching across the roadway. They were armed with three-foot riot sticks and protected by helmets and face shields. It was dark by now, and Cosgrove hoped the rioters would not see how small his force really was. In the back of the phalanx, he set up five arrest teams, each with five men and a police dog. The fifteen county policemen were kept in reserve to the rear.

"What I wanted to do was to cause people to believe we were well organized and coming in massive numbers so they would disperse before we got there," he said. "I hoped a show of strength, with riot batons and helmets, would be dramatic enough so we could avoid having a confrontation." By now the crowd was so unruly that Cosgrove decided he couldn't wait for the SWAT team and ordered his column to begin moving. "I started in, marching in cadence, with batons at port arms," he said. "I was up front calling out the cadence. Everyone was in step. It looked impressive, which is what I wanted it to do." And it worked. At the first glimpse of the solid blue phalanx, the rioters turned and fled. "What happened was that by the time we got to the Justice Building, the great majority of the crowd had cleared out. They just left, nearly 3,000 of them. Only a few stragglers were left."

As his men surrounded the building and firemen moved in to douse the fires, Cosgrove said a sniper opened up at them from the parking garage of the Cedars of Lebanon Hospital a block away. The policemen took cover. Cosgrove ducked down behind a burning police car, which chose that moment to explode, hurling Cosgrove and other officers to the ground but hurting no one seriously. With the arrival of the SWAT team, the sniper saw the wisdom of leaving the scene— and quite suddenly it was all over.

Calling in the Guard

Not until the eruption at the Justice Building did the two police departments become convinced that they might not be able to handle the disturbance on their own. Both departments had a mobilization plan that provided for an orderly increase of personnel in four or five steps. It called first for shifting on-duty police officers from one assignment to another, then for calling in off-duty officers and then for asking for help from outside police agencies such as neighboring departments, the Florida Highway Patrol and the Fresh Water Fish and Game Commission. The last phase was a request to the governor to send in the National Guard. Under the metropolitan form of government, this decision rested with Director Jones of the PSD, and it was under his local aegis that the Guard operated.

Three general problems attended the attempt to increase police manpower during the riot. First, the riot quickly grew to such magnitude that the early phases of mobilization made so little difference as to be meaningless. And, by the time police officials got around to asking for the Guard, it was too late to stifle the burgeoning riot. Second, the mobilization succeeded eventually in bringing in enough forces, but in the early stages there was no clear idea about what to do with them once they arrived. Third, the restrictions placed by Governor Robert Graham on the manner in which the Guard could be deployed—restrictions that officials felt necessary, considering the Guard's generally unprofessional performance during the riots of the 1960s—placed a serious limit, as we show later, on their usefulness to the police. Indeed, some police officers feel that when the rioting died down it was not so much a case of the police and the Guard stopping it as of the rioters simply running out of steam. "By the time we had all our tactics together," says Major Robert Windsor, a district commander for the PSD, "the riot had run its course."

At 9:44 p.m., Director Jones put in the call to Tallahassee to send in the Guard. A liaison officer did not arrive at the Central District command post until nearly 11, and the Guard did not begin showing up on the streets until 12:30 Sunday morning. Because the Guard was there under Jones's authority, the county got the lion's share, and also got it first. Only on Sunday night did Guard units begin appearing in force in the City of Miami. "I got to the command center that night and looked out the window to the north and the whole city was aglow," says Captain Mahoney of the MPD. "I asked the captain from the National Guard who was stationed there where the Guard was. 'They're out there,' he said. I said, 'No, they're not.' So we went out looking for them—all along 36th Street, all along 7th Avenue, and we couldn't find one of them."

The Guard did not reach peak strength until Tuesday, May 20, when the riot was just about over. By then, 3,900 troops were listed as being on duty in the area, of which more than half were support personnel; only about 1,500 were actually available to stand on posts— 1,000 in the county and 500 in the city. With twelve-hour shifts, these numbers were cut in half again, to 500 and 250, respectively, on the streets at any one time.

Another problem was that once the Guard and officers from other police departments arrived, there was no ready plan for what they should actually do. "Our mobilization plan is good but very general," says Chief Dale Bowlin, head of the Police Division of the PSD. "We can get a lot of people in in pretty short time, but then everything is left to the specific commanders as to how to use them." In the early hours of mobilization, confusion reigned at police headquarters, with many men standing around not knowing where to go. For a long time, the parking lot of the PSD's Central District was filled with Florida

Highway Patrol officers who had been given no assignment. "I knew we had a lot of them there," says Sergeant Carrel, "but for some reason they weren't getting out on the street." Neither did the police have available any special shock force to go in and help people under attack. In the PSD, the SWAT team, the likely unit for such an assignment, was spread through the shifts and never got itself together during the riot. And lives might certainly have been saved had the departments given prior thought as to where perimeters should be set up at the first sign of trouble. It was only after the riot that such a plan was given consideration. Says Chief Bowlin, "We need to look historically at sections of the city, at what our experience has been there, and then make up a tactical plan for the area."

One of the greatest missed opportunities was the failure of the police to take advantage of the lull in the riot that could have been expected to occur, and that did occur, in the early morning hours following the initial outbreak of violence. In this regard, the police might have profited from a reading of the Kerner Commission Report, which analyzed patterns in dozens of disturbances in 1967. The report showed that in each twenty-four-hour period of rioting a precipitous dip in the action came between roughly 3 and 9 a.m., followed, as full daylight arrived, by a resumption of rioting.[1] This same dip, as we showed in the graph in the last chapter, occurred during the Miami disorder. There, the riot hit bottom at 6 a.m., as measured by the decrease in police calls and in the number of arrests, and did not resume its full intensity until about 9 a.m. "You had looting going on, but it was relatively quiet," says Captain Green of street conditions early Sunday morning. "Then, as it picked up, we started to lose it again."

If the authorities could have moved the Guard, or any force, into the riot area during this crucial period—confronting rioters when they awoke with troops standing on their street corners—the riot, in the view of many police officers, could have been stopped cold. "Ideally," says Major Windsor of the PSD, "what you should have before going into an area are special tactical teams of, say, twenty-five to fifty men, to take back the restricted area a block at a time. Then you secure it and continue the sweep. Starting at six or seven in the evening, the rioters had the streets to themselves. When they got tired at about four or five in the morning and went to bed, ideally in that two- or three-hour pause is when we should have amassed the manpower to go in and take it back."

Even if the police had thought of filling Liberty City with soldiers, the orders under which the Guard was operating precluded its use in such a manner. When he sent in the troops, the governor was so fearful of what might happen when frightened and poorly trained Guardsmen, armed with loaded automatic rifles, came into contact with black rioters that he ordered the troops deployed only on the perimeter of the riot area, not inside. Wherever the Guard troops were assigned, he instructed they had to be accompanied by a police officer, even on the perimeter. If arrests were made, it had to be police officers who made them. Thus, not only were the police prevented from using the Guard to take back lost areas of the city, but they had to use up their own men to guard the Guards, as it were. "It was a real drain on our manpower," said Major Windsor. "We didn't want the Guard to go into armed combat in there. We just wanted them to stand sentry duty."

In the City of Miami, relations between police and the Guard were even more complicated because every piece of communication had to be funneled back through Director Jones at the PSD, under whose aegis the Guard operated, before it could go on to the Guard commander, Brigadier General Jean Beem. In matters needing interpretation, the general then had to check with the governor's aides. At one point, Captain Green of the MPD put Guard troops in patrol cars with his officers and sent them off chasing looters away from stores. "I asked the liaison captain to check if that was okay," he says, "and he checked back through the brigade and so on. The answer was eventually 'no', but by the time it came back my shift was over and I'd gotten what I wanted anyway."

Although the police were unhappy with the restrictions on the Guard, it is difficult, looking back, to say that the governor's decision was wrong, in that it did succeed in preventing a direct and violent confrontation between the Guard and rioting members of the black community. Had Guard troops been thrust into the middle of the riot and freed to shoot at anyone they considered dangerous, most public officials think a bloodbath would have ensued. "The Guard is filled with private citizens, not professionals," said Captain Green. "They're just ordinary people with uniforms and big guns to shoot off. In the riot they were scared to death. You put them out there and just hope they don't do anything silly."

And untrained though they were, it was the Guard that ensured the eventual end of the riot by smothering it with sheer numbers. "They finally did save the day," concedes Captain Green. "They saved it because they were warm bodies and they stood out there and they were seen by the people. They didn't stand very good, but they were there, and that's all that mattered."

Indeed, the role of the Guard in quelling urban riots is seen as so crucial that both departments are working on ways to bring it into use much faster if it is needed again. "You take your biggest hurt between the time you lose control and the time you get the National Guard in," says Assistant Chief Cosgrove. Police officers, he said, can quickly go in and take back territory lost in the initial riot stages, but they need the Guard to go in after them and stand there or the ground will be lost again. "We have a police captain working full time," Cosgrove said shortly after the riot, "on the problem of how to shorten the time frame between when the police lose control and when the Guard is mobilized and deployed here effectively."

Gassing and Shooting

Both the police and the Guard were plagued by equipment failures and shortages, including a general lack of shotguns, face masks, gas masks and riot sticks. The portable walkie talkies belonging to the MPD were often useless because of dead batteries. The battery rechargers, which had once been installed in police cars, had been taken out and put at central headquarters as an efficiency measure. But because during the riot the radios were in constant use, they could not be brought back for recharging. (After the riot, rechargers went back into police cars.)

The question of tear gas grenades—when and how to use them—also caused considerable confusion. The departments stocked different kinds of grenades, each with a different function, and the police officers didn't always know which kind they were using. One round, black grenade, called a "baseball," simply lets out a cloud of tear gas when hurled. Another, an incendiary grenade, grows red hot after it is discharged so as to discourage anyone from picking it up and throwing it back at the police. It can also start fires, which is just what occurred in a number of instances when police officers hurled them into stores as a way to drive out looters. A third, the "triple chaser," explodes on landing, throwing gas charges in three separate directions. "Some guy would throw a triple chaser," said Captain Hughes of the PSD, "and the damn thing would go all over the place, and then our guys would get gassed, too."

What's more, police in the two departments disagreed over whether gas was really effective. Some believed it worked well to disperse crowds; others feared that it drifted into residential areas and brought more people out onto the streets, making things worse.

The police also had problems controlling officers who came in to help from small outlying communities, some of whom viewed the riot as a circus. "They did not take an interest in preserving the peace," says Chief Bowlin of the PSD. "Our officers showed a great deal of restraint, but some of those from outside had the attitude of 'We're going out of town, let's have some fun while we're down there.' They threw gas indiscriminately, they shot indiscriminately." Indeed, according to one PSD official, the whole contingent of one outside police force had to be ordered out of the riot area after its men hurled gas into the Scott housing complex, causing people to evacuate their buildings.

The policy and the practice regarding use of deadly force differ among departments, but it seems clear that across the country the police revolver is coming to be regarded more and more as a defensive rather than an offensive weapon. This is certainly true in Miami, where the discharge of a weapon by a police officer results in a long series of internal reviews and investigations. The trend away from shooting—both shooting in the air in warning and shooting at people—is partly a result of pressure exerted on mayors and police commissions by leaders of minority groups whose members are shot more frequently than anyone else. The law courts are also beginning to hold police officers and their supervisors responsible for aggressive acts that go beyond what is seen as reasonable conduct. "It used to be, as Chief Headley used to say, that 'when the looting starts the shooting starts,' " said Chief Bowlin of the PSD. "But today it's a lot different. When you give orders you've got to be sure they're responsible. To turn police officers loose without control is only inviting those officers to be arrested."

Although at the time of the riot Florida state law allowed police officers to shoot anyone fleeing the suspected commission of a felony—a policy known as a "fleeing felon" rule—the PSD had placed more stringent controls over its men and women. Its policy allowed officers to shoot at people only to prevent death or great bodily harm to the officer or to another person. They could also shoot at a fleeing felon whom they knew was armed and dangerous. In other cases officers were instructed to use "the least amount of force necessary to make the apprehension." After the beating of McDuffie, for instance, the PSD classified a police officer's Kelite, the heavy flashlight that weighs up to four pounds, as a deadly weapon, to be used to hit someone only in situations where an officer might otherwise use his revolver. This policy has resulted in some grumbling and confusion on the part of police officers on the street. In one incident after the 1980 riot, a PSD patrolman was accosted by a deranged man whose car he had stopped for a traffic violation. The assailant was a bigger and much stronger man who in a fight would clearly have the upper hand. But because the man was unarmed, the policeman holstered his revolver and tried to subdue the man with his hands. In the end, the officer was beaten so badly he had to be hospitalized.

Assistant Chief Cosgrove of the MPD thinks the problem can be solved by giving men better training in the use of nondeadly force. Not only would this increase their self-confidence, he says, but it would give them a wider variety of methods for subduing people. "Hitting a person over the head with a Kelite is not the best way to bring him under control," says the assistant chief, who has a certificate on his wall attesting to his own expertise in Kodokan Judo Yon-Kyu "with police arresting techniques." "A collar-bone break is better," says Cosgrove. "Or hit him in the solar plexus; it knocks the wind out of him." Particularly effective is a chokehold, which prevents blood from flowing through the carotid artery in the neck, and which, according to Cosgrove, "brings about a quick cessation of activity by the individual." It also, when it was practised by the police in Los Angeles, brought about a number of deaths and instances of brain damage and is the subject of considerable controversy.

Until the May disorder, the MPD had had a fleeing-felon rule when it came to shooting, but changed it quickly on the second day of the riot to one allowing police officers to shoot only to prevent death or grave injury. The hierarchies of both departments were worried that as their men became increasingly angry at the rioters they might start shooting looters. "A lot of guys were getting tired and frustrated because they had lost it," says Cosgrove, who explained that the wording of the new MPD policy had been in preparation for some time. "What I was concerned about was that out of frustration they might use deadly force against a looter, as a strict interpretation of the statute allowed them to do. They might have ended up shooting a lot of women, children and teenagers." (The frustrations of the men did spill over Sunday night, when several Guard troops and MPD officers smashed the windows of twelve cars they believed belonged to looters in the parking lot of Zayre's Department Store and spraypainted them with the word "Looter.")

While the decision not to use deadly force against looters does, of course, save lives, it almost inevitably results in an increased loss of property. "The more they saw we weren't shooting them and we weren't arresting them," says Lieutenant McGee of the PSD, "the more they felt free to riot and loot." Indeed, police forces everywhere are grappling with the question of how much force they should use to quell a mass disturbance. Few police departments have armored riot vehicles or the big guns it would take to suppress a major disturbance quickly with sheer force. And even if they had such armaments, it is doubtful, for political reasons, that they would be allowed to use them. Police forces, after all, are not armies. A civil authority as opposed to a military one, the police must uphold the law as best they can, whereas an army's job is to battle a foe, using whatever methods it must to avoid defeat. The police officer, after the riot is over, has to go back into the area and resume his supposed role as the friendly cop on the beat. "The National Guard even talks a different language than we do," says Chief Bowlin. "They are combat-trained and they talk in terms of 'the enemy' and in terms of 'missions.' We are trained to look after the rights of the citizens of the United States. Right now, they may be in a riotous condition, but they are still citizens."

Sniping

As was the case with the riots of the 1960s, official police reports and news stories on the Miami riot were filled with accounts of sniping by black rioters at the police. Reports came in of heavy gunfire in the 62nd Street area when police tried to get the Kulps off the street; at the Justice complex, before the police went in to clear out the rioters; along 22nd Avenue in the vicinity of the Scott Housing Project; on 7th Avenue in the fifties and sixties, and at 27th Avenue and 54th Street, site of the large Norton Tire Company. One *Miami Herald* columnist, Joe Oglesby, even raised the spectacle of black Vietnam veterans attacking the authorities with guerrilla-style tactics. "Military tactics from Vietnam were used on 62nd Street on Riot Saturday," he wrote. "Search and destroy. Set a target. Hit and run. . . . ."

Evidence from earlier riots, however, should have warned everyone to regard sniping reports with heavy skepticism. Not only are such reports likely to be exaggerated—one instance of gunfire is often reported by several people hearing it and becomes several instances—but many are dead wrong. Firecrackers may be reported as sniper fire; firing by the police and National Guard troops may be reported as sniper fire; so may the explosions of tear gas grenades hurled by the police, particularly the triple chaser, which sounds like gunfire when it goes off.

Nevertheless, judging from eyewitness police accounts, there does appear to have been considerable gunfire coming from the direction of the rioters. How much of it was sniping at the police, however, is difficult to determine. Most of the firing seems to have been more an attempt to scare the police than actually to hurt or kill them. The only officials struck by hostile gunfire during the rioting were Captain Boemler and Lieutenant James Watson of the MPD and Steve Edel-

stein of the Miami city attorney's office—and all three were shot in
the same incident as they were searching for looters on 7th Avenue at
57th Street at about 5:45 p.m. on Sunday. (An MPD officer was also
wounded in the foot when a fellow officer accidentally discharged his
carbine). None of the hundreds of PSD officers who saw duty during
the riot was struck by gunfire. None of the thousands of National
Guard troops was hit, nor was any member of an outside police agency.
Many of the forces were stationed on the perimeter, a good distance
from the heavy riot action, but even when police officers went inside
the riot area—into the very heart of the turmoil—they escaped unscathed. When Sergeant Patrick Burns and his five men returned from
their harrowing run to pick up the bodies from 62nd Street, they described the scene as a veritable shooting gallery, with bullets hitting
the pavement all around them. Yet here were six policemen exposed,
for the several minutes it took to load the bodies into their vehicles,
to the thickest gunfire of the entire riot, and none of them suffered so
much as a scratch. Even in the shotgun incident, when, according to
Sergeant Burns, a man tried to shoot him from close range as he was
running for the patrol car, the assailant aimed so high as to hit only
the dome light on top of the cruiser. It would seem difficult indeed to
fire a shotgun at a man at such close range and miss him so completely—unless one were trying to.

From all this, it seems reasonable to conclude that the rioters were
not trying very hard to shoot the police—a conclusion that is shared
by many police officials as well. If the rioters were after the police,
says Lieutenant Billy Riggs, head of the MPD's SWAT unit, "then
they sure had a funny way of showing it, because the violence was not
directed against us. They didn't really want to get us. If they did, and
at one point we only had fifty or sixty police officers against 5,000 or
6,000 rioters, why was no one hurt?"

Major Dickson of the MPD agrees: "They harrassed the hell out
of us, but I don't think the main object of this riot was to retaliate
against the police. If it was, they could have picked us off at random
anytime they wanted to."

As for Oglesby's Vietnam veterans, they too seem to have been
a myth. In our dozens of interviews with people who witnessed the riot
from many vantage points, we found no evidence of organized or con-
spiratorial activity that went beyond the conduct traditionally associated with a spontaneous mass disorder. Few of the riot arrestees had
ever served in the military; the police confiscated no automatic weapons during the riot. And the two activities cited by Oglesby as evidence
of military-style involvement don't go very far to prove his point. They
amount to the rolling out of garbage dumpsters onto 62nd Street to

slow down cars driven by whites and the spreading of oil on the street to make cars skid into the curbs. Using dumpsters to block cars, as Captain Hughes of the PSD recounts of his troubles in the James E. Scott Housing Project, is an old ghetto trick in Miami, and was used in Coconut Grove and Overtown as well as in Liberty City during the riot. As for the oil slick, there was one instance of this: on 62nd Street, just before the Higdon car appeared, a crowd broke into the gas station on the corner and poured cans of oil on the street. According to Bernard Coates, a black staff member of the Community Relations Board who said he watched the episode from across the street, the oil-pouring was done by the same young people who were involved in the general panoply of riot activities, and not by a gang of former servicemen.

Fighting the Fires

The fire departments of the City of Miami and of Dade County were both swamped with calls during the riot, but they differed markedly in the way they responded to the challenge.

The Miami Fire Department, a 600-man force that in three days had to contend with half again as many fires as it normally handles in a whole month, tried to respond in some fashion to every fire during the riot. Rather than send in single pieces of equipment, the MFD organized itself into eight task forces, each consisting of two pumpers, an aerial ladder truck and a task force commander's car. On the way into the fire it would pick up an MPD police escort, and the group would proceed as a unit, thus giving the firefighters protection against attack. The principal drawback of the approach was that coordination between the MFD and the MPD was not always smooth, and because of the press of business the department could not respond effectively to every fire. Several shop owners, particularly those along 7th Avenue, reported firefighters leaving one fire to answer another call before the first fire was thoroughly extinguished. There is some reason to question whether the complicated escort tactic was really needed. As with the sniper fire, rumors of hostile actions against firefighters seem to have also been somewhat exaggerated. This is not to say that rocks and bottles were not thrown at fire trucks or that firefighters had no reason to fear for their safety—or to have their feelings hurt. "It's especially hard on firemen to get rocks thrown at them," said Fire Marshall Charles D. Fabyan. "We respond to everything—water leaks, childbirths, people hurt. You go in and rescue someone one week and then the next you get rocks and bottles thrown at you."

Nonetheless, when one looks at the injury statistics, it does not seem that firefighters were the target of much violence. Some eighteen members of the MFD reported injuries during the riot, but nearly all of these were back injuries and minor cuts and bruises of a sort and number to be expected from the fighting of so many fires. According to the MFD's monthly report, only two people suffered any riot-related injuries. And Fire Marshall Fabyan says there were several instances of people in crowds helping to protect firefighters from injury by telling teenagers not to throw anything. "At one fire in an auto parts store on 17th and 47th Street," he says, "I had a black man come out of the crowd and say my men didn't have to worry about getting rocks and bottles thrown at them from that crowd."

On the county side of the riot, the Dade County Fire Department put a policy into effect during the worst hours of the riot of not responding to fire calls at all. "They had a station in the immediate area of the riot and we'd call that station, but we couldn't get them to respond," says PSD Chief Bowlin. "We'd send in a squad to verify the fire, then call the fire department, but they just wouldn't go. With one place, a lumber company at 71st Street and 27th Avenue that was going up in flames, the director himself called, but they still refused to respond."

In theory, at least, the DCFD also had a task-force system for use during riots and a policy to answer fire calls if it was given a police escort. But policy did not carry over into practice. "We'd get them an escort and everything, and they would start in," says Captain Hughes of the PSD's Central District. "But then they'd hear gunfire and turn around and refuse to go any further."

Chief Edward Donaldson of the DCFD said his decision to limit his department's response to riot fires was an "ad hoc decision" made late Saturday night. Not only did he limit the response, but at one point early Sunday morning he ordered the abandonment of the DCFD firehouse at 27th Avenue and 64th Street in Liberty City—a decision he made over the strong objections of its resident firemen and its chief. He said his decision not to respond to fires that night was governed by his fear of what it would mean for relations between his men and the black community if a firefighter was seriously hurt or killed. "I have to worry about the long-term relationship," he says. "If a man is blown away or badly hurt when he's trying to help someone, it could seriously hurt service in the community in the future." As to the abandonment of the Liberty City firehouse, he says that the PSD had moved its perimeter several blocks to the west, leaving the station unprotected, and that he was worried about what his men might do if they were attacked by rioters and caught inside their firehouse. "I was concerned that if the people realized the fire station was alone and a mob formed, what would happen if there was a confrontation and the crowd began to throw rocks? I'm not naive. We have a policy of no weapons in fire stations, but that doesn't guarantee that there aren't any. What happens if a fireman is injured and there's some shooting? Do we want another McDuffie?"

Note

1. *Report of the National Advisory Commission on Civil Disorders* (1968), charts in appendix following p. 609.

Rioters and onlookers in Liberty City, May 18, 1980 (Miami Herald Photo)

5 Who Rioted?

Any tumultuous assemblage of three or more persons brought together for no legal or constitutional object, deporting themselves in such a manner as to endanger the public peace and excite terror and alarm in rational and firm-minded persons, is unlawful . . . and whenever three or more persons, in a tumultuous manner, use force or violence in the execution of any design wherein the law does not allow the use of force, they are guilty of riot.

—Instructions to the jury delivered by
Judge Charles P. Daly of the New York
City Court of General Sessions during the
prosecution of those arrested following
the May 1849 Nativist riot in Astor Place
in Manhattan.

Observing the May disorder, one could easily have gotten the impression that the streets were filled with a mass of people all involved in the general act of rioting. In reality, the Miami rioters were not a single mass doing a single thing, but many individuals engaged in different kinds of acts. The streets were filled with many people who may have looked as if they were rioting but who were doing nothing illegal at all. It is not a crime to yell insults at the police or to look on as a raiding party loots a store or to run wildly up and down. In this regard, at least half of Judge Daly's 1849 definition of rioting is no longer legally useful. Black youths running wild through the streets of Miami could all be said to "excite terror and alarm in rational and firm-minded persons," white and black, but this no longer forms the basis for legal prosecution.

Florida law, like that of many other states, uses the word "riot" to describe a set of conditions rather than a specific act. Thus, when the Miami rioters were arrested, they were charged not with rioting, but with homicide, burglary, grand theft, arson, battery on a police officer, incitement to riot, petty larceny, disorderly conduct, trespassing, carrying a concealed weapon, discharging a firearm, disorderly intoxication, resisting arrest, loitering, prowling, possession of stolen goods, reckless driving and violation of the "emergency procedure" or curfew law, which made it illegal to be on the streets after 8 p.m. While all these arrestees could be considered rioters, there was a considerable latitude in the severity of what they did, from capital crimes calling for the death penalty to misdemeanors engendering only a small fine.

Social psychologists tell us that a mob—which the dictionary defines as a moving crowd of disorderly people—exerts a psychological force strong enough to compel people to commit acts they would not commit under ordinary circumstances. Not only does the sight of so much lawbreaking remove normal social restraints, but the security of large numbers—and sometimes the absence of any immediate police reaction—convinces people they will face no consequences for what they do. This is not to say that every member of a mob can be made to do any kind of act. The degree to which people feel they can "let go" is still controlled by lessons learned during their upbringing and other moral constraints. Who they were before the riot governs what they do in the heat of the action. Thus, in Miami, there were people who threw rocks and bottles at cars but refused to join in beating people. There were people who admitted taking goods from stores but who had refused to help in the original breaking in or in the setting of fires after the merchandise was gone. Similarly, the black lawyer in a three-piece suit who found himself ripping antennas off patrol cars during the riot at the Metro Justice Building held back when it came to tipping the cars over and setting them on fire.

Indeed, as it is important to stress, the vast majority of black residents of Liberty City and other ghetto neighborhoods did not go out in the streets at all; they stayed at home during the disturbance and were just as frightened of the violence as were the white people in other parts of the city.

So the question remains: Who were the real rioters?

In Miami, opinions varied significantly as to who was the most responsible for creating the disorder. Many people supported Chief Harms of the MPD when he enunciated the familiar "riffraff" theory of rioting in a statement on July 8, 1980, before the Governor's Commission investigating the causes of the disturbance:

> While the total monetary and human loss associated with this tragedy made it one of the most costly in the history of our country, I urge this committee to remember that it was a *relatively small number of lawbreakers who were responsible for most of the damage and violence* [emphasis supplied]. Certainly, the actions of this small "criminal element" do not reflect the attitudes of the vast majority of the Black community. . . . The good people of our community of all colors

and backgrounds want quietude, respect and dignity and believe that indiscriminate violence and property damage is not acceptable in civilized society.

Others argued that the violence was not created just by the criminal element. In their view, anger over the McDuffie case caused a large portion of the normally "good people" in the ghetto temporarily to abandon their preference for quietude and either commit unlawful acts themselves or applaud loudly those who did. "The riot was when we got back our self-respect," said T. Willard Fair, president of the Miami Urban League. "Any black citizen who said he did not condone the rioting in this town is being dishonest."

From the viewpoint of government policymakers, the question of who actually did riot is not merely of academic importance. To describe the problem, after all, is to suggest the solution. If the Miami rioters came predominantly from the criminal classes who were just doing what they do ordinarily, only more so, then the solution has to do with tactics—with strengthening police measures and ensuring swift punishment. The same solution would obtain if a neighborhood were suddenly overrun by muggers and burglars. If, on the other hand, the riot was sanctioned, indeed joined, by many of the normally law-abiding people in the black neighborhood, then it deserves to be regarded in a different light. Rather than looking only at *what* they did, attention must also be paid to why—to the things the rioters might be "saying" by their actions.

Some comparative statistics do exist concerning the pattern of participation among the general black population in riots of the past. After the outbursts in Newark and Detroit in 1967, research teams working for the Kerner Commission made house-by-house surveys in the riot areas and systematically asked people whether they had been involved. In Newark, the interviewers talked only to males between the ages of fifteen and thirty-five—the group they had determined formed the core of the riot—and found that 45 percent of this group said they had participated in some way. In Detroit, the survey included 437 men *and* women over the age of fifteen. Here the level of involvement was put at 11 percent.[1]

After the disturbance in Miami, the *Herald* hired the Behavioral Science Research Institute (BSRI) of Coral Gables to do a study comparable to the Detroit survey. In a random sampling of 450 persons found within the riot areas, BSRI found that as much as 26 percent of the ghetto population aged sixteen and over said they had participated in some way, a figure more than twice that in Detroit. The accuracy of the Miami figure, however, is impossible to determine. The firm hired staff workers from the James E. Scott Community Association to do its interviewing, and whether they got truthful answers to their questions no one really knows. BSRI itself advised people to use the figures "with caution," because it was not possible to determine whether the people interviewed over- or underrepresented their involvement.

The Arrestees

Although the BSRI study may or may not suggest the true level of participation, it does not say much about who the people were. For this, we turn to data on the rioters we know most about, those who were arrested by the police. In 1980, the Dade-Miami Criminal Justice Council (CJC) initiated a study of some 855 arrestees.[3] The study asked many questions, but the one of prime interest to us was whether the riot arrestees had prior criminal records. Was the average arrestee liable to be someone who normally got into trouble with the police? If so, then the survey results would favor the riffraff theory of Chief Harms; if not, they would tend to support Fair's view that even the good people were angry enough to riot.

Before examining these statistics we must satisfy ourselves that the arrested rioters represent a roughly accurate cross section of the people who actually engaged in the disorder. Evidence from the New York blackout in 1977, for instance, suggested that it was not looters the police were arresting, but the losers—those who went into stores long after they had been broken open and the best merchandise stolen.[4]

In Miami, it is easy to tell who was not liable to be arrested, and therefore to identify the kinds of people who are underrepresented in the arrest statistics. Aside from the individuals charged in five of the riot killings, for instance, no one, except one white who was later let go, was arrested in connection with the other murders and all the beatings.

Another category seriously underrepresented is that of rioters who committed arson. According to the CJC figures, only nine persons were charged with arson, despite the fact that 102 buildings were destroyed by fire and the burning went on for three days and four nights.

This leaves the last general riot activity—looting. To see whether the losers or the looters were actually arrested, we looked at several figures, beginning with the calls being dispatched to the PSD and to the Dade County Fire Department from 911 communications operators. (The MPD has its own 911 communications system for the City of Miami. During the time of our study, however, several lawsuits were pending that involved the question of whether the police had responded quickly enough to rescue assault victims during the riot. To prevent tampering with the tapes of police calls during the period, the court placed a seal on them and forbade their release.) The county received some 22,000 calls from citizens in one eighteen-hour period of the riot, about three times the normal rate. Operators were told to relay only the most important calls to patrol cars, and only a few of these, because of the crush of business, actually got answered by the police. Among dispatches, we looked at three categories: fires, life-threatening emergencies and stealing, the last including reports of ringing burglar alarms, burglaries in progress, larcenies, vandalism and holdups.

We then examined the CJC data to see when the arrests were made. If there was a high correlation between the time the police were making the most arrests and the time when stores were broken into and when the rioters were assaulting, burning and looting, then we could regard the arrest data as providing a fairly accurate picture at least of the people doing the stealing and perhaps also of those involved in other riot activities.

In all four comparisons, there was, in fact, a high degree of correlation (see Figure 5-1).[5] Arson alarms began coming in between 9 p.m. and midnight on Saturday and hit a riot-high on Sunday at 6 p.m. Life-threatening calls had hit their riot-high much earlier—by midnight Saturday—but went up again Sunday night and on Monday. Looting dispatches hit three peaks during the riot: first from 9 p.m. to midnight on Saturday, again at noon on Sunday and a third time at 9 p.m. on Monday.

Looking at when arrests occurred, we can see the high correlation with riot levels. On Saturday night, the riot peaked at midnight; so did the arrests. As the riot activity abated on Sunday morning from 6 to 9 a.m., arrests also dropped. As riot activity rose to its peak Sunday evening, the arrest rate rose with it. Again on Monday, the police made eighty arrests, most for curfew violations, at the same time that the riot picked up again, albeit with abated force.

The high correlation of the Miami arrests seems especially meaningful when compared to the times that the New York City police made arrests during the blackout looting of July 13, 1977. In that disturbance, most of the stores were broken into by midnight on July 13. Yet by that time, the police had made only 4 percent of the more than 3,000 arrests they would make during the whole disorder. In Miami, between midnight Saturday and 3 o'clock Sunday morning, when many of the stores had been freshly broken into and riot originators could still be presumed to be on the scene, the police had made 15.4 percent of the

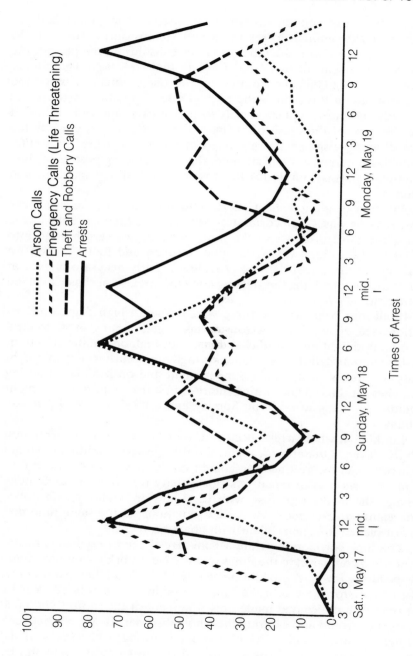

Figure 5–1. Dade-Miami Criminal Justice Council Arrest Data and Riot Call Data.

total arrests they would make during the whole riot. This rate rises to 21.6 percent if one doesn't count minor curfew violations in the total. By 6 p.m. Sunday, the police had made 44 percent of their total arrests, or 61 percent of the total, excluding curfew arrests.

One further piece of evidence involves the instructions given to police officers by their superiors during the riot. To avoid tying themselves up in red tape, officers were told to arrest people only if they were involved in flagrant violations. "I told my squad that if they don't have to make an arrest, then don't do it," says Sergeant Carrel of the PSD in a typical comment. "If you see people drop stuff and run, don't chase them. Just run them off and tell them to go home." This policy would seem to add weight to our conclusion drawn from the arrest correlations—that in the instances where arrests were made, they were not done frivolously or with little reason. In other words, it would appear that in Miami the looters, rather than the losers, were picked up by the police.

So what kind of people were arrested during the Miami riot? How do they compare with their counterparts in earlier disturbances?

Right away we can see that the riot in Miami seems to have drawn in a vastly different class of people than did the eruptions of the 1960s. During the Watts riot in 1965, more than 78 percent of the 3,435 adults arrested had had some contact with the police before the disorder, either as arrestees or suspects in crimes.[6] Some 74 percent of them had prior arrest records, and, of these, 71 percent had been convicted of a crime. In Newark, the Kerner Commission reported that of the 1,169 adults arrested, 867, or 74.2 percent, had a prior record. Another, broader survey of disturbances during the decade found that those arrested during riots had the same generally high rate of prior record as those who were ordinarily arrested in those cities on similar charges.[7] Thus, it could be said that the arrested rioters in the 1960s were in general people who normally did on their own what they did during the riot all at once.

The dramatic news about the Miami rioters is that their figures are almost exactly the reverse. Of the 855 arrests in the CJC survey, only 32 percent had been arrested before, against 74 percent in both Watts and Newark. And only 24 percent had ever been convicted of crimes, compared to 71 percent in Watts.

The police were quick to challenge the CJC data and, by implication, its suggestion that a large percentage of the "good people" rioted in Miami, as well as the riffraff. Officials of the PSD pointed out that the 68 percent of the arrestees who were shown to have no police record included those arrested for curfew violations, whom the police had no time to fingerprint before their arraignment in court and subsequent release, usually in custody of their family. This meant, the police argued, that in checking for a prior record the CJC researchers had nothing but the name the arrestee had given the court, not the positive identification established by a fingerprint. Many of these arrestees may well have given false names, the police said, thus inflating the figure for arrestees who had had no prior trouble with the law. But if this were true—that curfew violaters were more likely to identify themselves with "innocent" names—then that category should show a higher rate of no prior arrests than the norm. In fact, this is not so. Of the 259 curfew violations, 171, or 66 percent, had no prior arrest record, which is slightly lower than the average. And arrestees on more serious charges—the ones who were fingerprinted and positively identified—had in many instances a higher than average rate of no prior arrests. Of those arrested on burglary charges, 70.6 percent had no prior arrests; disorderly conduct, 68.6 percent; grand theft, 78.3 percent; resisting arrest, 70.5 percent. Thus, the inference from the CJC data still stands: In Miami, unlike the riots of the 1960s, an overwhelming majority of those arrested for riot activity were normally law-abiding people who had never been in trouble before.

We also compared the riot arrestees to those people who are normally arrested in Miami. According to George Yoss, chief prosecutor in the state attorney's office, about 8 percent of the people arrested and charged with felonies by his office are ordinarily diverted to the county's Pre-Trial Intervention program (PTI). This program admits only first offenders whom it counsels for several months, at which point, if they have stayed out of trouble, their cases are dismissed by the court. Of the 516 felonies charged to riot arrestees, 114 were referred to PTI. This is a rate of 22 percent, almost triple the rate among those arrested during normal times. Thus not only were the Miami riot arrestees less crime-prone than those of the 1960s, but they were only one-third as likely to have a previous record than their counterparts normally arrested in Miami during non-riot conditions.

To determine the economic status of the riot arrestees, we had hoped to get the same kind of employment information that was gathered by New York City after its blackout disorder. However, the courts in Miami were so taxed trying to process all the arrestees that weekend that they simply decided to scrap the elaborate pretrial interviews that normally verify a defendant's employment status and roots in the community for the purpose of setting bail. Instead, the judges interviewed the prisoners themselves and, depending on how they liked their answers, either set them free or held them on bail, with no firm idea about what kind of person was really standing before them. There is, however, one scrap of evidence, which, although not as good as the missing interviews, does at least suggest that some of the arrestees were not very badly off economically. This evidence comes from the number of felony arrestees who were accepted into a pretrial intervention program that offers jobs as part of its rehabilitation package. To qualify, a defendant must have no prior arrest record and no regular employment for the previous twelve weeks. Of the 114 PTI referrals eligible for the program on grounds of having no previous record, only 10 qualified on the grounds that they were also unemployed. This suggests that less than 10 percent of the PTI cases had no jobs, a figure that was much lower than the 17 percent unemployment rate then current among blacks in the Miami area. (Although these figures are intriguing, we cannot logically use them to generalize about all arrestees. First, the PTI referrals have no prior record and so represent the "cream" of the arrestees. Second, several of them were housewives and students who could not qualify for the employment program anyway.)

In the final analysis, then, the statistics do seem strongly to disprove the riffraff theory—that the riot was the work of criminals. It may have been criminals who started it, and it may have been criminals who did the hard-core killing, beating and burning and who opened up many of the stores to looting. But the figures suggest that the good people of the ghetto joined the rioting in large numbers and that a sizable proportion of them were willing to commit criminal acts and expose themselves to arrest. Just what made them step so far out of character is impossible to answer for sure. It was clearly anger over the McDuffie verdict that drove them into the streets on Saturday, May 17. But what kept them out there on Sunday and Monday involved other considerations that we will discuss later.

The Three Stages

What different kinds of groups were engaged in the rioting? According to the arrest statistics, the age level of the rioters fell generally within the historical norm for such disorders. The largest group, 363 of the arrestees, or 42.7 percent, were between twenty-two and twenty-nine years old. Next came the eighteen- to twenty-one-year-olds, with 204, or 24 percent; then the thirty- to thirty-nine-year-olds, with 179, or 21 percent. Finally, there were those over forty, with 99, or 11.5 percent.

Racially and ethnically, 777 of the 855 CJC arrestees were black; 43 were white, 25 were Hispanic and 4 identified themselves as Caribbean black. (The two largest Caribbean groups in Miami are the Jamaicans and the Haitians.) Of the whites and Hispanics, a dispro-portionately high number were arrested on gun charges. This seems consonant with the theory that they were trying to get into the riot area either to attack blacks, three of whom died at the hands of white civilians, or to protect their stores and property.

The most important thing we wanted to learn from the CJC data was whether the Miami disturbance followed the classic pattern for urban disorders in terms of when different kinds of people decided to join the rioting. According to research done on the 1960s riots by Russell Dynes and E. L. Quarantelli, riots tend to draw in three kinds of people at different stages.[8] Stage I rioters join in at the very begin-ning and consist of young street people who race around wildly smash-ing windows and creating an atmosphere of chaos and confusion. As the disorder settles down into more organized stealing, Stage II rioters tend to be attracted to the scene. These are largely people with criminal backgrounds who take the riot as an opportunity to organize into thiev-ery gangs and who go about the looting in a businesslike manner. After the riot has gone on for some time, it draws in the Stage III rioters. These are the older, noncriminal, working-class members of the com-munity who finally give in to the temptation to "dip in" and participate in the general looting. These people can also be considered the "los-ers," not only because by the time they come on the scene the good merchandise has already been cleaned out, but because by that time the police have amassed enough officers to begin making numerous arrests, and the Stage III looters tends to get caught.

The theory that riots draw in different people at different times does not mean that the streets belong exclusively to one group or another. It means that different kinds of people choose to involve themselves at the time their senses tell them is right, and that the "right time" is different for different kinds of people. Young males are more likely to jump in impulsively at the start and risk the possibility of arrest in exchange for a little fun and profit. Criminal types, who view the disorder more professionally, tend to hang back and wait until they are convinced the police can offer no serious interference. The older, more stable people—the most cautious of the groups—get drawn in only after the looting becomes the accepted community norm and the police still seem to be incapable of moving in and making mass arrests.

While the data on just 855 arrests cannot tell anything conclusive about the stages in Miami, they do tend to support the notion that the Miami riot followed the classic Dynes and Quarantelli lines (see Table

Table 5–1
Frequency of Arrest, by Age and Date

	JUVENILE	AGE 18 - 21	AGE 22 - 29	AGE 30 - 39	AGE 40 - ON	TOTAL
MAY 17/DAY						
FREQUENCY	0	0	3	0	1	4
PERCENT	0.00	0.00	0.35	0.00	0.12	0.47
ROW PCT	0.00	0.00	75.00	0.00	25.00	
COL PCT	0.00	0.00	0.82	0.00	1.01	
MAY 17/EVE						
FREQUENCY	0.00	28	31	16	3	78
PERCENT	0.00	3.27	3.63	1.87	0.35	9.12
ROW PCT	0.00	35.90	39.74	20.51	3.85	
COL PCT	0.00	13.66	8.47	8.84	3.03	
MAY 18/DAY						
FREQUENCY	0.00	20	41	20	8	89
PERCENT	0.00	2.34	4.80	2.34	0.94	10.41
ROW PCT	0.00	22.47	46.07	22.47	8.99	
COL PCT	0.00	9.76	11.20	11.05	8.08	
MAY 18/EVE						
FREQUENCY	1	69	121	60	35	286
PERCENT	0.12	8.07	14.15	7.02	4.09	33.45
ROW PCT	0.35	24.13	42.13	20.98	12.24	
COL PCT	25.00	33.66	33.06	33.15	35.35	
MAY 19/DAY						
FREQUENCY	0	14	28	14	3	59
PERCENT	0.00	1.64	3.27	1.64	.35	6.90
ROW PCT	0.00	23.73	47.46	23.73	5.08	
COL PCT	0.00	6.83	7.65	7.73	3.03	
MAY 19/EVE						
FREQUENCY	2	56	109	51	36	254
PERCENT	0.23	6.55	12.75	5.96	4.12	29.71
ROW PCT	0.79	22.05	42.91	20.08	14.17	
COL PCT	50.00	27.32	29.78	28.18	36.36	
TOTAL	4	205	366	181	99	855
	0.47	23.98	42.81	21.17	11.58	100.00

5-1).[9] Among the first arrestees picked up on Saturday night, when the riot was just getting under way, people between the ages of eighteen and twenty-one—the age group that would correlate with younger, Stage I rioters—were overrepresented. Overall, they accounted for only 23.9 percent of the arrestees, but between 6 p.m. and midnight Saturday, they made up 35.9 percent of the arrest population, or 50 percent more than they were supposed to. During the same period, all the other age groups were underrepresented, if only by slight margins.

Conversely, older people—those more likely to be both Stage II criminal types and Stage III stable types—tended to come up to their correct representation in the arrest statistics only as the riot moved into Sunday and Monday. The twenty-two- to twenty-nine-year-olds were underrepresented by three percentage points on Saturday night, but then over-represented the next day. Those thirty to thirty-nine were most heavily represented on Monday morning, and the oldest group, those over forty, were arrested most often on Monday night. This was the same period during which the young group had the smallest percentage of their number arrested.

To see what the CJC data could tell about the involvement of criminals, we compared the times of arrest for those with no prior record with the times of arrest for "priors." Here, however, the differences in percentage are so slight as to preclude any generalization.

Three Rioters*

The profiles of three Miami rioters that follow—their names have been changed—are offered as examples of the three types outlined by Dynes and Quarantelli. While we cannot say that they are absolutely typical of their respective stages, they do seem to exhibit enough of the necessary characteristics to serve as reasonable illustrations. Indeed, of the three, it was only the Stage III rioter, or "loser," who managed to get herself arrested. The other two, both of whom were much more involved in the stealing, and one in the violence, got away scot-free.

Stage I: Leroy J—

Leroy J—, eighteen, was a Liberty City resident with $1,500 in a savings bank account when he went out looting on Saturday night. His house, where he lives with his mother and twelve-year-old brother, is near African Square Park, so Leroy had the chance to be involved in the riot from the start. He watched people gathering on the street after the McDuffie verdict. He says he felt angry over the verdict but did not throw rocks or bottles at cars. Near African Square, he heard the rumor of the black child supposedly shot by whites who had driven off, he says, in a "white Cougar." And he was at the outer edge of the crowd watching the Kulps get stoned and beaten. Leroy "felt sorry" for the two boys. "They were innocent people that didn't know what was happening to them," he says.

After a while, he and some friends joined in the looting of a U-Totem grocery on 62nd Street and 11th Avenue. He says the store was hit because its owner had charged high prices to the community. "That

---

*Information in this section came from interviews the authors and their researchers conducted with the three rioters.

was like with a lot of the stores," he says. "Depending on how they treated you was whether or not you came in on them." About 10 p.m., Leroy and his friends went looking for a larger store. They ended up with the crowd that broke into the large Zayre's Department Store at 54th Street and 12th Avenue. (This was while Assistant Chief Cosgrove of the MPD, who would later drive the looters out of this very store, was still tied up at the Metro Justice Building.) At Zayre's Leroy got two portable television sets, which he later sold to a grown-up on the street for $300. He also stole a double-barreled twelve-gauge shotgun, which he wrapped in a piece of plastic and buried in a vacant lot near his house. It was two or three o'clock Sunday morning before he finally got home and he claims he did not go out again during the riot.

Far from boasting about his actions, Leroy seems somewhat taken aback by them, genuinely puzzled over why he had participated.

> When we went down to Zayre's, I had money in my pocket. I had $1,500 in the bank. But people would jump up and say, "Hey, let's do such and such," and we'd run off. I guess I was just doing it to be doing it. . . . We did it because we thought it would be so easy, that we could get things and get out. I didn't think it would be so easy after that night, and some guys went out again the next day and they got caught breaking into stores.

He told his mother nothing about his escapades, because he knew she would be angry. "She would have been shocked, because I don't do those things," he says. He talked of his aunts and uncles and about his mother's father, who, he says proudly, was a preacher. "They would all be shocked if they heard about what I did," he says. "Our family is not like that."

And his upbringing in Liberty City hardly seems typical of what one would expect of a budding criminal. Although his father, a cement finisher, divorced his mother more than ten years ago, he lives in a nearby city and still sees his son regularly. He takes Leroy to Miami Dolphin football games; he has the boy to his house on weekends, where the pair fish for catfish and turtles in a nearby canal. At Northwestern High School, from which Leroy graduated shortly after the riot, he played on the varsity basketball team, which reached the semifinals in the state playoffs. During his last year in school, Leroy worked every afternoon as an orderly at a local hospital as part of a work-experience program. This was how he acquired his $1,500 bank account.

In school, he read *Roots* and *The Autobiography of Malcolm X* by Alex Haley, and *Black Boy* by Richard Wright. His own choice of reading is a little less inspired, consisting of works such as *Bloodline* by Sidney Sheldon, but Leroy does like to read. And at home, his mother, who is a schoolteacher, subscribes to *Reader's Digest, Newsweek, Ebony, Sports Illustrated* and *Jet*. She also regularly takes him on trips to places like the Miami Planetarium and Seaquarium and, on Sundays, to a Baptist church.

While Leroy has never been involved with the police, he worries about his ability to stay clear of the law for much longer. In his mind, keeping out of jail does not so much involve a conscious decision to refrain from committing crimes as it does the act of removing himself from criminal temptations—which for him means getting out of Liberty City. "If I stayed home, I think I would be getting into trouble," he says. "It's pretty easy around here. Some of my friends are in college, but some are in the street and some are in jail." While still in high school he went to a dry-cleaning institute to learn the trade of pants pressing, and the summer after the May riot he signed up to join the Marines. "The Marines are tough," he says. "They give you a chance to prove yourself." After completing his military service, he hopes to become a computer technician and eventually to move to New York, Detroit, or Chicago.

Stage II: Willie T—

At the age of twenty, Willie T— seems already hermetically sealed into a life of street crime. He was raised in Miami as part of a loosely organized family; he has to pause and count on his fingers before he can say that he has five brothers and one sister. When Willie was ten, his mother was stabbed to death by a jealous lover, and he went to Georgia to live with a grandfather. Five years later he returned to Miami to stay with his father, a casually employed dock worker, and his stepmother, but he soon fell out with his father, who was constantly trying to get his hands on the child's death benefits from the federal government. On one occasion, when Willie's stepmother kept aside some of the checks to try to get Willie a ten-speed bike, his father got so angry he smashed a two-foot-high trophy Willie had won playing softball in a tournament sponsored by the Miami Department of Parks. After that, Willie left to stay with an aunt.

According to Willie's caseworker, who supervises Willie's probation (more of which shortly), he has a severe learning disability, and left school because he resented being put with "all the dummies." As a result, he cannot read or write adequately, and since age seventeen he has been making his living with now-and-then jobs and by hustling on the street. Dressed in a yellow polo shirt, cut-off khakis that hang below his knees, white sneakers and a yellow Caterpillar hat, he has a baleful expression and a mouthful of painfully crooked teeth. Day and night he hangs out at various "trees" in the Liberty City and Overtown sections of the city. A tree, in Miami, consists of a shaded street corner, usually next to a grocery store or bar, that gets known for the special kind of activity, often illegal, that goes on there. When he has stolen goods to sell, Willie goes to the tree on 2nd Avenue and 9th Street. When he is selling reefer or cocaine, he usually does so at the tree on 15th Avenue and 62nd Street. He said cocaine sells on the street in six-, ten-, twenty-five- and fifty-"cent"—that is, dollar—bags. Much of the business comes from whites. The police suspect that during the riot several of the whites who got beaten had come into Liberty City for drugs. Indeed, on Sunday night, Willie helped beat up a white man trying to buy drugs along 62nd Street.

Along with getting him a small amount of money, Willie's hustling provides him with a rich fantasy life. He sees himself as something of a master criminal who is so good at what he does as to be beyond detection. On the street, he encourages people to call him "Smarts" and relishes telling about his escapades. "If I do some wrongness, I don't do it in front of anybody," he says. "Ain't no one gonna see me when I do wrongness." Willie usually works with a partner, a young man called "Slimey." Together, they have contributed their share to the tremendous increase in street crime in downtown Miami, where they engage regularly in what Willie likes to describe as "pickpocket-ing" but which appears to be purse-snatching. "What you do," he says, "is you come at someone from opposite directions, like a lady walking on the sidewalk, and one of you bumps into her and the other grabs the bag or wallet or whatever and you take off." Smarts and Slimey can also be violent. Two weeks before the riot, Willie says, they mugged a man on 2nd Avenue and 54th Street. Slimey grabbed the victim from behind with a chokehold, and the pair dragged him into the bushes. There, they removed his pants and took his wallet. Willie then de-scribed how he took a .38 caliber revolver he carried, reared back to gain swinging room and struck the man on the side of his head with the butt.

Willie says the police are much too slow-witted to catch on to his wiles.

We were going to go into this store on 183rd Street in Carol City three days after the riot. Things had cooled off and everything. The way I do it, I'm sitting on the bench, smoking a little reefer. Then I get this feeling I want to do some wrong. I want to get paid. I want a pay day. So I go into the telephone booth and start watching the store to see when the time is right to go in and grab something. But I'm talking on the telephone so if the police come by, well, "I don't know about nothin', officer, I'm talkin' on the telephone." That's why they call me "Smarts."

According to Willie's probation officer, he depends for most of his slickness on Slimey, the smarter half of the pair. When left to his own devices, Smarts tends to pull things that are somewhat less than brilliant. In April 1979, while he was working as a kitchen boy at a branch of the International House of Pancakes, Willie went through the telephone book during his lunch break and picked a name at random. He called the person out of the blue and threatened to kill him if he didn't hand over $1,000. The man told Willie he would have to go to the bank to get the money; where could he call to arrange a meeting? Willie gave him the telephone number of the Pancake House. By the time the victim called again, Willie had gone back to the kitchen, and the person who answered the phone was the restaurant manager. After being filled in on Willie's noontime activities, the manager called the police. Willie got four years on probation for extortion, with the provisos that he stay out of trouble and get a job. Willie honors the first provision to the extent of trying not to get caught for any of his muggings. The second poses more of a problem because he is incapable of holding down even a casual laboring job for very long. Several months before the riot, he was fired from a job putting up sheetrock on a construction site because he insisted on smoking marijuana while he worked. Willie considers his dismissal a great injustice. "The foreman said it'd slow me down, but reefer never did anything to stop me from working. It slows other people down, but it speeds me up."

At the time of our interview, Willie had a job as a busboy in a chain-owned steak house. He disdained the pay, which was the minimum wage of $3.10 an hour, and kept the job only as a condition of his probation. "I can make a lot more money on the street than at any job by selling reefer and cocaine," he says. How long he will be tolerated at the restaurant is another question. When we dropped him off at work one day, he was so loaded up with Quaaludes that he had serious difficulty putting three or four words together coherently.

During the first night of the riot, Willie says, he stayed out of trouble because of the danger of getting caught and violating his probation. He did agree to help Slimey load up the trunk of Slimey's car with stolen goods, but he didn't steal anything himself. It wasn't until 2:30 on Sunday afternoon that he and Slimey got a "bag of reefer," climbed into Slimey's car and went looking for goods. Their first stop was not in Liberty City but over in Hialeah. "We figured all the rioting was going on here, so we'd go somewhere else," Willie says. "Slimey knew of this hole in the roof of a jewelry store where he tried to break in once. And we got a crowbar and everything and got in part way. Got some medallions, some watches."

At a tree on 2nd Avenue and 9th Street, known as a place to get rid of hot goods, Willie traded in the jewelry for a twenty-five-inch television set. Then the pair went to a gun store on 95th Street and 7th Avenue, where he said he stole a .357 magnum pistol with a silencer, six .32 caliber pistols and two .30-.30 rifles. "I got a pump, just like my grandaddy's—the kind he uses to shoot deer with." After that it was over to a drug tree to smoke a little reefer and participate in "stompin' crackers." It was about nine in the evening. The white man had come to the tree often before and felt himself in no danger during the riot. The way Willie describes it, Slimey started a fight with the man, and when Slimey started getting the worst of it others joined in. Willie did, too. He elaborately describes how he kicked the man's head, like a placekicker trying for the extra point.

Willie said he was angry with the man not because of the McDuffie verdict but because he was a stand-in for other whites who often came into Liberty City to harass blacks. "Whites come driving through all the time, and call you 'nigger' and such. Or they catch you at a bus stop all by yourself and then throw bottles at you. Call out 'Hey, nigger boy. . . .' I say, we beat that man half to death."

Stage III: Mrs. Willa J—

Mrs. Willa J— is a forty-seven-year-old mother of seven, a resident of Liberty City who was raised in Savannah, Georgia, and who had her first child at age fifteen. Although currently unemployed, she has worked most of her life as a presser "in just about every laundry in Miami." She was never in trouble with the police, she says, until Sunday of the riot, when she and her husband, a construction worker named Henry, who had also never been involved in trouble, were arrested and charged with grand theft for trying to loot a freezer from in front of a store selling frozen shrimp.

"My husband came home and said to me that there was a lot of fire and people in the street," she recalls.

> He said, "My God, Willa, so much fire it looks like the world is coming to an end." So we ate dinner and I said to him, "Well, take me for a ride." I said, "I want to see." We finished up dinner. I didn't

even wash the dishes; I just put them in the sink. That was on Sunday. I'll never forget it.

We first went down 17th Avenue. The first place we seen was Joe's Market. People was running with stuff out of Joe's Market. We got to around 48th Street; people was really running out with big boxes of auto parts and all. You name it, they had it. Then we came on down 7th Avenue. "My God, Henry, look!" Every place we looked was just burning, burning. Then I wanted to go over to 27th Avenue to see what they was doing over on that side. So we went over there, and just before we got to the shrimp place, near 75th Street and 27th Avenue, all those places was burning. We seen people was just running out with big boxes of shrimp.

I said to him, "Henry, look, a stove and a freezer!" So he said, "Oh, Willa, come on, you always wanting to stop and stuff." So I said, "Henry, let me get this freezer." It was right there by the street, you know. I said, "Henry, let me get this freezer." He said, "No, no, no!" I said, "Oh, please let me get the freezer." So finally he backed up to get the freezer. When he backed up to get the freezer, he said, "Wait, Willa, I have to let the tailgate down on the truck." And people was just . . . the police just ignored *them*. All the people was just getting stuff and running across the street. He was telling them to halt and they just looked back and laughed at him and kept on going. And me and Henry was the only ones standing up there with our mouths wide open. We hand't even put the freezer on the truck. And this cop comes along, and said "Halt." And that's what happened. "Halt." We didn't even put the freezer on the truck.

Mrs. J— says that when she went out with her husband she had no intention of taking anything.

On my mind was just going to see. After he said, "My God, it looks like the world is on fire," that was my main reason for leaving— to see what was all burning. And everywhere you looked it was fire. I had never seen nothing like that in all the days of my life. I had never seen so much of a place burning. Old people was just carrying chairs, lamps, you name it. Everybody was just really helping themselves. But what I feel about it, I feel it was wrong. It was wrong for me to even back up to think about getting that freezer because that wasn't mine. And I wasn't taught that way. And it was really wrong. But after seeing so many people just getting things off the street . . .

Mrs. J— and her husband were taken to the Dade County Jail at four in the afternoon and were kept there until six the next morning waiting to get released on their own recognizance. "This was an experience for me," she says. "And my sick mother was here and all. Boy, I'm telling you, I went through hell. I'll never experience that again. I was so afraid of going to jail and doing time and having a bad record and everything. I went over to the Beach, Miami Beach, and got a lawyer and he charged us $750." She paid him $200 on account, she says, but as it turned out, neither she nor her husband needed a lawyer. Because they had no prior record, their cases were referred automatically to the pretrial intervention program, which, if they stayed out of trouble, meant that their case would eventually be dismissed. "They told me to go to Room 282 and to continue with my counseling, and I wouldn't have to come back to court any more. But that lawyer is still aggravating us for the $550."

Mrs. J— has a quick and rich sense of humor and can now talk about her arrest with laughter. Her experience raising a family in Liberty City has been arduous and at times heartbreaking. Though married, she seems to have paid the bills, kept up the house and taken care of her children pretty much by herself. Only one of her six sons avoided getting into serious trouble with the police; he now works as an electrician for a company in Chicago. "He's even got stocks and things," she says. "He's really made something of himself."

Another son, Jimmie, was involved in the city's drug traffic and was shot to death by the police—unjustifiably, she says—in 1971 when he was twenty years old.

> I was going to sell this house to get justice for what happened, but nobody would take it. This big old crook lawyer, the one that takes all those black people's money and sends them up for fifty or sixty years, that's the one that didn't want to take the case. That's the one black people need to get out of his seat because he really does a lot of black people harm.

A third son is doing twenty years for shooting one of Mrs. J—'s former boyfriends, who, she says, had cheated her son out of $700. A fourth was beaten up by the police in her backyard.

> "Mama, mama," I could hear him out there. "They like to kill me out here." There's so many things. Black people have a *right* to hate. They really have a right. It's so many things these people do and get by with it. So many years they beat up poor people you'd think it would get better, but it's no better. I really had troubled boys but they're supposed to go to jail, not get beaten and killed."

Even so, Mrs. J— says, she does not think the mistreatment of blacks by whites justified the violence during the 1980 riot or her own attempted theft:

> I'm forty-seven years old, married and I would do no harm to anyone. Did you hear what they did? They cut off their ears on 62nd Street! My God, I thought that was the worst thing that I could ever

hear in my life! Regardless if you do somethin' to me, why should I go next door and cut somebody's ears off or hit somebody or run over somebody? I wouldn't agree with that. They're human and they're some mother's sons. You wouldn't want that to happen to your child, I don't care what color. I don't really hate nobody. I just hate what they did to my sons. I have a lot of bitterness in me, but I wouldn't take it out on nobody, and this didn't cause me to go out and say, "Well, they did this and they did that. Now I'm gonna take a freezer." No, no, I just happened to pass by and see the freezer and had seen other people doing it, taking things. And I just thought I could get by with getting me a freezer.

I don't see where it accomplished nothing anyway. So many old people have been hurt. All the neighborhood stores were burnt; now they got no place to cash their welfare checks to pay their light bills or water bills. I don't see where it really made sense. There's not a store around here you can get a pound of hamburger. You have to go to 93rd Street, and just imagine the people around here who don't have cars. If I was young, if I had went in those people's stores and looted, I wouldn't have burned them down. I would have gotten what I wanted, but not set them on fire. But the police burnt Sunny South [a grocery store] down. People saw them. People were in Sunny South looting, and they shot that stuff in there and the fire started right up. Blacks were looting it, and they couldn't get out all the stuff they wanted to get out because the fire started on them.

The only bitterness I really have towards the whites is, like my mama, my grandma and all those slave people back years ago. This is one of the reasons why black people are not educated like whites. For the simple reason, they had to wash their clothes, raise their kids, lay down with the men when their wives go to the store shopping and have these bastard babies. This is why you seen some brown-skinned blacks and some almost white blacks. It came back from slavery, you know. And I feel like, if they're gonna give—look at these Cubans. Giving all these Cubans things. There's so many damn rich Cubans in this town. Why haven't we got somewhere? What have the Cubans ever done for them? Our women done lay down and had those bastard babies. We done washed their clothes. They wouldn't allow us to read and write—our parents. Now, this is what we get for thanks. They go adopt some other nation. And set them free!

Mrs. J— thinks the reason her sons got into trouble was that she could never be home to watch over them and that when she was she was too tired to pay much attention:

When I came home every day, I had to wash the clothes and get supper, and I was so damn tired. I pressed at French Benzo, in just about every laundry in Miami. I worked so hard. I came home at night and I'm asleep by eight-thirty or nine. What happened and why they went wrong is that it was six boys and one girl and no father to help me. How it started was by me being tired. They would slip out at night and get into devilment or, in summer months, in the day.

But they never brought any of the stuff back here. They knew they'd
be in big trouble. They were afraid. So all they would do is get into
devilment and then hide it out. My kids were just as frightened of
me as a rattlesnake. I imagine a lot of things they wanted I just
couldn't get by being on one salary. I imagine that had a lot to do
with it, too. There was no food stamps then. You could have twelve
kids and get only $85 a month. I was down at the food stamp place
last month and there was so many Cubans and Haitians there the
American people were not getting any stamps. It looked like the
foreigners were getting their stamps first. Now the mothers get stamps
enough to get food and fruit in the house. All I could afford was the
major food for my kids.

But, I tell you, maybe the changes will come one day, you know,
in the stature of living, equal rights. I have a little pick-up and deliv-
ery, dry-cleaning. It's not real good now, but all I ever done in my
life was pressing. I got a friend over on 22nd Avenue. She got a
cleaners, and different people they usually bring me their laundry,
and I take it and do that. But right now I'm tired of sitting around
and I want a job. But you look in the paper every day and you can't
find a job. You used to find pressing jobs a dime a dozen. That's
right. You can't find a pressing job. Because I wanted to get out and
earn some money because I got nine grandchildren for Christmas.
But I can't find nothing.

Notes

1. *Report of the National Advisory Commission on Civil Disorders*
(1968), p. 128.

2. Study by the Behavioral Science Research Institute, Coral Gables, 1980.

3. Dade-Miami Criminal Justice Council, "Profile of Those Arrested During Miami's May 1980 Civil Disturbances" (unpublished report), March 1981.

4. Robert Curvin and Bruce Porter, *Blackout Looting!* (New York:
Gardner Press, 1979), Chaps. 1, 5 and 7.

5. Prepared from calls to 911 received by Dade County Public
Safety Department and from arrest data compiled by the CJC.

6. Anthony Oberschall, "The Los Angeles Riot of August 1965,"
Social Problems (Winter 1968), pp. 322-341.

7. Hugh Graham and Ted Gurr, *Violence in America: A Report to
the National Commission on the Causes and Prevention of Violence*
(1969), p. 326.

8. E. L. Quarantelli and Russell Dynes, "Looting in Civil Disorders: An Index of Social Change, *The American Behavioral Scientist,*
(March/April 1968).

9. Compiled by the CJC.

A burned-out tire store smolders in the northwest section of Miami, May 18, 1980 (United Press International Photo)

6

The Damage

Immediately after the riot, officials in Miami were quick to announce that the disorder was the worst in the country's recent history. Although more people had been killed during the riots in Watts, Newark and Detroit, they said, none of the disturbances approached Miami's in terms of sheer physical destruction. A week after the outburst, Dade County Manager Merrett Stierheim put the damage at more than $200 million, a figure far outstripping that for any civil disorder in this century.[1]

Surveys of the riot damage, however, disagreed, sometimes wildly, on both the number of businesses affected and the cost of the damage. In one count, reporters for the *Miami Herald* put the total number of businesses looted and burned during the riot at 190.[2] In another survey made right after the disorder, the community development agencies for both the City of Miami and Dade County came up with 240 businesses that reported being damaged. Neither of these counts included any of the damage outside the immediate Miami area. According to the county fire department, some forty cases of arson were reported in black areas of Perrine in the southwest and fifty-seven more in Opa-Locka, the largely black city to the northeast.

The dollar estimates of the loss vary even more dramatically. Figures for fire damage during the riot, as reported by the Miami Fire Department, ranged from one-third to one-tenth the estimates eventually claimed by owners of the businesses for insurance purposes. For example, in the cases of three stores destroyed by fire—Central Tile, Jay's Drugs and Magnum Furniture—the MFD came up with building losses of $30,000, $50,000 and $75,000, respectively. Owners of these stores, however, were quoted in the city and county surveys as claiming damages, including inventory, of $319,000, $230,000 and $221,000, respectively. In some instances the estimates were raised again when the *Herald* questioned the owners a month later.[3] In the city survey, Central Tile claimed damages of $319,000 for its building and $203,000 more for the contents, or a total of $522,000. In the *Herald* study this figure rose to an even $1 million.[4]

To make matters still more confusing, the fire department figures do not seem to be consistently low. The MFD loss figure for Farrey's Hardware was $1 million, very close to what the owner later claimed.

129

In the case of Grand Drug in Coconut Grove, the MFD estimate of $60,000 matched exactly with what the owner later told the *Herald*.[5]

To arrive at a total damage figure, the city and county sent questionnaires to the 240 businesses on their list. Of these, 174 replied and claimed a total bill for buildings and contents of $50.68 million. In its study, the *Herald* talked to 147 of the 190 stores on its list and came up with a figure of $59.25 million.[6] Assuming an equal distribution of damage among the stores not responding to either survey, the city/county figure would increase to $69.9 million and the *Herald*'s to $88.03 million. Splitting the difference—and assuming that owners' estimates were not grossly inflated—one could say that the property loss for businesses during the Miami riot was about $80 million.

Even correcting for inflation, the numbers do not support the claim that the Miami disorder was the worst in recent history. Miami's loss clearly exceeds the $10 million in damage reported in Newark in 1967. But the $45 million figure for Detroit in the same year, assuming a 150 percent inflation over the thirteen intervening years, would amount to more than $112 million in 1980 dollars. Even more destruction occurred during the blackout looting in New York City in 1977. There, a total of 1,576 businesses received at least some damage, compared to the 240 in Miami, and the loss was put by city officials at between $135 million and $150 million, almost double the Miami estimate, even in 1977 dollars.

On the other hand, the Miami riot does seem to have been far more intensively destructive than the outburst in New York. While the 240 businesses hit in Miami amounted to only 13 percent of the number of businesses looted in New York, the dollar loss in Miami was something around 50 percent of the New York figure. What this means is that the rioters in Miami were far more inclined to burn stores as well as loot them. And because of the ready availability of gasoline and the failure of the county fire department to fight many of the blazes in its territory, the buildings put to the torch tended to be destroyed. In Miami, 102, or 42 percent, of the 240 stores on the riot list were "totally" or "irreversibly" damaged. In New York, only 214, or 13.5 percent, of the 1,576 businesses were set afire. And because the New York City Fire Department was extremely active that night, only a small percentage of those were destroyed. To get some idea of the destructive force in Miami, one would have to compare it to the burning on Bushwick Avenue in Brooklyn during the blackout, which shocked New Yorkers by its intensity. When the ashes cooled, 45 of the 133 stores on Bushwick Avenue, or 33 percent, had been burned, and many of these were not destroyed. In Miami, the stores destroyed amounted to 42 percent of the total. An even greater proportion in Miami were burned but saved from total destruction.

The stores that were destroyed in Miami tended to be larger than the ones merely looted and left standing. In the city survey, the average square footage for stores suffering "irreversible damage" was 19,701. The area of stores with only "minor" damage averaged only 7,428 square feet. This is in line with the assumption that the bigger stores were large, outside-owned businesses with little, if any, ties to the community. The smaller ones would be more likely to have a personal relationship with their customers, and hence to be spared malicious destruction.

Another difference in Miami was that judging from the kinds of property that were burned, the rioters seemed often driven more by the desire to destroy than to steal. Many of the buildings put to the torch were manufacturing concerns that had little material to loot besides office supplies, machinery and specialized tools. As many factories were on the "totally destroyed" list as were furniture stores, drug stores and liquor stores. The Moss Manufacturing Company, which makes antique ceiling fans, was burned out completely. So were the DTC Tool Company, Clark Chemicals and Britt Metal Processing, the last of which overhauled jet aircraft parts. Some twenty-five others that were looted were service businesses, such as Welch Moving, or businesses not normally on a looter's list, such as a lumber yard, an electric parts wholesaler and a ceramic tile dealer.

One possible reason for hitting these businesses was anger over their having failed to employ a significant number of blacks. And compared to retail outlets, which in a *Herald* survey had a fairly high ration of black salespeople, the factories and services did seem inordinately low in black employment. Indeed, seven of the factories with total employment of 102 people listed no black workers.[8] All it took for a fire, after all, was one man with a grudge and a soda bottle filled with gasoline. "It was a time that if you didn't like someone, that's when you got him," says one former convict now with the ex-offender program run by the James E. Scott Community Association. "There's a lot of people around here carrying a lot of mad around with them."

Partly because of a heightened sense of the rage present in the community, and partly for other reasons, half the businesses in the riot area picked up and left after the disorder. Even some that had employed significant numbers of blacks before the riot decided afterwards that the area was too dangerous for future operation. The twenty-six-store Norton Tire Company, for instance, employed 60 blacks at its headquarters at 27th Avenue and 54th Street out of its work force of 100. When its large retail outlet was burned out early Sunday morning, the company lost a $250,000 computer located in the back of the store. On the heels of this, it decided to move its administrative center and most of its jobs away from Liberty City, leaving only a small tire store behind.

In many parts of Miami's black ghettoes, commercial life after the riot all but ceased to exist. This was most true in the city's Overtown section, a twenty-block community that was pretty bad off before the disorder. The riot, however, finished off the last of its stores: the Rexall Drugs, the furniture store, the supermarket, an appliance outlet. Overtown was left little more than a ghost city where the people—most of them unattached males—still hung out on the corners out of habit, but where one could go for block after block and find little to spend money on except marijuana, a home-barbecued rib, or a can of soda or beer. As for redevelopment plans, which had been proposed before the riot, they also received a severe setback. "Commercial revitalization improvements were under way prior to the disturbances," the city's riot survey read. "Now, it will be very difficult to recruit more businessmen into the program."

In Liberty City a year after the riot, with so many businesses gone—supermarkets, furniture stores, hardware outlets, automarts—one could drive for miles along formerly commercial strips in Liberty City and see nothing open for business but an occasional gas station, a blaring record store, a pool room, a bar, a cleaners, or the omnipresent corner grocery, the only business that is generally owned by blacks. In between, slowly growing up in weeds, were vacant lots filled with the rubble left after the city's demolition workers tried to sweep away all evidence of the riot. Large parts of Liberty City looked not so much like the proverbial bombed-out city as they did an empty lot.

The Looting of 7th Avenue

The part of 7th Avenue that runs through Liberty City begins in the north as a fast-moving stretch flanked by new and used car lots and auto parts stores. To the south, from the seventies to the fifties, it becomes lined with ramshackle dwellings typical of black Miami commercial strips. Half-abandoned before the riot, the avenue lost its large furniture stores, hardware stores and supermarkets during the looting and became largely barren of significant commerce. What stores remained have bunkered up their exteriors with cinderblocks, affording customers no view of what merchandise may be for sale until they step through the door. Display windows are a marketing device that ghetto stores can no longer afford.

After commercial enterprises fail along the avenue their buildings frequently are reborn as rickety houses of worship. At 62nd Street, for instance, a newly painted sign announcing the headquarters of "The Evangelical Crusade of Fishers Men" [sic] shows out beneath a broken tangle of neon that once read "Beer Wine and Liquor." Indeed, in what used to be the commercial heart of the avenue, storefront churches now account for nearly half the census. Here are the occupants of the western side of the avenue between 60th and 61st Streets: Captain Curry Bail Bonds ("Any Jail Any Time"); Al's Shoe Repair; Paradise Beauty-Rama, Wigs; Blood of Jesus Temple of Deliverance (whose display window is painted with a wooden cross dripping blood from its spar); defunct, no-name church; pool room; Full Gospel Evangelistic Tabernacle; Afro-Tone, Wigs; Fellowship Missionary Baptist Church. A block down is the Edison Center Shopping Mall, a mostly vacant four-block tract whose only sign of business activity is a large parking lot slowly being reclaimed by weeds, and the Dupont Car Wash, which sits like an outpost at the center's northwest corner. The lot was the site of Shell's City, a major food and liquor store whose closing ten years ago was a milestone in the area's decline. At 62nd Street, two other prominent department stores, J. Byron's and Jackson's, moved out at roughly the same time.

Nearly every corner has its mom-and-pop grocery, such as Frazier's or the G & C, the L & M, or the B & M, the initials usually standing for the first names of its proprietors. Their shelves are sparsely stocked with canned goods, beer, soda, Goody's Headache Powder, Chattanooga Chewing Tobacco. The jewel of most groceries is a little glass-encased ferris wheel carrying ninety-cent sausages past infrared heat. Dark, with no windows, the stores are stifling in the summer. Candy bars have to be stored in the refrigerator so they won't run all over the counter. The largest black businesses on the strip are Bottom Dollar Fish and King the Tailor, both at 62nd Street, Stay's Hardware, at 75th, and Burrough's, a substantial grocery. The rest of the larger stores are controlled by Anglos or Cubans.

The following is a store-by-store account of how the avenue was looted. Along with showing the pattern of destruction, it gives a peek into the commercial life of a Miami ghetto community and a feeling for the mood of those who live and work there. The interviews were conducted by Craig Rose, who came down to help us with our research two months after graduating from the Columbia University Graduate School of Journalism:

Washington's Grocery.* Thomas Washington, 53, a construction worker
by trade, has owned his store for six years. It is attended by his wife
during weekdays while he is at work; he's there on weekends. Inside,
it is a cut above most mom-and-pops, with a dropped ceiling, unfin-
ished concrete floor and air conditioning that is inadequate for the
space and allows the Kit Kat candy bars to show grease through their
wrapping.

Next door is a Cuban-owned liquor store that was looted and
burned out during the riot. Washington called his neighbor to tell him
his place had been broken into. The man came down, but then went
back home, resigned to being wiped out. A couple of years ago, Washington's store was firebombed after a Spanish-speaking person tried
and failed to buy the store, he said. He rebuilt it himself. During the
riot he had tried to fight the fire next door with a garden hose to protect
his own building. After the fire died out at 4 p.m. on Sunday, he was
nailing plywood over his neighbor's gaping windows when some policemen in an unmarked car drove by.

"What are you doing?" he said the cops asked him.

"I'm nailing the window shut," Washington answered.

"I don't give a fuck what you're doing," he said one cop said.
And as Washington was leaning down to drive another nail in, he said
he was hit on the head with the butt of the policeman's rifle. He spun
around, and heard one policeman say, "Hit him again, do it again,"
and they did, Washington said. After he was hit the second time, a
marked police car pulled up with black and white policemen. "Why
did you hit him?," they asked, but then drove off without waiting for
an answer, Washington said.

"If the cops see a kid of twelve or thirteen just running down the
street, they'd probably shoot the shit out of him," said Washington,
who went to the hospital and was given several stitches to close his
head wound. He later filed a complaint with the Miami police.

> You got a few nice police down here. But some of those white
> cops, when they get their buddies together, they put hell on a guy.
> If they catch a black man alone, forget it. There's really only a few
> bad ones. The rest are okay. . . .
> I'm thinking about selling out and going up North. You can't
> raise a family in this town. I got two daughters in college, and when
> they get out, I might leave.

Salvation Army Thrift Store. This store, on 56th Street, is managed by

---

*The name of the grocery has been fictionalized at the owner's request.

a black woman with two white employees and one black. Fred Holcomb, one of the workers, said it was hit on Saturday night. "They broke the front glass and ripped off the back door. They took 90 percent of the clothing and furniture and they tried to burn it. The only thing that saved this building were the old sprinklers." Holcomb said the smell of tear gas, which seeped into the walls and clung there, made it hard to work in the store a long time after the riot. It was in front of this store that two Miami policemen were shot on Sunday by someone firing from across the street in the alleyway between the Luxury Apartments and Sawyer's Upholstery.

Family Meat Market. This Cuban-owned meat store on 57th Street was hit at 2 a.m. Sunday. Luis Lazaro, the owner, said he had been at the location for four years and that he employs five workers, three of them black. "They took all the meat and all the equipment," he said. "The only thing they left was two pounds of lard."

He estimated his damage at $42,000 and had to close for three weeks making repairs. He chose not to apply for an SBA loan. "I got good credit. If I borrow from SBA, that's thirty years. By the time I pay it back, they hit me two, three more times."

He had expected trouble that Saturday and closed the store early. "We didn't even clean up. I said we'll come in tomorrow and clean up." Lazaro, who owns another meat market at 17th Avenue and 62nd Street, and he spotted a truck filled with meat at 103rd Street and 17th Avenue later on Sunday. "I asked the guy if he took that stuff from me. The guy just waved and said, 'I got it from everybody.' "

King the Tailor. "King," who is really William Calhoun, a soft-spoken black man with flecks of blond in his Afro, has been in business on 62nd Street since 1969. In 1974 his place burned to the ground during an apparent burglary, and Calhoun rebuilt it, partly with his own hands. Inside, it seems designed for better days. Some of the display racks are empty, and there is a lot of unused floor space.

About 11 p.m. Saturday he got a call at home from a street urchin telling him his shop was being broken into. He came down immediately, unarmed. "If I couldn't talk them out of it, I didn't think it was worth getting hurt over," he says:

> When I got to the store there were eight or ten of them in here. I recognized some of them from over on 55th Street, the guys who hang out playing dice at Duhart's Grocery. I said, "Hey, you ain't supposed to be in a black man's store." And then one teenager said, "Yeah, man, that's Calhoun. He's right," and they left.

They had pulled open the back window bars and opened the back door to get in. Calhoun had forgotten to set the burglar alarm that night. They had taken about $5,000 worth of merchandise. Calhoun stayed around in front of his store after they left and watched the same group move up to start the looting at Furniture World up the block.

> There got to be around twenty or thirty people just taking things, pushing things down the street, putting them on bicycles and in cars. There were Haitians, Jamaicans, blacks, young people, old people. Some people came by with pickups and vans, but most of them were using cars. Some tied their trunks open by running a rope from the front bumper to the trunk latch. After they filled up the trunk, they piled stuff on top. There were a couple of arguments. One guy got part of a couch set, but by the time he got back, somebody else got the other part of it. There was some lady in her fifties who went into the store barefooted, over all the broken glass. She came out pushing a dresser down the sidewalk, but it caught in the cracks and so she moved it out into the street and pushed it away.

After the crowd spent about three hours looting Furniture World, Calhoun was worried they would burn it down. "I told 'em, 'You all don't burn down the place 'cause I'm gonna burn also if you do.' " The core group from Duhart's had moved on to break the glass window at the Royal Castle luncheonette nearby but stopped when they were told it was a black-owned business.

Calhoun also watched the looting of Eagle Discount and saw the people carrying goods away from Pantry-Pride. "There were people carrying bags of groceries, pushcarts, shopping carts and bicycles. There were adults who had children with them. There were youngsters running to and fro with bags and loose merchandise. I called the cops several times for Eagle, and they would send people to run them off, but they'd come back."

Active in community affairs, Calhoun worked on the Model Cities Advisory Board and is involved with the Tacolcy Center, a multiservice agency nearby. At one point he went to Atlanta with Model Cities people in an unsuccessful attempt to change the plans for I-95, which parallels 7th Avenue a block to the east. Calhoun and other businessmen wanted the access ramp put at 54th Street instead of at 62nd, where they are located. "Now people just use the street as a thoroughfare. Traffic used to slow up but now it just goes by. We went all the way to Atlanta, but they said they had already spent the money."

Bottom Dollar Discount Fish Market. A black-owned store on 62nd Street, Bottom Dollar was not struck by looters during the riot.

Eagle Discount. To judge by the half-block-long vacant lot left behind on 63rd Street after it was destroyed, Eagle was a big store. James Goodman, owner of the G & C Grocery across the street, stayed in his store all night watching the looting of Eagle but didn't want to talk about it. He said that at one point the police watched, too. "The looters, they didn't bother black people during the riot 'cause we had nothing to steal."

Brenda's Flowers. This black-owned business on 63rd Street was hit. Brenda Jackson said the store was broken into Saturday night and wedding accoutrements and some bamboo baskets were taken. Total value: $2,000. She had been in the neighborhood for two years and had just expanded by breaking through a wall and annexing the store next door. "My husband wanted to come down on Sunday, but I didn't want him to because there was this sniping," she said. "I'd really like to leave the neighborhood." All the store's windows are now boarded up, and the two employees she had before the riot, both black, were laid off while she made repairs.

Susan's Market. This meat store on 64th Street was probably the first business hit along 7th Avenue. Julio Bermejo has owned the place for two years. The number of his employees varies from four to eight, and there were some blacks working alongside Hispanics behind the counter. It's a clean, modern-looking place with the standard glass meat cases and signs advertising its specials in hog maws, pigtails, goat meat, cow feet, ox tails and other cuts of meat. On the back walls are taped-up pictures of Muhammed Ali, some sexy-looking black women and some black leaders. Barmejo said his alarm went off at 8 p.m. and that by 11 p.m. half his merchandise was gone. Total loss was about $23,000. A small, slightly built man, he came down to the store in response to the alarm but couldn't protect it because he was unarmed. He called the police but said they wouldn't come.

U-Totem. The store on 68th Street closed at 9:30, "just after the rocks and bottles started flying in the neighborhood," said its black manager. He said it is a white-owned store and was hit before midnight on Saturday and lost all but a few canned goods. "They had to have three or four men with a hand truck to take the safe out of here," he said. "They never took the safe before." He said the store was broken into again three times in the two months following the riot.

Edison Furniture. Signs outside the 69th Street Edison Furniture announce: "Where customers send their friends: 3 rooms of furniture,

$549.95. No interest or carrying charges." This white-owned business is operated by Homer Stembridge, a talkative born-again Christian who operates another furniture store with his brother in Homestead. It employed eight to eleven people before the riot. After it was burned out all but three or four of them were transferred to the other store. "I'm not angry at anyone," said Stembridge as he walked through his gutted building, his feet squishing on the water-logged remnants of the store's carpeting. "I'm a born-again Christian and I've learned to hate the sin, not the sinner. I've always tried to do right by people. You know the only thing I saved out of here was a family Bible." On the site for twenty-five years, Stembridge says he plans to rebuild.

Miami Appliances. This windowless orange and brown cinderblock fortress on 69th Street was broken into on Sunday between 1 and 1:30 p.m. The business deals in appliance parts, not an item high on the looters' list, but they took adding machines and some parts that the owner, Fred Locasio, who inherited the business from his father, said they couldn't sell. The firm employs fifteen people, none of them black. Locasio said he was told the doors of the Edison Furniture Store were blown off with shotguns.

M & J Foreign Car Repair. In this small place on 70th Street most of the work is done outdoors under a corrugated tin canopy on a concrete floor hidden under layers of dirt and grease. It is owned by Michael Nicholas, a Haitian, and serves mostly Haitian customers. At about 6 p.m., he said, "I heard some shots, looked up and saw this guy running down 70th Street west. I just closed the gates and got the hell out of here." Nicholas's business was not touched until Monday, when someone cut the padlock on his iron gates and took tools, an air compressor, jacks and a battery charger, total value $7,000.

Convention Contractors Inc. Owned by a white named John Elko, this 71st Street business employs six people, two of them black, and makes its money setting up displays for conventions held in downtown Miami or in Miami Beach. Elko said he had heard nothing about the riots until he went down to his shop at 6 a.m. on Sunday to do some work and passed by the Edison Furniture Store as it was burning.

> I went inside to make myself a cup of coffee and then went back out to watch the fire. Then a cop came up to me and said, "Get out of here. Don't you know there's riots?" I got some plywood to board up the front of my building. While I was boarding it up, three cars pulled up in front of Farrey's with six people. They took a sledge and busted the front door. They went in and started bringing out light

fixtures and everything. Then the next thing I knew I saw a fire started. The fire department came and they parked here in front of my office. They fought the fire for about a half hour and then they rolled up the hoses and started to leave. I asked them, "Aren't you going to fight this fire?" And they said, "No, we have other fires to go to." There's no other building around, so they just figured let this one burn.

About 1 p.m. he heard pounding on the walls, went outside and saw that the noise was coming from a crowd pounding on the doors of Allstate Office Furniture two doors to the north. Elko called the police and says he was told: "We can't stop them. As long as no white people are in the building then nobody's going to get hurt."

At this Elko called his wife and had her go to Hallendale, a town outside the curfew area, and buy him a shotgun. "The guy guaranteed that this shotgun she bought could blow a hole in a concrete wall at 100 yards. I said, 'That's the gun for me.' " Meanwhile, he called the Allstate owner at home to say they were breaking into his store. "He said, 'I'm not coming down there, you're crazy.' " Mrs. Elko had the gun dropped off at Elko's office by one of his trucks coming back from a convention job at the Diplomat Hotel for more supplies. "I had two black men working for me, and while they were loading the truck, three cars pulled into my back driveway and some big colored woman said, 'Oh, you broke into that place, too.' But my worker said, 'No, it's just empty crates.' Then I came around the corner with the double-barreled shotgun, and they got back in their cars and took off."

Elko thinks it was sometime around 2 p.m. when two cars pulled up to E & J Liquors on 70th Street.

Again, out came the sledge hammers. They smashed in and took what they wanted, then took off. By then, the police cars were driving up and down, and everybody was scared to go in. But they'd look around and when they'd see no cops, they'd go in and come right back out with something. It wasn't large crowds; it was in twos and threes as they were passing by.

Two black guys passing by while I was on the corner said, "Hey, white man, get off the street." I threw up my arm and gave them the black power salute, and they said, "Right on, brother," and I went back inside. They said it to me in a friendly way.

At Allstate Office Furniture, he said:

The cops ignored people wheeling furniture down the street. They said, "Until they're doing bodily damage, we're instructed to do nothing." The first two cars loaded up with typewriters and calculators, the small stuff, and then they left it open for the rest of the people—whatever they wanted. They were pushing chairs down the street with desks on top. It was all young kids; they were running up and down the street. I'd say the kids were from twelve to twenty-seven or twenty-eight—in that range.

Talking about doing business in general in the area, Elko said:

> I'm staying until I can find another place. They've scared all the whites who employ blacks here. I can't hire decent office help because they say they won't come into the area. A white client told me, "John, I hope you move soon, because I don't like to come into the neighborhood." He said four to five black people every day come looking for a job, but that he does all his hiring through a union hall.
>
> I won't stay in this neighborhood with the thought that if there's another big racial incident and a white policeman shoots somebody the riot's going to start all over again. It's kind of hard every time you wake up in the morning and your wife says should I pack you an overnight bag? Are we gonna live like this the rest of our lives? I can't see it, so within the next year I will be moving. Prior to the riot I felt safe here. We used to go to Jumbo's [a fast food place up the block] for breakfast, but now we go over to Biscayne Boulevard. Right here is very convenient for me because we service all the hotels and all the major convention centers. We service Marco Island, we service West Palm Beach. The location is ideal because we're right near the expressway—we can go north, south, east or west. But even if it comes to the point where it costs me more money for gas for traveling from Fort Lauderdale to service the Miami area, I do know this: within the next year, I will be moving.

Since the riot Elko has installed a high Cyclone fence around his building, but his wife doesn't feel safe anymore. "The black people don't want us here," she said. "The government doesn't understand that. Even with the fence up out there you see them out there smoking and snorting. The men pee up against the building. The minute I get off the expressway at 69th Street I come right to the office. I don't stop. If the light's turning red, I move. I'd rather get a ticket, because you just don't know. Especially a woman, a white woman. They just come up to the car and that's it."

*Joe's Liquors.** Joe Aran, the Lebanese American who runs and owns Joe's Liquors, has made his store into a little fortification. It has solid steel doors, and Aran deals with his customers through a wall of bulletproof glass. Bottles of wine and liquor and money are exchanged through a small space hollowed out under the glass or, if it's a large

---

*Name of store fictionalized at owner's request.

order, through a metal passageway that allows Aran to put the fifth or quart into the opening and then close a door behind it. He also keeps a .38 caliber revolver behind the counter.

As well as being a liquor store, Joe's also serves as a makeshift outdoor night club. Aran has a jukebox next to the outside wall of his building surrounded by steel bars to prevent its being stolen. People drop money in the slot, then drift over to sit on a broken couch under a tree to listen to the music and drink.

Aran is a short, stocky man who sits sweating under the inadequate air-conditioner rigged with a flap of cardboard to direct cool air in his direction. The customer zone is not air-conditioned. Aran closed at 9 o'clock on Saturday night after a black friend stopped by with a warning: "Joe, there's a riot. They're killing whites." According to Elko, they did not hit Joe's until 2 p.m. Sunday, when they took all Aran's stock, his refrigerator and his lights. The total loss, he said, was $18,000.

Aran does cash checks, but only if the customers buy a bottle, and he does extend some amount of credit. One day two months after the riot a black man came in to complain about being overcharged.

"How come you charged me twenty-four dollars for that stuff?" he asked.

"Good," Aran answered.

"I only bought two fifths and that small bottle. I'm gonna get you, mother-fucker."

"Good," repeated Aran.

Finally, they recalculated the bill, and the customer agreed that what he had been charged was correct and left.

Allstate Office Furniture. The only surface not cinderblocked-up at Allstate is the door, which is kept locked by a mechanically sprung bolt. Customers cannot get in unless "Doc," the retired teacher who now acts as bookkeeper and armed guard, pulls a chain that removes the bolt. The owner, who moved from the New York-New Jersey area because "I didn't want the unions to tell me what to do," has had the store on 72nd Street for ten years. A few years ago he actually bought the building, a move he now regrets, since the riot resulted in $147,000 worth of inventory loss and damage to the building. "Would you buy this building?" he asked. "If I could get out of here I would." He was out of business for four weeks after the riot and was not insured for most of his looted merchandise. Since the riot, he takes all his office records home at night in the trunk of his car. He also bought a German shepherd that patrols the property at night. And, like Doc, he wears a revolver on his hip while selling furniture. Before the riot, he said, there were no guns in the store. "Now I go to the bank with a gun in my hand."

No-Name Pawn Shop. Who says white businessmen are afraid to come into the area? Frank G. opened up this brand-new business two months after the riot. Frank is a native Philadelphian. It is supposed to be a pawnshop, but unlike most pawnshops in Miami it seems to be a one-way business. There's plenty of empty floor space and a fifteen-foot display cabinet, but hardly anything for sale. Frank runs the operation from a desk behind the counter. A shotgun stands within reach. Neighborhood residents say Frank is a fence, and that he opened up the shop to soak up the loot stolen during the riot.

Intercoastal Roofing Materials and Hardware. This white-owned wholesale business is on 72nd Street. Its manager says it employs fifty people, forty of whom are black. At 9 a.m. Sunday, looters broke in by smashing down a steel door held in a wooden frame. They took power tools, hand tools and an air compressor. According to Fred Downs, a black man who owns the Borinquen Grocery across the street, looters were about to burn Intercoastal down until he told them that the company had gas tanks on the premises and the fire would endanger the Edison Housing Project just behind it.

Stay's Hardware. In terms of inventory value, this is the largest black business on the avenue. It is a spacious store on 75th Street that employs five persons, all black except for a white manager. Jim Brewington, the owner, keeps a guard dog in his parking lot. A former maintenance worker for the New York City Board of Education, Brewington closed up at about 5:30 p.m. Saturday. "Nothing was happening then but horn-blowing and people telling me to keep my windows down so they could see I was black." He came back with his wife on Sunday at noon, armed with a shotgun. "I saw my wife taking this brown wrapping paper and writing 'black business' on it. I thought it was tacky. I'd been in the neighborhood long enough for people to know me." He said pictures of the sign later appeared in one of the national news magazines. That day he stayed on his roof with the shotgun. His store was left unscathed.

Harley-Davidson. Ace Armstrong, the parts manager, said the 77th Street store closed at 5:30 on Saturday and everyone went home. Armstrong, who has a graying goatee and wears jeans, a thick leather belt and T-shirt, said the police called him at home at 2:30 a.m. Sunday to say the store had been looted. He had a good relationship with the police, he said, because the shop services MPD motorcycles and also does work on the officers' private bikes. Ace and three employees got down to the store at about 3 a.m. A policeman was parked in front waiting. Most of the front window glass had been broken out. All the accessory cases had been looted, office equipment stolen, two motorcycles gone and one left hanging half out the front door. Ace boarded up the front windows, dropped the hurricane awning and stayed in the store until Sunday noon. At 7 p.m. Sunday the store was hit again and four more bikes stolen.

Like the rest of the businesses on the avenue, the store is broken into regularly, about once a year in the ten years Ace has been there. It is a customer of Farrey's Security, a silent alarm company located behind Farrey's Hardware, which was burned down during the riot. The store employs eight persons, two of them black. "I just don't feel the same about this neighborhood since they took out their frustration on the businessmen who serve the community," says Ace.

> Now I carry a shotgun back and forth to work with me. We installed Lexan glass and we drop the awnings at the first sign of trouble. A lot of customers have called to ask if it's safe to come down here. A lot of people didn't want to come into the area. If the police were allowed to do their job when the riot got started, you would never have had the trouble. Why take it out on the businessmen who are employing people? It was nothing but thieves who were in here. They couldn't eat or wear what they stole.
>
> I didn't agree with the McDuffie verdict either.

The Dilemma of Black Businesses

When it comes to the treatment of black businesses in a civil disorder, what the Miami riot made clear—and what was also true of the blackout looting in New York—is that when the people of the ghetto go on the rampage their outburst is an "equal-opportunity" event. It is true that out of 102 stores burned down completely in Miami only one was owned by a black—and that was a beauty shop under the same roof as a white-owned pawn shop. Generally, however, where black stores had merchandise worth stealing, and where they were left unguarded, they fell with everybody else—the only distinction being that they were not as readily burned out. There was at least one exception. As we have just seen, Mr. Brewington, the black owner of Stay's Hardware on 7th Avenue, thinks his store escaped being looted on Saturday night because people knew it was black-owned. But on Saturday night looters had plenty of other stores to go into that were owned by whites and brimming with attractive merchandise. Two blocks on either side of Stay's were the Allstate Furniture Store and the Harley-Davidson shop, both of which were looted. By the time the white stores were cleaned out, on Sunday, Brewington was standing in his doorway armed with a shotgun, his guard dog patrolling the parking lot. There is no way of telling whether, had he not been there, his store would not have fallen with the rest. The black-owned Firestone Tire shop on 27th Avenue and 84th Street was looted. So were the black-owned auto parts store on 22nd Avenue and 79th Street and the black-owned Leonard's Clothing Store on Grand Avenue in Coconut Grove.

In every riot since the one in Watts, black businessmen have sought to play on racial loyalty to persuade rioters to spare their stores. When trouble is expected signs saying "Soul Brother" or "black-owned business" pop up in store windows, and owners stand in their doorways to fend off looters. But evidence over the years, including the Kerner Report and the Curvin-Porter study of the blackout looting in New York City, seems to suggest that black businessmen, particularly the successful ones, are becoming perceived by ghetto residents as little different from the whites.[9] They are not always regarded as fellow members of a racial group whose success in life should be applauded by the community. Indeed, what seems evident from our discussions with black store owners and customers is that the opposite is true. To the very degree that black merchants achieve commercial success—and follow policies of charging high prices and turning away bad credit risks that help ensure that success—they are perceived as having become just as bad as the white merchants. Thus, the price of solvency for the black ghetto merchant is often alienation from his own community. The dilemma this poses for black economic development is obvious. What it means for blacks trying to make it in a ghetto business is they are resented if they do make it and broke if they don't.

No one sees the paradox better than Samuel Watts, a thirty-three-year-old black Miami merchant whose well-stocked clothing store was cleaned out on Saturday night of the riot.* "In a community business like this, you've got to carry a lot of people," he says.

> They need pants or underwear and they come in and say, "Mr. Watts, I got a check coming in at the end of the month." You can't *not* let them have it. But it's not that you can let everybody in the community have an account. You just can't. You'd go broke. . . .
>
> Then a lot of them can't get Sears or Master Charge cards or go to the big stores because they can't get credit. But then they complain

---

*His name has been fictionalized at his request.

about the high prices in community stores. People complained about the furniture store here in Liberty City, how he charged more than Burdine's and the other big department stores. And he does, it's true. But he can't buy in quantity lots like they do. And he also has to carry a lot of people out of his pocket.

Watts, an articulate man with a soft-spoken and deliberate manner who serves as the assistant pastor of his Baptist church, found out about the riot while he was in Georgia to give a sermon as a visiting preacher at another church. The call came sometime between eleven o'clock in the evening and midnight from his brother back in Miami. Rioters, his brother said, had driven a car through the scissor gate of Watt's store, shattering the plate glass, smashing the store fixtures and proceeding to loot the entire contents of the store, from the white gloves and black suits that Watts rents out for weddings and funerals to the work pants bought by day laborers. Someone had even tried to set fire to one of the walls, but the blaze never caught. Total damage was somewhere around $50,000. "I remember exactly what I said at the time," he recalls. "It was 'Lord have mercy. The Lord giveth and the Lord taketh away. Blessed be the name of the Lord.' "

Raised and educated in Liberty City, Watts lives in the town of South Miami and has owned his store since 1968. The word on the street that night was that people looted him in the belief that it was a white man who "held the paper" on the store—in other words had Watts so much in his debt that he was merely a front, not the real owner. The truth is that Watts bought the store in 1968 for $52,000 from the previous proprietor, had owned it mortgage-free since 1973 and at the time of the riot considered it worth twice what he had paid. "That thing about the white man owning the store was just an excuse," he says. "They knew I owned it, but these people out there are good at making things into what they want them to be. It was the criminals out there who took the lead in this thing, but it was also done by the other people who were not very strong-willed and who said, 'I'm in it now, and so I might as well finish it.' "

What angers Watts even more is the fact that the Miami police stood blocks away and watched it all happen from behind a barricade set up to keep white people from driving down his street and getting themselves beaten up. "They were just standing there, as if they were telling the people, 'Take your best shot. We're not going to do anything.' " It was not until about 2:30 a.m. that the MPD felt it had sufficient forces to sweep through the block and chase away the looters. By that time all the stores in that section had been cleaned out.

A religious man, Watts believes there is good and bad in both races, and he seems somewhat ashamed that the blacks in Miami could have caused so much damage. "I didn't think that what they did to McDuffie was right, and I didn't think the rioting and burning was right either. White people believe that most black people are part of that element that's no good. But you got black people who cried out to God to intervene and stop it. And I really think God answered them, because this whole town would have been burned down."

Watts, who has a wife and three children, aged three, twelve and eighteen, first began working at the store when he was in high school, sweeping the floor, polishing the display cases. It had been owned for twenty years by a middle-aged man named Isaac Friedman who had three daughters and no sons, and who saw Watts as his successor. "When I started work there," Watts recalls, "he said, 'Sam, I never had a son. And so I'm going to teach you the business.'" Friedman taught Watts about accounting, how to take inventory, how to run stock, how to wait on customers. "You just don't walk up to everybody who comes in and say 'Can I help you.' You have to know when the time is right. When someone comes in you have to be able to tell when they just want to look around at the merchandise, when it's time to back off and let them alone, and when to go over and see if they need help." Friedman also took Watts on two- and three-day buying trips to New York City. "We'd have a good time there," Watts says. "We'd stay in a hotel, the Howard Johnson's Hotel, and we'd go out and eat dinner and go around the town. He'd take me to the garment district and teach me about the different kinds of fabrics, about which ones to use for different kinds of suits. He'd introduce me to the key people to deal with."

When Watts took over the store, he said the biggest problem was changing his role from that of employee to the person in charge. As owner, he has hired a tailor, a salesman and a boy to do the sweeping. "You have to adjust from having a boss to being one," he said. "You just can't go out whenever you want to. You have to keep checking back to see how everything's going." After the riot, Watts replaced his scissor gate with a self-standing cage of metal bars that keeps passers-by well back from the display window. "I would like to have nicely trimmed windows and have people come by and windowshop in my store. But you've got the criminal element out there who will do anything to get something for nothing. So I can't do that."

White Businesses

In the Coconut Grove section of the city, a merchant who also had to change the looks of his store front because of the riot was Irwin Sklar, a white pharmacist who runs Grove Drugs. A native of Hartford, Connecticut, and a graduate of the University of Connecticut, Sklar owns the drugstore in partnership with another man and has been at that location for twenty-one years. In the 1968 riot, Sklar's store was looted clean, after which he sealed up his plate glass front three-quarters of the way to the top with cinder blocks. That didn't stop the looters during the 1980 riot, so Sklar now has closed the entire front with cement and cinder blocks and also covered the front door with a sixteen-inch-thick steel plate. His store is located only about 100 yards from McDonald Avenue, the dividing line that separates the Black Grove from the White Grove. There is no physical barrier at McDonald Avenue but walking that distance is like crossing a hemisphere. On the white side sits a Rexall Drugstore whose window display is filled with merchandise behind gleaming plate glass. By contrast, Sklar's drugstore is a brown-painted concrete bunker.

Sklar hires only black help, including a black pharmacist, but he has no illusions about how he is regarded in the black community. "To a certain extent, I'm accepted," he says. "I'm liked by some but if those who wanted to could do me in, that wouldn't bother them at all, although this wouldn't be true of the community as a whole since some people care what happens to me. Just my being here to some people means I'm here to exploit them. That's the way they feel." Sklar heard it was the criminal element that first broke into his store, the eighteen-to twenty-five-year-olds who hang out at the "tree" alongside Pinkney's Market a block or so away. "Their profession is stealing and dealing in drugs," Sklar said. "Once they broke in and got what they wanted, then it was open house. Everyone came in."

Dealing with ghetto customers is much different from selling to whites, Sklar says. Sales in the Black Grove tend to be in small lots, one purchase at a time rather than items on a list. Black customers also tend to take whatever they're given and to pay the price. There is little questioning or comparison shopping. "The people in the white areas, if it's ten cents cheaper down the block, they'll go there," he says. "People here buy what they need and don't ask questions. They don't bother to find out if it's cheaper someplace else. When I did offer sales or better prices over the years it didn't make any difference. They don't demand the kind of service here they would in a white area. I like to tell people about the drug they're buying and what it does and all, to talk about this drug and that drug. But here I don't have to give out a lot of information about prescriptions. The people here who are coming up, the ones from the good families, they'll travel farther to find a bargain. But most of the people here are not sophisticated shoppers."

Most ghetto residents do not have checking accounts, so Sklar is often called upon to cash paychecks and government checks. Like most store owners, however, he makes them buy something at the store in return. "I don't want to be in the business of being a bank," he says, "and even the banks charge fifteen cents." This prerequisite, however, is resented among some Black Grove residents, who feel that Sklar should cash checks for free in return for making a living in the area.

In considering what the future might hold for most of his customers, Sklar does not express much optimism.

> I've seen three generations in the twenty years I've been here. I see the grandmothers, the mothers and the children—the kids that all end up on drugs and welfare. I see it on my Medicaid cards, the families with six and seven children, each with a different father. You can see when they're born what they're going to be. They're different—the values. It's almost like they come from Mars—a completely different culture. A certain percentage can rise above all this. They go to college, teach school, and their kids get better and become doctors or lawyers. But not most of them. And the people from good families, they don't stay around here. They're gone.

He said he understands the history of discrimination and considers it a major factor in the situation he perceives. "Most people get cynical working here," he says. "But I try not to."

Any store in a ghetto neighborhood with attractive merchandise that survived the Miami riot intact must have possessed a considerable deterrent force. Such a store was T.J.'s Pawn Shop on 17th Avenue and 79th Street. Offering "$ Instant Cash $" Monday through Saturday, T.J.'s gets a lot of attention from criminals even in ordinary times. As one clerk, a lanky black man named Bill, put it: "We have guns and gold and we deal in cash. That's enough to entice anyone."

In the April before the riot, the store experienced eight burglary attempts and five more in the month following the disorder. Around back of the single-story, white-washed cinderblock structure, three body-size holes have been patched with concrete. They had been made in the building's walls where burglars tried to knock their way into the building. Bullet holes pockmark an area around a spotlight bracket up on the roof, showing where would-be burglars have tried to shoot out the light to protect their activities. "Our riot started way before the stuff in May," says Bill, "and it's still going on."

The pawnshop sits back from the road amidst two pool halls, another pawnshop and two bars. T.J.'s does the normal pawnshop trade in jewelry, cameras, musical instruments, portable television sets and small appliances, and charges 20 percent a month for loans, or 240 percent a year. A mainstay of its trade is guns—rifles, shotguns and handguns—most particularly "Saturday night specials," which are not carried by most regular gunshops in town. Traditionally, the special has been a small-caliber weapon, often a .22. At T.J.'s they are mostly .38s and .357 Magnums, the latter being popular among Miami's street criminals for its legendarily hard hitting power. But whereas weapons of this caliber would cost between $300 and $400 if made by an established firm such as Colt or Smith & Wesson, the specials at T.J.'s are assembled in this country from parts cast in West Germany and Brazil and sell for $60 or $70. The castings are so cheaply done that not only is the gun's owner in danger of blowing himself up along with his victim, but he has to be pretty careful how he handles the weapon generally. "If you drop it on the sidewalk, it'll break," says Tony Alvarez, manager of the shop.

Security at T.J.'s, is fairly tight. The front of the building is entirely sealed up with cinderblocks except for the front door, which is fitted with one-way glass. From the outside, it looks like a mirror. Inside, there are display cases on the right and left; straight ahead is the cashier's cage, which is fenced off and enclosed in more sheets of one-way glass. Taking out or paying off a loan, all one can see is a hand moving in and out of the opening to give or receive the money. Behind the glass, several employees watch customers warily. A rifle and two riot guns are racked nearby, ready for use. Nestled in the cash drawer is a little .25 caliber automatic pistol among the bills.

The night of the riot, the clerk, Bill, and two other employees locked the shop at seven and drove off. They hadn't gone far, however, when they stopped the car. "All of us had sort of a gut feeling that we ought to go back," he says, and they turned the car around. When they got back to the shop they saw half a dozen burglars in the back, trying to find a way through the cinder block walls. Others were on the far side of the building, another on the roof. "We got out of the car shooting," Bill said. The man on the roof was caught and severely beaten. A call was put in to the manager, Alvarez, a Nicaraguan who says he worked for exiled President Somoza "in the area of security."

When Alvarez arrived he directed his men like a squad leader, stationing two on the roof and several down around the building sides. He was armed with an M-1 carbine, the others with assorted rifles and shotguns. "We'd see them run through the fields across the road. It looked like the women and the children were doing the stealing, and the men doing the burning," he said. "I'd go 'pow, pow, pow' with the M-1 and they'd scatter and take off. Then I'd hear the 'blam, blam' of the shotgun. If they started coming in our direction, I'd fire over their heads to see if they'd stop. 'Pow, pow.' We didn't really want to hit anyone.''

Alvarez and his men remained in the pawnshop all weekend. He estimates that they fired off between 400 and 500 rounds to keep the looters at bay. Had they not been there, T.J.'s would surely have shared the fate of Lenny's Pawn Shop across the street, which was looted clean. Three months after the riot the only sign of Lenny was a notice tacked on the plywood nailed over the place where his steel shutters had been. It announced hopefully: "Will reopen soon."

The largest gunshop in Miami is the Tamiami Gun Shop, a Cuban-owned store located well outside the riot area on the Tamiami Trail, or Southwest 8th Street. The store manager said he experienced a tripling of gun sales in the weeks following the riot, and that salesmen were kept busy cutting down the long unwieldy barrels of shotguns to make them more suitable for "personal defense." In dealing with customers, one salesman said he recommended different kinds of weapons, depending on whether the buyer wanted it for his house or his store. "For shooting in the house," he said, "we recommend the twelve-gauge pump. This way you've got a large capability for damage, but the pellets will be contained by the walls of the house. This is much more preferable than a rifle that can go through the wall and hit a neighbor or someone." For shooting at someone in a store, however, the best weapon would be a .38 caliber revolver, he said. Not a pump? he was asked. "No, no," he said. "There'd be too much chance of damaging the merchandise."

Notes

1. "Assessing the Damage," *Miami Herald,* May 25, 1980, p. 1B.
2. "Riot Survey: What Firms Will Do Now," *Miami Herald,* June 22, 1980, p. 1F.
3-6. Idem.
7. Robert Curvin and Bruce Porter, *Blackout Looting* (New York: Gardner Press, 1979), pp. 21-35.
8. *Miami Herald,* op. cit.
9. *Blackout Looting,* pp. 47-55.

Clean-up begins at a looted and burned-out Miami meat market (Miami Herald Photo)

7 The Aftermath

In their aftermath, riots seriously change the patterns of people's lives. Inside the ghetto, residents are often forced to travel farther to find supermarkets still doing business, or else to shop at the more expensive neighborhood groceries. Merchants—those who haven't moved out altogether—shored up their storefronts with concrete and steel, resigned to doing business under more or less permanent siege. Whites who traveled through the community to work or recreation drive out of their way to avoid the area, newly conscious of its potential for violence.

In studying riots it is important to look at how the larger community responds once order is restored. How, for instance, does the justice system treat the arrested rioters? If they are dealt with harshly, it would suggest they are considered no better than common criminals; if leniently, then it might mean the judges felt they had some justification for what they had done. What about the high unemployment and poor social conditions that are generally perceived to be the ultimate cause of the disorder? Almost invariably, following the 1960s riots, the atmosphere was filled with rhetoric, from blacks and whites alike, to the effect that the larger community had a responsibility to help improve things in ghetto neighborhoods. This kind of talk was frequently heard in Miami. Indeed, following the riot, hardly a week went by without an announcement of some new economic development scheme from the public or private sector. What was the difference between the promise and the performance? What actually got done?

Prosecuting the Rioters

Historically, the tendency of judges and prosecutors responding to disorders is to crack down unusually hard on arrested rioters while the disturbance is fresh in the public's mind, then to become increasingly lenient as it recedes into the past. Those arrested during the episode of looting in New York City's blackout of 1977, for instance, were three times more likely than people arrested for similar crimes at other

times to face demands for high bail and to spend time in jail awaiting
court appearances—a state of affairs that amounted to informal punishment by the system. "You know these guys won't be punished later,
so we're gonna get them now," a New York judge was quoted as saying
by a Legal Aid lawyer.[1] And once the looting defendants got to court,
their chances of being sentenced to jail terms were 50 percent greater
than other defendants charged with the same crime. On the other hand,
riot defendants who could make the generally high bail imposed,
and thus delay their return to court until weeks or months later, were
much more likely to have their charges reduced or dismissed.[2]

In Miami, however, right from the start, the prosecutors and the
courts demonstrated considerable leniency toward riot defendants. Not
only were almost all of them released on their own recognizance (ROR)
or in the custody of their families—with no effort by the court to
determine whether they had sufficient roots in the community
to ensure their return—but when they appeared several weeks later
for sentencing, they were usually given the lightest sentences possible.
Even more remarkable, of 1,100 felony and misdemeanor charges filed
against 855 arrestees, according to the study by the Dade County Criminal Justice Council (CJC), only three cases resulted in jail terms.[3]

One reason for the high incidence of ROR (the normal practise
in Miami is for defendants charged with burglary, which was the charge
most commonly filed against looters, to be held in lieu of $2,500 bail)
was that the Federal District Court had put a cap on the Dade
County Jail population, which simply had no room for a large number
of riot arrestees. At the time of the riot, the jail had an inmate population of about 750, with room for only 90 more without violating the
court order. According to jail officials, however, had the courts truly
wanted to retain custody of the riot-related defendants, there was am-
ple room in the jail's exercise yard and, for that matter, in the Orange
Bowl, which was then housing Cuban refugees.

A more important reason seems to be that the judges simply didn't
consider the rioters to be real criminals.

"We were dealing with an unusual set of facts," said Chief Judge
Edward Cowart, of the Dade County Circuit Court, who set the tone
for the judicial response to the riot. "We were dealing with a mob
situation where, nine times out of ten, the people were doing things
they wouldn't normally do. What you had . . . were people charged
with things who are not normally involved in the criminal process." In
the case of one defendant, Judge Cowart agreed to release him on bail
for whatever amount he had in his pocket, which turned out to be
twenty-five cents.

The CJC data on the disposition of the riot cases (see Table 7-1) show how light the ultimate sentences were. Aside from the three defendants who were sentenced to jail terms, five were given jail terms but then had them suspended and were released on probation. Twenty-seven were sentenced to time already served in jail, which in most cases amounted to being locked up overnight while being processed for court appearance the next day. Eighty-nine defendants were given probation with "adjudication withheld," meaning they would have no record of a felony conviction, though there would be a record of an arrest. In effect, the sentence says: "You are not guilty of anything, but don't do it again."

Adding it up, and even throwing in those sentenced merely to probation, only 135 riot defendants, or 13.5 percent of the 997 cases that went through the system, were sentenced at all. According to

Table 7–1
Individual Disposition Frequency

	Frequency	Percentage
State filed no information (case dropped)	239	21.532
Nolle pros (case dropped)	165	14.865
Pretrial intervention programs	114	10.270
State abandoned	2	0.180
Dismissed, witness unavailable	29	2.613
Dismissed, without prejudice	25	2.252
Acquitted by court	1	0.090
Sentenced time served	27	2.432
Sentenced to probation	5	0.450
Sentenced to jail	3	0.270
Sentenced alter program	4	0.360
Convict/fine + CST	7	0.631
Adjudication withheld, sentenced to probation	89	8.018
Other	11	0.991
Found not guilty-bench trial	2	0.180
Found not guilty-jury trial	5	0.450
Warrant issued, defendant did not appear	261	23.514
Awaiting trial	113	10.180

William Moriarty, director of the Criminal Justice Coordination Division of the CJC, the percentage of defendants who normally end up receiving at least some kind of sentence from the court is about 32 percent, or two and a half times as high.

Conversely, about 85 percent of the riot defendants had their cases dropped by the prosecutor or dismissed by the courts; qualified for a pretrial intervention program, in which case, if they stayed out of trouble for several months, their cases were also dismissed by the courts; or simply never showed up for their trial, in which case a warrant was issued for their arrest.[5] Considering the leniency granted those defendants who did appear and also the ways in which Miami policemen were overburdened as it was, it seems unlikely that the warrants will ever be served.

The number of no-shows—of the 1,116 charges, 261 involved cases in which the defendant failed to appear following arraignment—the numbers are also much higher than normal, according to Moriarty. A major factor contributing to the high rate of nonappearance was the failure of the courts to order the traditional prearraignment interviews with arrestees. The purpose of these interviews, usually conducted by a special detail at the Dade County Jail, is to verify a defendant's identity and determine whether the defendant's roots in the community are sufficient to guarantee court appearance. Otherwise, the defendant is held under bail. The result of the failure to order interviews was that the judges who made decisions to release defendants on their own recognizance had little or no knowledge of the people they were dealing with. "For all we knew," said Stephen Levenson, a statistical analyst in the state attorney's office, "we could have had escaped murderers in custody and been releasing them back into the community."

All in all, then, the prosecutors and courts in Miami responded to the riot in a much more lenient fashion than did the criminal justice systems in other cities after other riots. Just why this was the case would be hard to determine. One is tempted to theorize that psychologically the apparatus of justice was suffering collectively from a guilty conscience. Considering how the black population of Miami had already been served by the system, it may not have seemed fair to crack down hard on the rioters for expressing their anger. A criminal justice system ultimately reflects the majority outlook of public opinion. The tough prosecutorial stance of New York City following the 1977 blackout reflected the general outrage over the looting that was felt by the nonpoor residents of the city. What the powers-that-be in Miami seemed to be saying—by their actions, though certainly not by their words—was that the rioters had considerable justification for what they did and should not be too severely punished.

The Killers

In the months following the riots, a series of emotionally charged, riot-related trials was held in Miami.* Defendants were identified with the assistance of Liberty City residents who cooperated with the police and the state attorney's office in the intensive, and eventually successful, investigation of the Kulp, Owens, Barreca, Higdon and Munoz murders, most of which occurred in areas near the Liberty Square housing project on 62nd Street soon after the riots began.

In October 1980, two black male defendants, James McCullough, eighteen, and Frankie Lee James, twenty, were tried by a racially mixed jury on second-degree murder charges in the death of Jeffrey Kulp and the attempted murder of Michael Kulp. The precise time of the beatings was a key issue in the trial, in that the state's key witness, Mary Kinsey, a thirty-five-year-old black woman, suffered from night blindness. The state established the time of the beatings as late in the day but still during daylight hours. In addition to Kinsey's testimony, the state used a statement given by McCullough himself, in which he admitted to police that he had "kicked Kulp once in the chest." On October 28, McCullough was found guilty of manslaughter and on December 11 was sentenced by Dade County Circuit Court Judge Mario Goderich to fifteen years in prison. Because of the defendant's age, the sentence was later overturned and he was then sentenced to four years in prison and two years of "community control," a sort of probationary period back in his community. Frankie Lee James was acquitted on all charges.

In February 1981, four young black men—Leonard Capers, his brother Lawrence, Samuel Lightsey and Patrick Moore—were charged with first-degree murder and tried by another racially mixed jury for the murders of Benny Higdon, Robert Owens and Charles Barreca, who had also been dragged from their cars and beaten to death. Lightsey made a taped admission to the police that he had pulled Owens from the auto after it had been forced into a parking lot. He said he had "punched Owens a few times" as he lay on the ground. Moore admitted on tape that he had stood over Higdon with a .25 caliber automatic pistol and fired point-blank three or four times. The Capers brothers did not deny that they were at the scene, but along with Lightsey they accused two other black youths, Nathaniel Lane and Lonnie Bradley, of being the main attackers in the fatal beatings.

On the evening of February 6, 1981, after more than five days of

---

*All information on the trials came from an interview with Assistant State Attorney George Yoss.

deliberation, the longest in Dade County history, a jury that included three blacks found Lightsey guilty of second-degree murder. He was sentenced to life in prison. The Capers brothers were found guilty of three counts of third-degree murder and received three consecutive sentences of fifteen years in prison. Moore was acquitted. Assistant State Attorney Jeffrey Raffle, a prosecutor in the case, declared the state "satisfied with the verdict."

In early March 1981, the trial of Lonnie Bradley, eighteen, and Samuel Williams, thirty-two, both black, was slated to be held in Miami. Both men were charged with second-degree murder in the slaying of Owens, Barreca and Higdon. The charges against Bradley and Williams were dropped when the state's two key witnesses claimed to be unable to identify Williams in a police lineup and when another witness recanted her earlier statement implicating the defendants. Nathaniel Lane, eighteen, described by other defendants as the chief culprit in the beating deaths of Higdon, Owens and Barreca, was tried in April 1981, on charges of first-degree murder. The key witness against Lane was Doris Jones, a black woman who lived in an apartment overlooking the parking lot in which the murders occurred. She knew Lane and testified that she recognized him as a key figure among the mob that beat the three white motorists. The trial resulted in a hung jury. The panel of nine whites and three blacks split racially, with the whites voting for conviction, the blacks for acquittal. The state decided to keep Lane in jail and try him again.

His second trial in July 1981 also ended with a hung jury split along racial lines. The state made the unusual decision to try him a third time in December. This trial, too, was heard by a biracial jury, and, although not split along racial lines, it again was unable to reach a verdict. The state finally gave up and Lane was released.

On July 16, 1982, Lane was back in jail, this time charged with shooting an unarmed black youth in the neck in an attempted robbery at a rock concert in Overtown. The victim was paralyzed as a result. Lane was identified by several witnesses, all of them black, but denied the charges, claiming that he, too, had been the victim of an attack. Lane was convicted of attempted first-degree murder and armed robbery and sentenced on March 29, 1983, to two life sentences, the terms to run consecutively.

On March 7, 1982, after three and a half hours of deliberation, a Dade County biracial jury found Ira Lee Pickett, a black man, guilty of first-degree arson and burglary with assault in a mob attack that left Emilio Munoz, a sixty-six-year-old Cuban refugee, burned beyond recognition after his car was torched at the height of the riot in Liberty City. Pickett, a former garbage collector, signed a confession in which he stated that he set the car afire. His defense attorney made an unsuccessful attempt to discount the confession, claiming that because his client's IQ was only 67, he had not understood what he was signing. Pickett was sentenced to fifteen years in prison.

Three blacks were also killed in the course of the riot by white civilians. The killers cruised the black northwest area of the county in what witnesses described as a pickup truck or van and randomly shot at blacks. Nearly a year after the riot, one white man was arrested as a suspect, but he was ultimately released after the state said it could find no hard evidence linking him to the shooting. As of the spring of 1984 no additional white persons had been charged with murders.

Riot Relief

Shortly after the ashes cooled in the Miami riot the time came for what people called "economic recovery," which, according to the Carter administration, was to be carefully planned and coordinated. Local, state and federal agencies, as well as local leaders, were expected to cooperate in rebuilding the areas of the city hardest hit. Federal money, however, was not to be merely thrown at the problem; the local community and its leaders were expected to carry their share of the burden.

The general expectation was that debris in the riot-torn area would be removed and jobs would be created for young blacks. Businesses— new ones, as well as those destroyed or damaged by the four-day carnage—would be established or reestablished. Blacks would be significantly involved in this process as entrepreneurs. More and better public housing was needed. Old housing projects would be upgraded and recreational facilities expanded or created. Attempts would be made to reduce the crime rate and improve black political power and governmental representation.

Local Response

The response to the riot at the local level should be considered in the context of actions taken by Dade County, the City of Miami, the private business sector and various civic groups. Immediately after the riot, the Dade County and the City of Miami commissions, as well as local leaders, limited their initiatives to writing or speeding up grant applications to the federal government. Expressing a local consensus, Ray Goode, then president of the Chamber of Commerce, sent a telegram to President Carter four days after the riot asking for "extraordinary help in the situation—soon and in large amounts." When it became clear that Washington wanted local leaders to take their own initiatives, Dade County and Miami began looking elsewhere. One thing they did was to bring in the Janus Corporation, a minority-owned concern from Washington, D.C., that specialized in economic-development planning. The corporation was hired by the city and county under a $100,000 contract, with funds provided by the Economic Development Administration. The contract charged Janus with providing an economic-adjustment plan within six months. In effect, it was asked to tell local officials what had to be done to bring blacks into the economic mainstream of the community.

By March 1981, the Janus Corporation was halfway through its work in Miami. First, it identified the kinds of businesses growing the fastest in Dade County. Next, it examined the pool of black labor to determine how much of it was included in the area's mainstream economics. Its preliminary findings in late 1980 showed that the Dade County area as a whole was experiencing an economic boom. Trade and commerce were expanding, office buildings were going up, support services were growing, retail businesses were profitable, and finance, insurance and real estate were healthy. John Gloster, director of Janus's study, said he was interested in identifying these broad areas of opportunity "in order also to identify related areas into which blacks may be incorporated. We also wanted to see if there are barriers to blacks entering these areas." He pointed to the Harlem Commonwealth Council and the Bedford-Stuyvesant Restoration Corporation in New York, and to the East Los Angeles Community Union as examples of the kind of organization Dade County needed. He pointed particularly to the Chicago Economic Development Corporation, which is supported by banks and city money and could serve as a model for Miami. The black economic-development organizations that Dade does have—such as the James E. Scott Community Association Center, the Belafonte-Tacolcy Center and the areas's Opportunities Industrialization Corporation program, all operating in Liberty City—are concerned primarily with training in skills. Others—such as the New Washington Heights Community Development Corporation, which operates in Overtown—are community and social service organizations. The overall problem, said Gloster, was that no one had yet found a way to bring in large sums of money to build a sound overall economic base for the black community itself.

After about a year of planning efforts in Dade County, the Janus group submitted its plan to local government officials. What impact did the plan have? So far, the answer seems to be, none. William

Cullom, current executive director of the Greater Miami Chamber of Commerce, says that no action was ever taken based on the Janus study.

Another effort was initiated by the Miami-Dade Chamber of Commerce, a group of black businessmen who tried to package loans to bring business back to Liberty City. One thing it did was to draw up a Liberty City Plan that carried a $242 million price tag and called for a massive infusion of dollars into Miami's ghetto areas. In announcing its plan, the black Chamber challenged, almost angrily, those who would grapple with the recovery effort: "The black community in Miami needs united leaders with realistic goals and workable plans. It does not need more fragmentation, lecturing on organization, dreamy-eyed do-gooders, or political fanatics. The black community needs to get down to business."

The white Miami business establishment, however, dismissed the black Chamber's plan as a "dream list" and pressed its own plan to bring in another group from outside to try to get things moving. At the urging of Alvah Chapman, head of the Miami Herald Publishing Company, the Greater Miami Chamber hired City Ventures, Inc., a subsidiary of the Control Data Corporation of Minneapolis, and paid it $40,000 to develop plans for the economic revitalization of riot-impacted areas—principally, Liberty City. "That's the problem," said Lester Freeman, former Chamber executive director, pointing to a ten-inch-high stack of letters, memos, proposals and studies, all pertaining to the riot. "All of us are fooling around. Duplication. Redundancy. Outright thievery. No one is giving us our assignment. That's why we went with City Ventures. They can put everything under one umbrella." This time, he said, the private sector would really act. "The economic vitality of this community is threatened. They've finally gotten the message. If they don't shape this thing up, they're going out of business. I can tell you from my heart, the commitment is there and it's not out of altruism. It's the old pocketbook issue."

Unlike the minority-owned Janus Corporation, which believed in relying on government funds to get private companies interested in black areas, City Ventures focused its efforts on using the private sector. In March 1981, the firm presented a preliminary plan calling for a large infusion of private capital into the Liberty City area. Among its proposals was one for a large business and technology consulting center to cost more than $6 million, with 25 percent of the cost being put up by Control Data. The center would provide 500 jobs upon opening, with hundreds more to be provided later. City Ventures asked for $380,000 from the Chamber to move ahead.

Chamber officials and a handful of other corporate leaders told City Ventures to press on; they would raise the money. City Ventures, however, had been running into problems with the black community. Some black leaders were complaining that the Minneapolis-based group was an outsider that did not understand local problems. The organization was accused of not seeking suggestions from the grass-roots community, although City Ventures claimed it had called several community meetings and only a handful of people had shown up. The local NAACP and the black-run *Miami Times* also charged that City Ventures had no business in black Miami, because its parent company, Control Data, had ties with South African business interests.

In April 1982, the Chamber of Commerce decided not to renew its contract with City Ventures. The "essential problem with City Ventures," said Cullom, "was one of distance. . . . The decision-making process was being slowed down by the need for City Ventures' people in Miami to clear decisions with Minneapolis." There was also a serious question regarding the firm's credibility with blacks. The Chamber had chosen City Ventures because of its reputation for working with inner-city businesses in Minneapolis. According to Cullom, though, when the Chamber looked more closely at what the company was actually doing in Minneapolis, it discovered that of sixty-two businesses in Minneapolis with which City Ventures had worked, only one was black-owned.

The Chamber then took the revitalization of Liberty City into its own hands and set a goal of $5.4 million to be raised from businesses belonging to the Chamber to fund the effort. In a little over two months, Chamber members had contributed $6.9 million, an accomplishment in which the Chamber takes great pride (according to Cullom, 15 percent came from Latins, 2 percent from blacks and 83 percent from whites). The money was to be used to increase black employment by helping place blacks in newly created jobs. Another goal was to increase black ownership of businesses by creating a business-assistance center that will provide technical support and training to blacks opening businesses or expanding them. The center, located at 6600 Northwest 27th Avenue, opened in September 1982.

In late 1982, the Chamber also worked with an organization called the Miami Free Zone to purchase land in the Opa-Locka area for the setting up of a "free trade zone." The idea of such zones, which are favored by the Reagan administration and referred to as "urban enterprise zones," is to attract businesses by allowing them to pay lower wages and to operate under fewer restrictions from regulatory agencies. As proposed in Miami, however, the plan was expected to face rough sledding. Blacks, for instance, object to its provision for paying workers within the zone less than minimum wage, as well as the provision for relaxing safety standards on the job. Radical relaxation of zoning regulations also ensures some degree of opposition from county officials as well as environmentalists, who are almost certain to oppose the easing of pollution standards that may be recommended as part of the plan.

State Response

Florida's capital city of Tallahassee is located in the Florida panhandle, more than 300 miles from Miami. Typically, state governments work slowly until the closing days of a legislative session, when the capitals become a frenzy of activity, with a large number of bills, both major and minor, moved to passage quickly and not always with careful deliberation.

The Florida legislature was in just such a state in 1980 when the violence erupted in Miami, and it had just two weeks in which to decide on a response to the crisis before the session ended. The governor was already moving on a few ideas of his own, but if the state was to respond effectively to a riot in its largest urban area, the legislature and the governor would have to do so together. Meanwhile, several problems were developing. Representatives of the Greater Miami Chamber of Commerce wanted the legislature to create a powerful revitalization board for the Dade County area that would have the authority to levy a countywide one percent sales tax. Estimates of what this could raise annually ranged up to $100 million. The revenue would presumably be used to rebuild and develop the areas affected by the riots. This suggested use of the money, and the frantic way in which the concept was presented to the legislature, proved to be major stumbling blocks to creating the board and establishing its taxing authority.

According to Sandy D'Allemberte, a prominent Miami lawyer, confidante of the governor and a leading member of the Miami downtown legal establishment, the leaders of the Florida House and Senate, though cautious, were at least willing to discuss the concept. The leaders made it clear, however, that the full support of the Dade County legislative delegation was a critical prerequisite. D'Allemberte had been asked by the governor to work up the legislative language for creation of the board and was a central figure in the unfolding drama surrounding the new sales tax. The governor, having been approached by the Chamber of Commerce, announced his support of the tax the Friday following the riot. The tax had not been widely discussed in Tallahassee during the week; it was only on Monday, May 26, following a long

Memorial Day weekend recess, that members of the legislature, including the Dade representatives, were introduced to it. Because the governor had already publicly declared his support of the tax, many Dade representatives felt the Chamber had intentionally bypassed them and gone straight to the governor. "The local delegation felt excluded," says D'Allemberte. "They felt the business community had somehow not acted in good faith. There was also a general negative attitude that the business community was suggesting a sales tax. Why didn't they suggest a corporate profits tax, too?"

For his part, William Sadowski, then a Dade representative and one of the most influential and liberal members of the Florida House, also criticized the plan, saying that no one had spelled out precisely how the tens of millions obtained from the tax would actually be spent. Like many other legislators, Sadowski was worried that the new tax would be viewed as a "reward" to the rioters. These feelings were especially evident in the Florida Senate. According to Sadowski, some senators felt that if they provided that much money, "the message would be that you could get dollar relief from government if you conduct yourself in this way." The main problem, however, appeared to be a strong reluctance to give tax-levying authority to another body. The real power of a legislature lies in its power to tax, a power legislatures do not readily yield. There was also the matter of timing: 1980 was an election year. Dade County legislators were hesistant to create a body that would levy a new tax in their county so close to voting time, and several balked immediately at the idea.

The legislature had less objection to the idea of a revitalization board itself, which had gained currency throughout the United States as an efficient mechanism for handling the economic problems of distressed areas, and finally voted in the closing hours of the session to create a twelve-member board for Liberty City. It withheld the controversial taxing powers, however, and made the group an economic advisory body to the governor rather than an independent entity.

The legislature passed three other riot-related measures. One was a bill awarding corporate tax credits to businesses that hired people from poor areas. Another allowed tax credits to businesses that located or expanded in economically distressed communities. The third bill gave companies a 50 percent credit on their corporate state income tax for contributions made to local community-development corporations.

What happened?

The revitalization board—composed of six blacks, five whites and one Hispanic—met for the first time on August 11, 1980, and erupted immediately in conflict. The superintendent of the Dade County school system, the county manager, Miami's city manager and the federal coordinator for riot relief were designated ex-officio members. The board's first meeting was scarcely over before some members tried to redefine its mandated role. For example, Georgia Ayers, a black social worker and community activist, wanted the board to deemphasize its economic advisory role in favor of looking at broad social issues. Another problem was that once the board was established, it was expected to start doing something. But what was it supposed to do? There was no economic plan for revitalizing Liberty City. It had no control over who received state funds made available to Dade County's community development corporations, which were quickly organizing to apply for state riot-relief funds. That power was retained by the Florida Department of Community Affairs. The board had the right merely to advise the state as to which applicants seemed the best risks. Moreover, because of bureaucratic delays, the board had to operate for nearly a year after its establishment without a permanent staff. Governor Graham appointed John E. Smith, a prominent white attorney and a member of the downtown legal establishment, to serve as the board's chairman. As Smith views it, the board's purpose is to "serve as a broker, a catalyst, to identify possibilities, to publicize those possibilities to interested parties and to provide support. . . . Moral persuasion is important, even if we don't have authority to do some things." Smith said he was wary of the revitalization board creating more expectations than could be fulfilled. I feel that a lot of people for the first time want to help, but it's dangerous to hold out hope and not be able to deliver. We must not let ideas that may not fly ever see the light of day. The first major project we try had better work."

The board could hardly be accused of moving ahead too hastily. As the first anniversary of the Miami riots approached, it still had no permanent executive director and the State of Florida had allocated no money for the recovery of riot-impacted areas. By its second year, the revitalization board got a director: Newall Daughtery of Opa-Locka. Its key concern by then was the coordination of the eleven community-development corporations (CDCs), each of which had received about $100,000 in state funds to use for economic development. Board members expressed concern that some of the hastily organized CDCs were weak and had no definable goals. At least one high-ranking black member of the governor's staff who attended some board meetings also expressed the state's concerns about the possibility that the $1.1 million in funds given to the CDCs would "go down the drain."

The board seems to have a better record in some specific efforts and projects—for example, playing a key role in the establishment of Dade's first black-owned bank, monitoring City of Miami and Dade County minority set-aside programs to ensure more black participation in publicly funded projects and pressing for black involvement in the redevelopment of downtown Miami.

Dade State Representative Barry Kutun, chairman of the State House Committee on Finance and Taxation, said in March 1983 that if the board had generally not fared well it could be due to the fact that it has not been aggressive enough in seeking legislature support. Said Kutun: "I've had a staff member at every board meeting. I haven't seen material advances. I can't fault the board members personally. They may need powers they don't have but they never came to us. They never submitted a legislative proposal. They only asked for money for their existence. The ball got dropped."

In response to the legislature's two tax-credit proposals to encourage business relocation into the riot area, one year after the riot two corporations had announced plans to move facilities into Liberty City. Southern Bell Telephone, a company whose rates are regulated by the state, placed a customer-service center about seven blocks from where the Kulps were beaten. Alcoa Aluminum, after some arm-twisting from Frank Borman of Eastern Airlines, agreed to build an aluminum can recycling center in the area. These two companies employ fewer than fifty people in these ventures.

There were no takers at all, as of two years after the riot, on the legislature's offer to give tax credits for corporate contributions to local community-development corporations. Indeed, the general response by private companies was such that Chairman Smith of the revitalization board questioned the advisability of offering only tax credits to induce any kind of corporate behavior toward black neighborhoods. "I don't know of any significant efforts by corporations to locate in inner city areas for tax credits alone," he said. "I don't think someone will go into Liberty City solely in the expectation of getting tax credits down the line."

Indeed, there seems to be a reluctance among businesses not only to relocate to Liberty City but to anywhere in Miami. A survey by the Chamber of Commerce of out-of-state businesses did show that more than 50 percent based their relocation decisions at least partly on the availability of tax credits. But when it came specifically to relocating in Miami, the survey found a decided reluctance. Some 62 percent of the companies said they feared locating in Miami because of its crime, the waves of immigrants and racial tensions in the area. "Fifteen years ago," said Freeman, the Chamber's former head, "90 percent would have wanted to come." As if to underscore his point, on June 9, less than a month after the riots, Miami was advised that it would not get a 1,200-job electronics corporation. The reason given was that national and international perceptions of Miami were too heavily negative.

Federal Response

Concerned that the violence in Miami might spread to other cities, as it did during the racial disturbances of the 1960s, the Carter White House took the position that the riot was caused by circumstances unique to Miami. The turmoil resulting from the large influx of Cuban and Haitian refugees was given as a major contributing factor (although in a survey of blacks in Dade County conducted by the *Miami Herald* about a month after the riot, only 4 percent of the blacks interviewed thought the influx had contributed to the riots[6]). Officials in the Carter administration also expressed the view that the rapid succession of racially explosive cases in the criminal justice system in Dade County was unusual and specific to the Miami area.

As the week of the riot was winding down, the president dispatched Attorney General Benjamin Civiletti to Miami. His assignment was to make an assessment of the charges from Miami blacks that the criminal justice system was racist and to consider intervention by the U.S. Department of Justice. On May 21, Civiletti announced that civil rights lawyers from the Department of Justice had moved into Dade County to look into thirteen police-brutality complaints, including the deaths of six blacks shot by the police during the riots. "This is a serious situation and . . . is one substantial area we can address with concrete steps," the attorney general said upon his arrival. "We will have a sustained federal presence."[7]

The White House also established a special task force to develop an economic recovery plan for Miami, headed by Frank Jones, domestic expert and general counsel to the Community Services Administration. Jones was to coordinate the federal effort with state and local initiatives, devise an overall plan and submit the plan to the president. Jones told a delegation of Florida business and political leaders several weeks after the riot that the president wanted the Miami recovery plan to be a model for other cities needing to recover from civil disturbances.

The work of the task force involved several visits to Miami by its members. A number of local leaders—primarily blacks and elected officials, most of whom were identified with Carter's reelection effort—were called to confer at the White House. It was decided that the president himself would visit Liberty City on June 9, the same day he was to deliver a speech to a national convocation of the Opportunities Industrialization Corporation in Miami Beach.

The federal task force and the president's local supporters selected a small group of business and political figures to meet privately with the president at the James E. Scott Community Association Center (JESCA) in Liberty City. The group included Frank Borman, president of Miami-based Eastern Airlines; Alvah Chapman, president of the Miami Herald Publishing Company and one of the most influential men in Dade County; Mayor Ferre of Miami; Athalie Range, a funeral-home director and highly respected black leader; and about a dozen other prominent blacks and whites.

That the president was coming was well known, and a large crowd of blacks gathered early outside JESCA's headquarters. There was considerable confusion, however, as to the meeting's purpose. Some who were to meet with President Carter inside the building assumed that he had come to announce how much federal money Miami would receive to aid the rebuilding, and exactly when. It was also widely assumed that Carter had come to tell them how far he was prepared to go to help the community recover. The president's idea for the meeting was quite different. He had not come to talk but to listen. He wanted to hear about initiatives being taken by local leaders in both public and private sectors. Before committing federal funds, the president wanted to know specifically what the community was doing to help itself. But since, at this point barely three weeks after the riot, there were no local initiatives to speak of, the president was bound to be disappointed.

In the meeting itself, Carter called the local leaders on the carpet for having no recovery plans to tell him about. He warned them, according to several participants, that they should not expect the federal government to carry the entire financial burden. In response, the Miami leaders complained that no one had ever told them to have plans ready to talk about. "Our people weren't asked to prepare anything," says Lester Freeman of the Chamber of Commerce. "They were just called and asked to show up."

The meeting broke up after ninety minutes; the president left the building and entered his limousine. As the motorcade pulled away, several bottles and rocks were tossed by young blacks standing in the rear of the crowd outside the center. A few missiles struck the president's limousine, providing the local leaders with an embarrassing exclamation point to an already depressing day.

Ultimately the federal response consisted largely of loans made available through the Small Business Administration (SBA). Of about $40 million targeted for first-year use in the riot area, only a little more than half was ever successfully applied for. What's more, nearly 90 percent of the $22 million actually loaned to businesses by the SBA in response to the Miami riot went to whites or Hispanics, according to an SBA officer, and fewer than half of these people ended up reopening their establishments in the riot areas. Thus the impact of the SBA loans during the year following the riot was to facilitate the reestablishment of numerous businesses affected—but not in Liberty City. Indeed, the real impact of the loans seems to have been to help drain riot-damaged businesses away from Liberty City, rather than to keep them there.

According to the Greater Miami Chamber of Commerce, some new businesses had opened in the Liberty City area by July 1982. But most were small, service-oriented businesses, not the larger manufacturing or retail businesses that had been there before the riot.

The federal government also increased support for its Comprehensive Employment and Training Act (CETA) program in Miami. CETA made available substantial sums of money to train the unemployed and, in some cases, to support them in their jobs for a predetermined period, following which their employers were encouraged to hire them as regular employees. In one form or another, more than $6 million in federal riot relief was spent in this manner, with mixed results. A major problem of one of the CETA programs, for example—the short-term jobs-for-youth program—was the unavailability of jobs once CETA support for trainees had been terminated. More than $2 million spent on that project was largely wasted, according to one administrator, because few if any of the hundreds of young people who started in the training project ever found work.

Although drafted by the Carter administration, the federal aid package was left to be implemented by President Reagan. That has caused additional problems, one of the most serious of which has been the Reagan administration's effort to cut back or terminate the CETA program and the Economic Development Administration (EDA), an agency that was supposed to figure prominently in redeveloping the riot area. EDA did dispense nearly $10 million in riot relief funds in Dade County, but while some of its programs were operated in conjunction with other federal agencies that are still alive, its demise has seriously set back an already sluggish recovery effort.

Measured against the standard of Carter's promise to construct a "model" of governmental riot response, then, the federal plan does not seem to have been a resounding success.

Notes

1. Robert Curvin and Bruce Porter, *Blackout Looting!* (New York: Gardner Press, 1979), p. 106.

2. Op. cit., pp. 97-109.

3. Dade-Miami Criminal Justice Council profile study of those arrested during Miami's May 1980 civil disturbance, March 1981.

4. Idem.

5. Idem.

6. "Survey Reveals Unprecedented Black Bitterness," *Miami Herald,* June 22, 1980, p. 23A.

7. "Civiletti Reveals Plan of 'Concrete Steps' for Justice in Miami," *Miami Herald,* May 21, 1980, p. 15A.

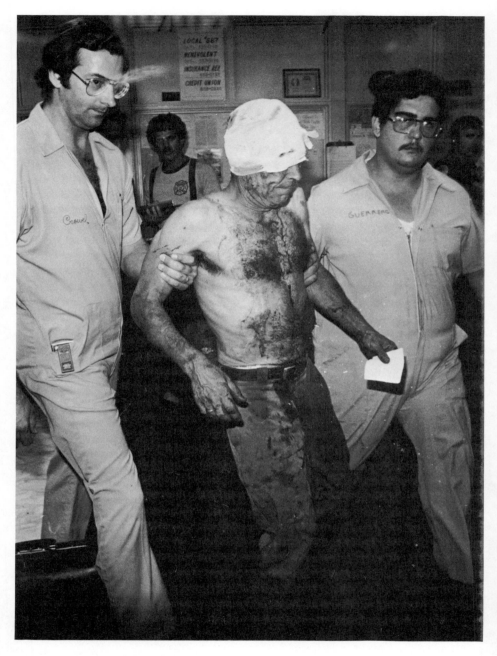

An unidentified man, beaten and stoned by rioters, is led to an ambulance at a police command post, May 17, 1980 (United Press International Photo)

8 Miami: Crossing the Bounds

What claim the Miami riot has to a significant place in the history of racial unrest in the United States does not, as we have seen, spring from its having been the most costly riot in terms of property loss. Nor did it result in the most deaths; seventeen people lost their lives in Miami—eighteen, counting a police officer who suffered a fatal heart attack—whereas thirty-five died in the Watts riot, twenty-three in Newark and forty-three in Detroit. Rather, Miami surpassed the previous disorders in two other ways. The first was the manner in which the disorder erupted, which varied considerably from the pattern of the 1960s and which was something the police did not seem to appreciate until it was too late. The second, and more important, difference concerned antiwhite violence. Whereas the violence in Miami was not as broadly destructive as it was during the biggest riots of the 1960s, it surpassed Watts, Newark and Detroit in its intensity. Indeed, to find a precedent for the random killing of whites, one would have to reach back before the twentieth century, to the Nat Turner-style slave rebellions before the Civil War, when blacks rose and killed the whites at hand.

Riot Patterns

From the first volley of rocks and bottles on 62nd Street at about 5 p.m. on Saturday, the Miami riot followed a dramatically different course from the disorders in the 1960s. Riots, of course, are tremendously complicated events, with many different kinds of activities going on simultaneously in different locations. Any attempt to define a general pattern for such disorders must begin with the warning that it is highly general, almost impressionistic, and should not be taken as a rigid description. But even given the risky nature of the endeavor, several researchers, most prominent among them those at the Lemberg Center for the Study of Violence at Brandeis University, detected a pattern in the 1960s disorders, an apparent progression through four separate phases of activity.[1]

Phase I consisted of the precipitating incident, usually sparked by the police and involving the shooting or beating of a black person or an inflammatory arrest. Phase II involved an angry street confrontation between blacks and the police, during which blacks made angry speeches and engaged in other hostile, but not yet violent, conduct. At this point, the police had a chance to cool things off, to appease black anger by granting concessions. Usually this was not done; the police tended to make matters worse at this juncture, either by acting too aggressively or by refusing to do something black community leaders desperately wanted them to do. Not only did this refusal further exacerbate black anger, but it weakened the influence of black leaders over incipient rioters by exposing the leaders' powerlessness when it came to dealing with the white establishment.

This led to Phase III of the riot, known sometimes as the "Roman holiday" or "carnival" phase, during which young black males took control of the situation from community leaders and began throwing rocks through store windows, setting cars on fire and engaging in wild cat-and-mouse chases with the police. Phase IV was "war." Here, the slightly hysterical atmosphere, the skylarking, deteriorated into serious violence when the police and agencies such as the National Guard arrived in force and tried to suppress the disorder by military force. This stage resulted in the greatest amount of burning, killing, looting and general destruction. "In Phase IV, I don't think anything can cool things off," wrote Dr. John P. Spiegel, director of the Lemberg Center. "The riot has to run its course, like a Greek tragedy. The initial motivation in the ghetto has to be exhausted until fatigue sets in or until there are no more stores left to loot."[2]

Measured by Spiegel's phases, the Miami riot burst out in the very beginning at the top level of violence—the war phase—and stayed there for about thirty hours, roughly from 6 p.m. Saturday to midnight Sunday. Unlike the rioting in the 1960s, the immediately precipitating incident was not a confrontation with the police but the verdict of a jury. The death of McDuffie five months earlier had been an event to which the police would seem to have reacted in an appropriate manner—by arresting the police officers involved. Indeed, by not rioting after McDuffie's death, blacks in Miami seemed willing to give the criminal justice system a chance to work. Acquittal by the all-white jury in Tampa, then, amounted to the second provocation, an unbearable event that was almost ordained to bring on the disaster as the news became generally known. Once the action began, it skipped over Phase III, or the Roman carnival, and went right into the killing, or Phase IV.

At that point, there seems no way to have stopped it other than for the police to have gathered as many officers as possible and moved them in immediately to confront the rioters. The police, however, presumably having learned the lessons of the 1960s, read the signals differently. They interpreted the outburst on 62nd Street not as the ultimate riot but as merely the preliminary behavior, the comparatively harmless action that comes during Phase II. Thus, rather than try to move in with large forces to suppress the violence, they pulled back to try to cool things off and avoid a worse situation. As Chief Harms of the MPD was quoted as saying earlier:

> It was not unusual for cars to be rocked and bottled on a Friday or Saturday night—it was business as usual. . . . If you stand there and make a confrontation, you'll escalate it; it can easily get out of control. Our typical response is that if there's any significant violence, stop the traffic and keep people out instead of having officers going in and stopping and chasing kids. Time and time again when making arrests in a black area, the possibility of conflict is escalated.

Pulling the patrol cars out of Liberty City, however, seemed to have the opposite effect from the one intended. Rather than cool the riot down, the show of no resistance to the growing disorder demonstrated to rioters that they faced few consequences as a result of their actions; the authorities had created a vacuum that was quickly filled with the mounting violence. Having failed at first to offer even token resistance to the riot, the police faced a situation less than two hours after its onset in which it was already too late to suppress the disturbance with anything less than a full-scale military operation.

The Violence

Unlike the wildfire manner of riots in the 1960s—researchers counted no fewer than 1,893 disturbances between 1964 and 1969—the Miami riot erupted as an isolated, spontaneous expression of anger that came after ten years of relative national calm. The disorder in Miami also differed from its earlier counterparts, in that the rioters had little reason to believe their actions would result in better living conditions for themselves. The 1960s disorders, on the other hand, came during a widely publicized tide of rising expectations, when government efforts to relieve poverty were on the rise. Although anger and frustration were certainly factors in the disorders of the 1960s, many rioters also certainly hoped to "gain something" through the rioting, in terms of increased government attention to ghetto problems.

By 1980, the situation was different. The War on Poverty had virtually been called off. Public enthusiasm for improving conditions in the ghetto was muted. The feeling of rage among Miami rioters was unmixed with the hope that the rioters' action would in any way improve living conditions in the black community. This difference in attitudes was striking to people like Archie Hardwick, director of the James E. Scott Community Association, who had observed both the 1968 riot in Miami and the one in 1980. "In the Miami riot in 1968," he said, "people did it because they thought, 'Maybe now we'll get results. Something will happen.' But this riot was a lot different. It was brutal; it was done out of pure hostility, out of intense hatred. They weren't out there to get something. They wanted to hurt people."

And it was the killing—the manner of the killing and who was killed—that most clearly separates Miami from the earlier riots. Of the thirty-five victims of the Watts riot, all were black and none were killed by the rioters. Of the twenty-three who died during the Newark riot, only two were whites, a policeman and a fireman, both struck by bullets fired by someone unknown. In Detroit, whites accounted for ten of the forty-three victims. Of these ten, two were themselves looters who were shot by a storeowner and a police officer, one was a policeman shot by mistake by a fellow officer and four or five others died accidentally. According to the Kerner Report, only "two or three" whites were killed by rioters, and they died at the hands of someone firing at random from a considerable distance.[4] Of those killed in all the disorders of the 1960s, by far the great majority were black. What few white deaths could be attributed to rioters seemed to occur more as a byproduct of the disorder than as its sole object.

Again, as we have shown, Miami was distinctly different. Of the seventeen victims, seven were white; an eighth victim, a light-skinned immigrant from Guyana whose body was discovered Sunday morning, may well have been taken for a Cuban—in other words, for a white. Four of the whites were taken from their cars and beaten to death; two others were stoned to death as they sat trapped in their vehicles; one was set afire. This list does not count the Kulp brother who barely escaped with his life or another victim who was beaten so badly he was left paralyzed. It also does not count the approximately 250 whites who were sent to hospitals suffering injuries ranging from cuts and bruises to concussions and serious internal trauma requiring surgery.

Some of the antiwhite violence in Miami can be attributed simply to geography. Sixty-second Street in Liberty City, Grand Avenue in Coconut Grove and other streets in the ghetto are major north-south or east-west thoroughfares, used as much by whites as by blacks. And unlike Watts, Newark and Detroit, where the riots built slowly and whites had at least some warning to stay clear, in Miami many whites found themselves caught in the middle of a riot that suddenly erupted all around them.

Still, whites were also caught in the 1960s riots, and quite frequently. In those instances, however, according to Anthony Oberschall of Yale University, blacks tended to show remarkable restraint when it came to causing the whites lethal harm. In his study of Watts, Oberschall writes:

> There is considerable evidence that the rioters observed certain bounds, that they elected appropriate means for the ends they intended to obtain. The fact that no deaths resulted from the direct action of rioters is evidence that they observed certain bounds and limits. The first two nights, when white motorists were dragged out of their cars and beaten and when newsmen were severely roughed up, none were beaten to death or killed, as might easily have happened, since the police were unable to offer protection at the time. . . .[5]

To find prior incidents where blacks attacked and killed whites, one would have to look back to the race riots following World War I that occurred in East St. Louis, Chicago and other cities. However, according to an analysis of those disorders by Dr. Spiegel of the Lemberg Center, blacks were found to have acted generally in self-defense.[6] Spiegel found that every black-white clash during the period grew out of either black residential encroachment on white neighborhoods or white fear of competition for jobs from blacks migrating north from the South. In all instances, he said, the violence was initiated by white gangs or groups of whites who went into black neighborhoods and attacked blacks. "While policemen stood by and National Guardsmen joined in the attack," he wrote, "whites viciously assailed Negroes, clubbing, shooting and hanging any black person they could catch."[7]

Prior to the World War I disorders, there is no precedent to blacks killing whites unless one goes all the way to the sporadic slave rebellions that occurred before the Civil War. And even there, if one counts the blacks on the periphery of the uprisings who were hanged or shot for the actions of their fellow slaves, most of those who died as a result of the rebellions were also black.

None of this is intended to claim that every black on the streets during the Miami riot had murder in his or her heart. At no time did more than a tiny minority of blacks engage in the actual beating or stoning of people. Probably as many blacks tried to save whites from harm as caused them harm. The crucial factor, however, did not lie in the specific numbers but in the general air of approval that pervaded the scenes of violence. Relatively few people did the beating; many, many more stood watching, doing nothing to stop it. By all accounts, hundreds watched the beating of the Kulp brothers, hundreds looked on as the three whites in the Higdon car met a similar fate and hundreds lined Grand Avenue in Coconut Grove as white men and women were beaten and stoned.

"It was the crazies who did it, we all know that," said Major Clarence Dickson of the MPD. "But those who wanted to be violent felt very confident in exercising that violence. They thought that, generally, the black community would support them one hundred percent by not turning them in to the police. They felt they could actually commit murder in the streets while everyone was watching and that not even the Uncle Toms would report them.

"And for a time there they were right."

The real significance of Miami, then, seems to be that it was the first time in modern history when blacks crossed those certain bounds and limits that governed their conduct in civil disorders of the past. It may well be, as others have argued, that the looting and burning of white-owned stores in the 1960s rioting really amounted to vicarious attacks on white people themselves. But even if so, Miami still represents the first time that antiwhite rage built up among blacks to the extent that they were no longer satisfied with attacking images, but needed to go after the real objects of their hatred.

No one can say, of course, whether the beating and killing in Miami will have introduced a new style to urban disorders of the future—whether crossed once, the bounds will be easier to cross again—or whether the event was an isolated aberration unlikely to be repeated. Whichever the case, the lesson brought home most vividly by Miami seems to be the same one offered up by the earlier riots, no matter what level of violence they achieved. The lesson is that keeping blacks in a position of economic and social isolation and of political disenfranchisement and where they feel deprived of basic human justice can be allowed to continue only at greater and greater peril to the health, safety and peace of mind of every member of American society.

Notes

1. Dr. John P. Spiegel, director of the Lemberg Center for the Study of Violence, Brandeis University, in "Race Relations and Violence—A Social Psychiatric Perspective," a paper presented at the December 1967 meeting of the Association for Research in Nervous and Mental Diseases, Hotel Roosevelt, New York City, pp. 8-11.

2.   Idem.

3. *Report of the National Advisory Commission on Civil Disorders* (1968), p. 107.

5. Anthony Oberschall, Yale University, "The Los Angeles Riot of August, 1965," *Social Problems* (Spring 1968), pp. 322-341.

6. John P. Spiegel, "Violence and Social Order," *Journal of Religion and Science* (September 1969), pp. 222-237.

7. Idem.

A man whose business in Miami was burned by rioters on the night of May 17 surveys the damage (Wide World Photo)

9 Some Reasons Why

In most studies of urban disorders—such as the Kerner Report, in 1968, and the Report to the National Commission on the Causes and Prevention of Violence, in 1969—researchers have noted that riots often have two sets of causes—one that is immediate and obvious; the other that lies in the background and is more difficult to identify. The immediate cause of the McDuffie riot, as we discuss later in this chapter, was the McDuffie verdict. Had the four policemen been found guilty, there would obviously have been no disturbance. The verdict, however, was seen by blacks as merely the latest in a series of miscarriages of justice that every black resident of Liberty City could recite on demand. Indeed, the readiness with which street blacks "packaged" McDuffie with other police transgressions raises the question of whether the riot would have occurred had the McDuffie case been an isolated event. McDuffie seems to have affected people as much by its symbolic value as by the particulars of the case.

In this regard, the onset of the Miami riot followed closely the pattern of several disturbances in the 1960s. The riots in Watts, Newark and Detroit were also sparked by precipitating events involving the police. The events were also viewed as being representative of a general pattern of oppression. Sometimes the events themselves were next to trivial. The 1965 Watts riot was precipitated by the arrest of a twenty-one-year-old black youth for running a red light.[1] The arrest grew into an argument between the police, the youth, his brother and his mother, which led to the arrest of all three. A crowd gathered to watch the shouting match, and after the trio was taken away a woman in the crowd spat at the police. She, too, was arrested. Quickly the rumor spread through the black community that the woman was pregnant and that the police had beaten her, neither of which was true. Blacks poured into the streets, and the riot was on.

It is the willingness, even eagerness, with which blacks generally believe the worst of the police that provides the emotional thrust behind the violence. Deep down, the crowds do not react to what the police are doing in the current situation as much as they react to what the police have done in the past—to what they "always" do in a given set of circumstances. Thus, as Captain Hughes of the PSD said of his preriot confrontations with blacks in Liberty City, it often matters little

181

whether the police act responsibly in a particularly situation or not; the crowd has already condemned them because of their actual or alleged misconduct that has occurred before. In this sense, riots are caused not so much by the precipitating events as they are by a general pattern of perceived oppression. The precipitating spark merely provides an occasion for blacks to try to "get even."

In the year preceding the Watts riot, California voters had turned down an important fair-housing amendment; the Los Angeles police chief, Tom Parker, had taken his police officers off the streets and put them into patrol cars, distancing them from the people; and a series of police-brutality charges had made a proposal for a civilian review board into a heated issue. "Prior to the start of the riot," wrote Anthony Oberschall, "Negroes in South Los Angeles were subjected to considerable strain due to unemployment, low income, poverty and similar factors. . . . A widespread belief in police brutality had existed for some time and was coupled with deep hostility against the police."[2]

In Newark, the precipitating event was the arrest of a black cab driver on the night of July 12, 1967.[3] Blacks suspected he was being beaten in back of police headquarters, and when the police chief refused to produce the man for inspection, a crowd of 300 to 500 threw rocks and Molotov cocktails at the building. The riot was on. But before that, according to the Kerner Commission Report, there were at least five incidents or issues that had greatly increased black hostility toward the police and whites in general. These ranged from the police shooting of an eighteen-year-old black youth two years earlier to the forced relocation of blacks from the construction site of a new medical-dental building.

Eleven days after the Newark riot started, the police in Detroit raided a party in an after-hours club, or "blind pig," at 3:45 a.m. and arrested some eighty patrons.[4] Blacks saw the raid as overzealous law enforcement, especially because the party was in honor of two servicemen who had just come back from Vietnam. The riot was touched off when someone threw a bottle through a police car window, but two other serious incidents the month before had already created bad feelings among Detroit blacks. In one, a black prostitute was shot to death on her front steps. Blacks suspected a white vice-squad officer, but no arrest was ever made. In the other, a black man on a picnic was shot to death while trying to protect his pregnant wife from an assault by seven white youths. The woman later miscarried; only one of the youths was even charged with a crime.

In the case of Miami, as we have already seen, the pre-McDuffie incidents involving Jones, LaFleur and Heath and the assault on the eleven-year-old girl had caused anger and resentment to smolder in the black community before the McDuffie trial even began.

Determining the underlying causes of the riot is a more difficult task. What was there in the history and social environment of Miami that increased the likelihood that some of its black residents, once provoked, would explode in so deadly a manner? In the vast literature on the causes of riots compiled by social scientists, it has often been noted that economic deprivation is a necessary but not sufficient precondition for civil disorder. In other words, poverty alone does not make people riot. This is not to say that economic factors play no part, as we shall shortly see. People who are relatively well off, after all, do not generally take to the streets, even if sorely provoked. But while being poor may impel someone to join a riot once it has commenced, the condition of poverty has not been determined to itself be capable of inciting people to violence. Blacks across the nation, after all, are beset by problems of unemployment, poor housing and ineffectual educational systems. But if such conditions did in fact cause rioting, blacks in the United States would be in a continuously riotous state.

Indeed, one of the more striking findings of this study was the degree to which the riot in Miami appeared to have drawn in the "good" people of the community. Judging, as we have seen, from a comparison of the Miami arrest statistics with those of Watts, Newark and Detroit, the Miami rioters by no means came exclusively from the ranks of the poor or unemployed or the criminal classes. Many held jobs, were normally law-abiding and did not otherwise fit the stereotypical image of a "rioter."

In their study of American riots from 1913 to 1963, Stanley Lieberson and Arnold R. Silverman found that the unemployment rate was higher in a group of selected cities that had experienced *no* disturbances than it was in those that had.[5] The team put more causal emphasis on three other conditions the riot cities did share but that had no direct relationship to income. They were (1) the employment of few black policemen; (2) a low frequency of black store ownership; and (3) election of public officials on a citywide, or at-large basis, rather than by individual districts, a system that effectively deprives blacks of representation in local government. Thus, in their view, riots are caused not so much by people being economically deprived as by those conditions that make them feel left out of the system, that make them feel victimized rather than served by the social order. "We suggest that riots are more likely to occur when social institutions function inadequately or when grievances are not resolved or come to be resolved under institutional arrangements. . . . Normal social controls are greatly weakened by lack of faith in community institutions."[6]

Practically the same conclusion was reached again three years later in a survey of the Detroit and Newark riots done by the Institute for Social Research at the University of Michigan. In their study, Nathan S. Caplan and Jeffrey M. Paige distinguished between disorders that could be characterized as rebellions and those that are riots. In rebellions, they said, people seek to destroy the system and replace it with another; in riots, they seek to gain entrance to the system from which they feel excluded. "One is led to conclude," the study said, "that the continued exclusion of Negroes from American economic and social life is the fundamental cause of riots."

As a description of black attitudes in Miami at the time of the McDuffie verdict, the exclusionary thesis suffers only from understatement. And on all three points of the Lieberson-Silverman findings— few black policemen, little black store ownership and political disenfranchisement—Miami fits the riot-prone profile with remarkable exactitude.

Black Policemen

Black police officers in both the county and city forces had filed discrimination suits in federal court, and at the time of the riot the departments were trying to increase the proportion of black officers on their rosters so that it approximated the percentage of blacks in the general population. Ironically, the department closest to the goal was the Dade County Public Safety Department, whose men were involved in the beating of Arthur McDuffie. In an out-of-court settlement in 1973, the PSD agreed to bring the numbers of its blacks and Hispanics to within 70 percent of their proportionate levels in the county-wide population. This meant building the force to 10.5 percent black and 24.5 percent Hispanic. (The 10.5 percent figure was based on blacks accounting for 15 percent of the county population. The 1980 census showed them at 17.2 percent, which would presumably increase their level in the PSD to 12 percent. The Hispanic 24.5 percent is based on their being 35 percent of the population, which is currently accurate.)

Shortly after the agreement, however, the county imposed a hiring freeze that limited affirmative action to the filling of positions left vacant by attrition. For every four white policemen who left, only one white would be hired. In this fashion, the PSD built its ranks to the following ratio as of 1980: the number of blacks increased from 55 in 1974 to 107, or 7 percent of the department; Hispanics from 42 to 150, or 10 percent; and white females from 37 to 102, or 7 percent.

Blacks had also been underrepresented in the upper ranks. At the time of the lawsuit, the PSD had only a few black sergeants, with no blacks in the higher orders. To amend the situation, the department created a new appointive rank of commander. The rank, which is a staff job rather than one concerned with actual patrol, lies above that of lieutenant but requires no competitive examination, and to qualify, a person need be only a patrolman. Of the first ten commanderships, six went to blacks, three went to Hispanics and one to a white female. The juggling succeeded in adding gold to the collars of more blacks, but the moves were seriously resented by rank-and-file white officers, who saw the affirmative action effort as creating obstacles to their own police careers and who tended to deride the new commanders behind their backs. However, the PSD's budget freeze was lifted in 1980, allowing the force to hire 200 more police officers. This would also create more openings for sergeants and lieutenants and would perhaps alleviate the bad feelings.

In the City of Miami, the MPD has had a more difficult job reconstituting itself along similar racial and ethnic lines. For one thing, the city has a much higher percentage of blacks and Hispanics for the department to match. At the last census, the population count stood at 55.9 percent Hispanic, 25.1 percent black and only 18.9 percent white. For another, the MPD has a smaller pool than the PSD of qualified black applicants from which to choose. As part of its affirmative action overseerage, the U.S. Department of Justice mandated that all affected departments must find their new recruits from within city limits. The rule was made to increase the chances of blacks by preventing whites in the suburbs from competing for the jobs. In Miami, however, as we shall detail shortly, the black demographics in the categories of education levels, poverty rates and single-parent families have seriously declined in the last ten years. Upwardly mobile blacks have tended to move out of the city into suburban Opa-Locka, Carol City and Richmond Heights, leaving the poorest and most socially disorganized elements behind. Hence the department has complained of being unable to find an adequate pool of black recruits with the necessary qualifications. To help remedy this, Chief Harms has been trying to get the Justice Department to allow him to recruit blacks from all over the county.

For whatever reason, the number of blacks on the force remained almost unchanged from 1975 to 1980, despite an increase in the black share of the city's population. In 1975, there were 83 blacks; in 1980 there were 88, or 13 percent of the 660-person force. The number of black males actually decreased during the same period, from 73 to 69, with the gap being filled by black women. Hispanics made out much better, increasing their number from 80 in 1975 to 131 in 1980, or 20 percent of the force. As with the PSD, the MPD has also been given permission to increase its roster, in its case from 660 to 810. This will certainly act to increase black representation, but because of the re-cruiting problem it is difficult to say by how much.

Black Representation in Government

The elected government for Dade County consists of a nine-member board of commissioners and, for the City of Miami, a five-member board of commissioners. (The twenty-six other incorporated munici-palities within the county have their own forms of government.) Al-though some county commissioners are required to live in particular districts, all commissioners in both jurisdictions are elected at large, meaning by all the voters in the city or county. Once chosen, the commissioners hire the county and city managers, who act as the chief executive officers. The respective mayors are elected by the whole population.

The political power of any racial or ethnic group to elect members to this all-important body depends on its strength in the general pop-ulation. Until now, blacks have usually managed to elect one member of each commission, but the new census numbers give at least some reason to question whether they can maintain even this much strength in the future. As of January 1980, there were 711,210 registered voters in all of Dade. Of these, 116,363, or 16.3 percent, were black; 127,357, or 17.9 percent, were Hispanic; and 467,490, or 65.7 percent, were white. Of these three groups, the whites are overrepresented on the voter rolls, compared to their strength in the general population; the Hispanics are greatly underrepresented and blacks have about the same proportion of voters as they do members of the general population. Of the Dade County total population of 1,626,000, whites account for 764,591, or 47 percent; Hispanics, 581,030, or 35.7 percent; and blacks, 280,379, or 17.2 percent.

This means that the greatest potential for increase in voting strength lies among the Hispanics, who currently have the lowest percentage of their population enrolled to vote (21.9 percent, compared to 41.5 per-cent for the blacks and 61.1 percent for the whites). Among the reasons offered by local officials for the low Hispanic registration rate is the feeling, particularly among Cubans, that the United States is only their temporary home, and so their involvement in its politics is tentative. This feeling, however, has been rapidly changing, according to Oliver Kerr, statistical director of the Dade County Planning Department. As their cultural roots in the U.S. deepen and as their economic impact grows stronger, he forecasts, they will begin to play more of a role in local government. Then, too, the 1980 figure leaves out the approximately 120,000 Cubans in Miami who came over in the exodus from Mariel Harbor. This increment brings the Hispanic population in Dade almost to the white level. While it will be some time before the new arrivals get placed on the registration lists, they will certainly count heavily in the future political mix.

Except under extreme conditions of political pressure, such as the threatened loss of the one City of Miami Commission seat held by a black, blacks in Miami often seem unwilling or unable to exploit what strength they have. This lack of assertiveness is what most impresses, or, rather, depresses, black professionals who move to Miami from other parts of the country. "Blacks in the other places I've lived are not as tolerant as they are in Miami," says Terry Percy, a black lawyer in Miami who has also worked in Chicago and other cities in the North. "There are a lot of indignities imposed on the community here, where under similar circumstances elsewhere the community would have erupted a lot sooner. Among the blacks here there is a preoccupation with reaching individual plateaus rather than looking at problems as a whole in a collective sense." Ron Lopez, a Miami social service worker in Overtown, who came to Miami after working in Newark and Boston, says he noticed some of the same things. "People here seem like sheep with no shepherd," he said. "When I came here, the first thing I noticed was that blacks were not as organized as they were elsewhere. There's no Overtown Political Club, no Liberty City Democratic Club. You don't have anyone to go to if you want to get things done—no district leader, no councilman who represents you. There's no one to see if you want to get a traffic light on your street or a building inspector to come down. Here, you've got to go down and plead your case to the commission. You have to throw yourself at their mercy and hope they'll listen."

Even if blacks were to get themselves effectively organized, the city-wide electoral system in Miami tends to undermine their political influence both inside and outside the black community. A system where officials are not elected by the people from specific districts encourages candidates to run on broad platforms, to try to appeal to a wide variety of people rather than a particular group. To get themselves elected in Miami or Dade County, black candidates must be careful not to alienate white and Hispanic voters. To the extent, however, that they soften their advocacy of black issues in order to increase their broad appeal, they are perceived by many blacks as selling out, as having been politically co-opted by the white establishment. This means that although they may hold high elected or appointed positions, they may not command much respect among large segments of the black community, especially the poorer people that are the most alienated from the political system.

By participating in the political game to the degree they do, however, blacks have succeeded in winning a significant number of government jobs and have also risen to power in the federally funded antipoverty structure. But here again, as local blacks are quick to point out, these positions are all held by the grace of the white community. "When I hear about 'power,' " says Hardwick of the James E. Scott Community Association, "I think in terms of money and influence. Real power is being able to help yourself and help your friends, and we don't have any of that here. All the white establishment has to do is to put no more financial support into this agency, and it's all over. Or they say to Bob Simms at the Community Relations Board, 'Bob, you're fired,' and there's nothing any of us can do about it."

Blacks in Business

Blacks are even weaker economically than they are politically. "The opportunity for blacks to enter the economy of Miami is practically nonexistent," says Michael Wallach, a federal executive and expert on minority business who served as the White House coordinator for riot relief after the May disturbance. "The black business community is so far behind economically here that I shudder to think how it could possibly be turned around."

In 1972, according to a study compiled by the Dade County Planning Department, blacks owned 1,530 businesses in the county grossing $80 million. Five years later the number of businesses increased to 2,480, or by 40 percent, but the gross climbed to only $94.8 million, or by 18 percent. This meant that the growth took place in small, marginal businesses, the kind least likely to succeed. It also meant that the average gross for each business actually declined during the period, from $52,287 to $44,178. Considering the rampant inflation during that period, the real gross declined even further. The study also showed that of the 2,148 businesses in 1977, only 18 percent, or 386, had any employees at all. The vast majority, 82 percent, were operated by only the owner. Of the hundreds of bars and liquor stores located in ghetto neighborhoods, few, if any, are owned by black permittees. One of the two black-owned clothing stores in the city was looted during the riot. There is just one black hardware store, and only one black-owned bookstore.

Similar statistics show up for the number of black professionals in Miami. According to the 1980 directory compiled by the Dade County Office of Black Affairs, there are only thirty-two black doctors in the county, twelve of whom have offices in one of two buildings. Only fifty-seven black lawyers are listed, a quarter of whom work for government agencies, and only eighteen dentists. All this for a black population of 280,379! As shown in Table 9-1, we compared these figures to the number of doctors, lawyers and dentists elsewhere and found that in urban communities in the North and South with black populations of similar magnitude, there were between two and five times as many professionals.[8] Cleveland, for instance, a severely depressed city compared to Miami and with 30,000 fewer blacks than in Dade County, has more than twice as many black doctors, more than three times as many dentists and more than four times as many lawyers. St. Louis, a city with even more problems than Cleveland, contains 73 percent as many blacks as Dade County, but half again as many dentists and doctors and more than twice as many lawyers.

In the area of black corporations at the time of the riot, the picture is equally dismal. "The blacks in Miami don't own or control any

Table 9–1
Doctors, Lawyers and Dentists Serving the Black Populations of Seven U.S. Cities

City	Black Population	Doctors	Lawyers	Dentists
Miami	280,379	32	57	18
Atlanta	282,912	130	200	40
Cleveland	251,347	70	260	59
Dallas	265,594	50	110	25
Memphis	307,702	45	80	40
New Orleans	308,136	100	175	25
St. Louis	206,386	50	120	30

capital institutions; there's not even a sizable credit union," says Al Hope, president of the Economic Development Corporation of Dade County.* Jacksonville, with a much smaller black population, has a black bank. Orlando, smaller even than Jacksonville, has a black savings and loan association. The accumulation of capital, Hope points out, does not require a wealthy population as much as it does planning and determination:

> In the town of Belle Glade, a small Florida farming community, they started an investment club with just community folks getting together and putting in their savings. Now it amounts to two or three million dollars. They were also smart enough to leverage it, turn it over and spin off a little finance company, a mortgage company. Folks up there now have somewhere to go to borrow when they want to expand a business or buy a house. They're able to keep the capital and their savings in the community to reinvest.

Although he has gathered no specific figures, Hope suspects that Miami banks with branches in black neighborhoods use the communities' savings for investments outside the ghetto. "If the people realized how much money banks are taking out of the community and putting into places like Coral Gables and Miami Beach, they'd go bananas," he said. "It amounts to millions and millions of dollars. They'd see the amount of capital that even a poor community has."

Although the condition of poverty alone is not seen as causing riots, it certainly encourages wide participation once the disorder begins. And in terms of general economic deprivation, things have not improved at all for Miami blacks in the last decade; in some cases, they have gotten considerably worse. According to an interim survey done between censuses by the Dade County Planning Department, unemployment in the county's Model Cities area, a section roughly following the boundaries of Liberty City, increased from 6 percent in 1968 to 17.8 percent in 1978. The percentage of young people past school age who had not completed high school rose from 26 to 29 percent during the same period. Persons living below the poverty line, measured as $3,000 in 1968 and $5,860 in 1978, nearly doubled, from 28 to 52 percent. Social disintegration, as measured by the number of children in families with only one parent, also got significantly worse. In 1968, 40 percent of Liberty City children under eighteen were living in single-

---

*In 1983 blacks in Miami organized the city's first black-owned bank on the outskirts of Liberty City.

parent families. Ten years later, the planning department found that 50 percent of the children under fifteen were in similar straits. Assuming that between the ages of fifteen and eighteen a child would tend more to lose a parent than to gain one, the 1978 figure of 50 percent would be even higher were it applied to eighteen-year-olds. As it is, the 50 percent rate is still much higher than the national figures for whites, which is 12.6 percent, and for blacks in general, which is 42.6 percent.

Why?

It is one thing to point out some of the conditions that would seem to make blacks in Miami poorer and more dispirited than blacks elsewhere; it is another to speculate about why this is so. Why do blacks in Miami seem to be lagging behind blacks elsewhere in the nation? One kind of answer, of course, is that essentially they are not—that the differences are of degree, rather than of kind. It can be pointed out that despite several black mayoral victories in large cities, black political power flagged in many urban areas during the late 1970s. According to the Joint Center for Political Studies in Washington, D.C., the rate of increase in black elected officials declined steadily from 1975 to 1982, when it began to pick up again.[9] One reason for this, it has been noted, is that black leaders drew their power from anti-poverty agencies whose budgets could be—and were—suddenly decimated by Congress, rather than from grass-roots political organizations that drew their strength from numbers of voters. It is also true that blacks on police forces in most cities are not up to the racial levels of the populations they serve. And black business everywhere lags behind white business.

But looking at the statistics for Miami, particularly those pointing to a serious lack of business people, professionals and politicians—the very classes that provide ethnic communities with their power in the outside world—it still seems that the city's black social order is significantly worse off than it is in other parts of the country. So the question stands: Why?

Generation Gap

One reason in the minds of many people is that Miami has often had a go-slow mentality when it came to blacks pushing for advancement. According to T. Willard Fair, president of the local Urban League, some of this has its roots in the nature of the black population that migrated to the area from other parts of the South in the 1920s and 1930s, and again in the 1960s. "It's important to remember that black folks came here to work for white folks," he says:

> Blacks from the South who migrated south had a different set of expectations of their relationships with white people than did the blacks who migrated to the North. If you went north to Chicago or New York, you expected things to be different. But blacks who migrated here didn't expect any differences; they were moving to an area that was still segregated and dominated by whites in the same way it was in the place they left. You were just moving for a better job. But if you moved North, you went for a better way of life. And that's a big difference.

Like Terry Percy, the lawyer for the City of Miami who spoke of a lack of assertiveness among Miami blacks, other blacks who move to the city are struck by what they see as a sense of defeatism among the locals when confronted by the possibility of trying things that are new. "The Jim Crow laws operated here until not long ago, and people have the sense of just now getting free," says Kimberly Parker, twenty-eight, a native of the Bedford-Stuyvesant section of Brooklyn and a graduate of Howard Law School who works as a special assistant to the director of the city of Miami planning department. "A lot of black people here still have that 1950s mentality of 'Oh, we can't do that,' or 'Oh, they won't lend us the money because we're black,' or 'Oh, I can't get that job.' So they didn't try." Ms. Parker, for instance, who specializes in land development law, said she surprised black lawyers when she joined a white law firm instead of a black one:

> The inroads by blacks into the white community and structure were not made here as they were elsewhere. Here, one generation didn't piggyback another generation into the structure. Blacks here didn't develop that sophisticated network; the positions they held were too often only token positions, so they didn't have the economic or political leverage to pull someone in behind them. New York City, for instance, has its Hundred Black Men and Hundred Black Women, who are there to help younger blacks get a toehold.

One consequence of this, she says, is a serious generation gap in Miami, one that has resulted in a dearth of bright, young black people with the training needed to help build the community's economic base. Until recently, she says, promising young blacks left Miami to go to college and, for lack of local opportunities, tended not to come back. "We're missing a whole generation of people from about twenty to thirty-five," she says. "A lot of energetic black people tended to leave town and go to places where the doors were quicker to open." She said the cadre of professionals in her age group is so small that they all know each other intimately and refer to themselves collectively as "we," or "us."

Negative Effects of Integration

Another factor, only now beginning generally to be perceived, involves the negative effects of the move toward racial integration and the tremendous damage it did to the stability of the black community. Desegregation allowed members of the black middle class to escape to their own suburban enclaves, leaving the old urban neighborhoods to be occupied solely by the poor, shattering the many cultural institutions that held the community together and destroying a large number of thriving black businesses. Before the big push toward desegregation in the 1960s, blacks in Miami were not allowed to eat at white restaurants; they paid their taxes at a special window at the Dade County Courthouse. According to the late Reverend Theodore Gibson, a black Episcopal priest and a prominent leader during the civil rights movement, blacks were not even allowed to use the elevators at Burdine's, the city's largest department store. They could buy clothes, but they were prohibited from trying them on. "It was look but don't touch," he said. The beaches—Miami's great claim to international fame— were also off-limits to blacks. "We had to go all the way to Broward County to swim in salt water," he said.

But painful as the rigid segregation was to black individuals, it left black businessmen in an enviable position. "Segregation was wonderful for black businesses," says Professor Jan B. Luytjes of the School of Business and Organization Sciences at Florida International University. "Blacks had to stay at black motels and hotels; they had to eat in black restaurants and shop at black stores. But when desegregation came along, suddenly all that business went away. For the black businessman, that captive clientele was no longer there." Wallach, the White House coordinator of riot relief, thinks that it was at this juncture that something should have been done to help black businessmen survive:

> When integration became law is when we should have helped in the transition from a segregated market to an integrated market. Before, black businesses didn't have to worry about being competitive. As a store owner, I wouldn't have to clean up the place, make it attractive, put in good lighting and do all those things a good busi-

nessman does. So when the blacks could come to the stores downtown, there was no way the minority businessmen could compete.

On the contrary, as we've pointed out, in many instances an unhealthy tension was created between the few black businessmen who
managed to survive and their customers. Because they pay higher prices
for insurance, cover costs of pilferage, carry many customers on credit
and buy merchandise in small rather than large quantities, they had to
charge higher prices than the larger stores in adjacent neighborhoods.
"So there developed an animosity between the black entrepreneur and
his black clientele," Luytjes says. "There was not that cohesive relationship between a business and its customers that you need to become
successful. The tendency of blacks was to be envious of the black
entrepreneur, to say that they were ripping the community off."

Indeed, for some middle-aged and elderly blacks, looking back at
the old days in Miami is like conjuring up memories of a lost civiliza-
tion. This was especially true of Overtown, now a ghostly urban neighborhood but one that used to boast proudly of being the "Harlem of
the South." "Ten or fifteen years ago it was a live and prosperous
place," says Cleve Turner, president of the local branch of the International Longshoreman's Union, which is located above a poolroom on
2nd Avenue, the main street of Overtown. (Besides skycapping at the
Miami International Airport, dock work is the only general occupation
controlled largely by blacks.)

> People would come into the area from all over. It had nice clubs,
> nice places to eat and drink, to stay at. The Sir John Hotel on 7th
> Street and 3rd Avenue was famous throughout the South. Its dining
> room had linen tablecloths. Sarah Vaughan sang there, Duke Elling-
> ton played there. There was also the Carver Hotel, a fine hotel. It
> was the only place blacks from out of town could sleep. There was a
> lot of money there, people walking around at night. It was alive. The
> whole neighborhood was like that. Then came desegregation. I tend
> to think that desegregation was one of the worst things that could
> happen, because all the money left the neighborhood.

The Cubans

The same stresses, of course, occurred during the 1970s and 1980s in
black communities throughout the South and the North. The more
successful the civil rights movement grew, it seemed, the more deteriorated became the black restaurants and nightclubs in Harlem as well
as in Overtown. Jackie Robinson making the Brooklyn Dodgers sig-
naled the end of the Negro baseball leagues. In most cities, how-

ever, blacks occupied center stage in the desegregation process. Their social and economic problems were given space in the press; they were of concern to public officials; they were discussed by black leaders; whites listened. And in most cities, blacks received much of the anti-poverty and community development money allocated to help relieve the situation. In Miami, however, the process of integrating blacks into the dominant culture was greatly complicated by the arrival of hundreds of thousands of Cubans and other Hispanics from Latin America and the islands of the Caribbean. Many of them middle-class and looking as white as the Anglo population, the new arrivals were considered to be members of a minority group by virtue only of their foreign language. Given this status, however, they succeeded not only in diverting attention from Miami blacks during the crucial integration period, but also, by virtue of their greater social acceptability and entrepreneurial skills, in winning the lion's share of public and private money available for minority economic development. "Prior to the 1960s," says Professor Luytjes, "you had blacks in all the traditional businesses, just like in any other southern city. But here, just as they were ready to come out, the Cubans arrived and exerted a downward pressure on the blacks."

Much has been written about how the Cubans took away the service jobs and other clerical work from the blacks. And, indeed, looking at a comparison prepared by the County Planning Department between the kinds of jobs blacks held in 1968 and those ten years later is like seeing economic progress suddenly thrown into reverse gear. Blacks who held jobs as clerical workers dropped from 13.3 percent of the black population to 11.1 percent. Machine operators went from 10.3 to 2.2; service workers, from 23.1 to 18.8; household workers, from 11.2 to 6.5. At the same time that blacks holding white-collar and semiskilled jobs declined, those doing general labor, at the bottom of the economic heap, rose dramatically. It went from 12.4 percent of the black population to 25 percent.

But as devastating as was the job takeover, even more disastrous from the black viewpoint was the apparent ease with which the Hispanics rooted themselves financially in the economy of the city. This was especially true in the establishment of those small businesses that act as steppingstones for any people trying to break out of a pattern of dependency. Not only did Hispanics set up businesses in their own ethnic enclaves, but they also moved into enterprises formerly run by blacks. According to one survey by Professor Luytjes, in 1960 some 25 percent of all the gas stations in Dade County were owned by blacks. In 1979, the figure had dropped to 9 percent, while the number of Hispanic-owned gas stations rose from 12 percent to 48 percent in the same period. Hispanics also began opening up businesses in black neighborhoods: meat markets, laundromats, dry cleaners and franchised groceries such as U-Totems. Overall, in its survey of business growth from 1972 to 1977, the County Planning Department found that while black businesses increased in number and gross by 40 percent and 18 percent, respectively, the number of Hispanic businesses rose by 70 percent and their gross income by 35 percent. With 8,248 businesses grossing $509.9 million, this meant that the average gross for a Hispanic business was $83,890, or nearly twice that for the average black-owned business.

The surge of Cuban economic activity should be not surprising considering that it was a largely professional and entrepreneurial group that had fled Castro's island in the 1960s. And the working class element that joined in the exodus tended to share the historic willingness of other immigrant groups to take on the lower order of jobs—the jobs that were often spurned by black Americans who felt they deserved something better.

Particularly galling to blacks was the fact that much of the capital that Hispanics needed for their business success was provided by the U.S. government. Because the Hispanics qualified as a minority group, their businesses got special consideration from contractors who did business with the federal government and had to use a certain proportion of minority-supplied goods and services. For instance, in the construction of METRO, the rapid transit system that will eventually serve most of Dade County, minority contractors got $318,105 worth of business during work on the project in fiscal 1978. Of this, $168,528, or 53 percent, went to Hispanic firms; $111,240, or 35 percent, to firms owned by women; and only $38,337, or 12 percent, to black-owned businesses.

An even greater disparity exists in loans granted over the years by the U.S. Small Business Administration (see Table 9-2).[10] From 1968, when the agency first began keeping racial and ethnic statistics, to 1979, Hispanics received $47.3 million, or 47 percent of the total, over the twelve-year period. (We did not use the figures for 1980 because of the distortion created by the number of loans granted to businesses destroyed in the rioting.) Whites got $46.8 million, or 46.5 percent; blacks got $6.5 million, or 6.4 percent. Comparing the money each group received from the SBA with its representation in the general population, one sees that blacks, whose strength in the population is half that of the Hispanics, received only one-seventh of what the Hispanics got from the SBA.

Table 9–2

Loans by the Small Business Administration to Miami Businesses, 1968–1980, by Ethnic Origin, Dollar Amount and Number

		$	#			$	#
1968	Black	82,600	9	1975	B	137,200	8
	Hispanic	1,078,950	72		H	6,437,195	293
	Anglo	3,356,875	118		A	3,157,000	58
1969	B	658,750	23	1976	B	321,200	16
	H	1,630,645	111		H	4,430,380	200
	A	4,364,798	73		A	3,323,850	85
1970	B	510,750	27	1977	B	321,700	12
	H	938,600	69		H	4,608,960	192
	A	1,130,600	27		A	6,527,150	99
1971	B	957,000	47	1978	B	289,100	10
	H	3,535,600	180		H	3,793,400	115
	A	2,689,650	44		A	4,041,300	67
1972	B	1,036,105	40	1979	B	1,084,500	14
	H	4,820,210	238		H	3,095,500	74
	A	3,448,250	68		A	6,234,600	65
1973	B	735,650	34	1980	B	1,193,500	42
	H	7,085,100	325		H	4,259,516	99
	A	4,933,180	75		A	19,201,392	149
1974	B	378,685	22				
	H	6,166,120	305				
	A	4,154,520	70				

Totals (Excluding 1980)

Black	6.3%	6,458,240	262
Hispanic	46.9%	47,677,660	2,174
Anglo	46.6%	47,361,773	849
	99.8%	$101,447,673	3,285

The McDuffie Verdict

Dade County blacks did not riot in response to the brutal beating leading to the death of Arthur McDuffie; rather, they erupted months later when a criminal justice system failed to prosecute successfully those they viewed as responsible for McDuffie's death.

Some essential questions remain to be answered with respect to the McDuffie case. Did the criminal justice system fail, and if so, why? Were the jurors racist in voting for acquittals? Are there lessons to be learned which can be applied to other communities in the United States?

Some blacks believe that justice is routinely denied blacks in the United States because the criminal justice system in their community is racist. In one sense, they are absolutely right; a system of justice that allows those in a position where they can determine guilt or innocence—members of a jury, for instance—to be selected or excluded on the basis of their race is a racist system on the face of it. A system in which those who act as prosecutors, defense attorneys and judges are overwhelmingly white, while those processed through the system are overwhelmingly black, adds to the appearance of racism, even if individual prosecutors, defense attorneys and judges are themselves not racist in their dealings with those who come before the system.

In defense of the exclusion or selection of jury members on the basis of race, some district attorneys argue that when they are prosecuting a white person for victimizing a black, they prefer a predominance of black jury members. Although these prosecutors may not readily admit it, when they accuse a black of victimizing a white, they often prefer a predominance of whites on juries. "For lawyers on either side, the objective is to win," says Tom Petersen, chief administrator to Dade County State Attorney Janet Reno. "Such is the result of an advocacy system of justice." To increase their chances of winning, Petersen implies, attorneys often insinuate the defendant's or the victim's race into the minds of jurors. For the same reason, lawyers may want to include or exclude whites or blacks from juries. Although they excluded blacks from the jury in the Johnny Jones case, prosecutors in the McDuffie case did not try to exclude black jurors; the defense did. Some of those defense lawyers had community reputations as liberal thinkers, yet, as advocates for their clients, they joined in an agreement to ensure that no black sat on the jury.

Says Prof. Gary Moran of the department of psychology at Florida International University, a recognized consultant to attorneys in the psychology of selecting jury members: "When it comes to excluding blacks from juries by use of the peremptory challenge, it is almost always the state that does so. They do this because they tend to feel that blacks are less likely to vote to convict. In the unusual instances in which the defense excludes blacks, it almost always involves defense attorneys who are defending white police officers accused of abusing blacks."

But even if the system of jury selection is blatantly racist, it does not necessarily ensure a racist outcome. In the McDuffie case, the evidence presented by the state was so confusing and contradictory that the six white male jurors who heard the case, though themselves selected through an arguably racist process, could hardly be blamed, considering the rules they were told to follow, for finding the police officers not guilty.

To that extent, it might be argued that the criminal justice system did not fail in the McDuffie case. On the contrary, as noted by Robert Hardin, a Miami writer whose examination of the media's role in the riot was featured in the Columbia Journalism Review, the system may have done precisely what it was designed to do—exonerate those charged with a crime when the evidence presented in court did not establish in the minds of the jurors the guilt of the defendants beyond a reasonable doubt.

One is left to conclude, however, that if the criminal justice system did not fail to do what it was supposed to, and yet the result was clearly an act of gross injustice, then the system necessarily contains basic flaws when it comes to dealing with matters involving race. Indeed, in following the letter of the law in the McDuffie case, those who operated in the system—the defense lawyers, the prosecutors, the jury members—almost guaranteed that they would end up violating its spirit.

Evidence of such flaws continued to crop up in Dade County repeatedly after the 1980 riot. In the three-year period following the disorder, four new cases of white police officers accused of killing blacks were heard by all-white juries, with blacks having been eliminated by use of the peremptory challenge. In two instances the officers were acquitted; in a third the accused was found guilty. The fourth and most volatile case involved the shooting of a black Overtown youth in a games arcade that resulted in another riot in December of 1982. The policeman charged in the case was acquitted as work on this book was being completed.

What was demonstrated by the McDuffie case and those occurring subsequently is that in racially sensitive cases, the appearance of justice is as important as the fact of justice. It is not enough that the lawyers and judges who operate within the criminal justice system know that the system is fair; the system must also appear fair to those outside it. With respect to blacks whose history in this country is steeped in abuse inflicted on them, often with no consequence to the guilty parties, it is all the more important that in the present-day United States there be a sense of confidence that—while discrimination may exist in many aspects of their lives, from employment to housing to health care and education—at least in the nation's courts each will be treated as equal to all other citizens. When this does not happen, whether in fact or in appearance, a dangerous potential for violence will always exist.

Conflict between the law-enforcement establishment and those who live in America's ghettos is, of course, not unique to Miami. It is a pervasive problem, compounded by the abandonment of the ghettos by middle- and upper-income blacks who might have served as a moderating force or as a buffer as tension grows between poor young blacks and the law-enforcement officers who try to police them. Many urban communities have their McDuffie cases. In assessing the potential for reactive racial violence in these communities, it is not necessary to examine the level of black unemployment, or the extent of overcrowding in public housing, or the expected temperature range during July. One need look only to see whether justice was done—and whether it was perceived to have been done by the first young black one sees on the street. That person's response is perhaps the most accurate gauge of those dark stirrings of violence that can push a community into the abyss.

Notes

1. *Report of the National Advisory Commission on Civil Disorders* (1968), pp. 37-39.
2. See Chapter 8, Note 5.
3. Report of the National Advisory Commission, pp. 56-69.
4. Ibid., pp. 84-108.
5. Stanley Lieberson and Arnold R. Silverman, "The Precipitants and Underlying Conditions of Race Riots," *American Sociological Review* (December 1965), pp. 887-898
6. Idem.
7. Nathan S. Caplan and Jeffrey M. Paige, "A Study of Ghetto Rioters," *Scientific American* (August 1968), pp. 15-21.
8. Table prepared by the authors from information obtained from professional associations and societies in relevant cities.
9. "Sharp Gain Found for Black Elected Officials," *New York Times,* January 9, 1984, p. B8.
10. Table furnished by the Small Business Administration, Washington, D.C.

Index

About the Authors

Bruce Porter, formerly the urban affairs editor of *Newsweek,* is director of the journalism program at Brooklyn College and an adjunct professor at the Columbia University Graduate School of Journalism. He is coauthor, with Robert Curvin, of *Blackout Looting!,* a study of the disorders that took place during the New York City blackout of July 1977. He lives in Brooklyn, New York.

Marvin Dunn, Ph.D., is an associate professor of community psychology at Florida International University and director of an alternative school, the Academy for Community Education, in Miami, Florida. He lives in Miami.

DATE DUE

DEMCO 38-297